subterranean TWIN CITIES

GREG BRICK

SUBTERRANEAN TWIN CITIES

University of
Minnesota Press

MINNEAPOLIS
LONDON

For information about previously published material in this book, see Publication History on page 219.

Published by the University of Minnesota Press
111 Third Avenue South, Suite 290
Minneapolis, MN 55401-2520
http://www.upress.umn.edu

Library of Congress Cataloging-in-Publication Data

Brick, Greg A.
  Subterranean Twin Cities / Greg Brick.
      p.   cm.
  Includes bibliographical references and index.
  ISBN 978-0-8166-4597-8 (pb : alk. paper)

  1. Caves—Minnesota—Minneapolis. 2. Caves—Minnesota—St. Paul. 3. Underground areas—Minnesota—Minneapolis. 4. Underground areas—Minnesota—St. Paul. 5. Minneapolis (Minn.). 6. St. Paul (Minn.). 7. Minnesota. I. Title.

  GB605.M6B75 2009
  551.44'709776579—dc22

                                                                                    2008053782

Design and production by Mighty Media, Inc.
Text design by Chris Long

Printed in the United States of America on acid-free paper

The University of Minnesota is an equal-opportunity educator and employer.

15 14 13 12 11 10 09   10 9 8 7 6 5 4 3 2

PUBLISHER'S NOTE

The underground areas described in this book are illegal to access and extremely dangerous to visit. Neither the author nor the publisher assumes any liability for readers who explore these places anywhere beyond their imagination.

CONTENTS

ACKNOWLEDGMENTS

THE AUTHOR would like to thank the following persons: the Bremers, for hospitality during my visits to the Wabasha Street caves; Dave Dickhut, late of St. Paul Public Works Department, for assistance while I was conducting research there in the 1990s; Don Empson, for sagacious advice and encouragement over the years; Lisa Hiebert, president of the St. Paul Jaycees, for assisting my project in the Tunnel of Terror and introducing me to their enthusiastic volunteers; Virginia Kunz, late editor of the Ramsey County Historical Society, for encouraging me to write cave articles; Larry Millett, for suggestions; Mike Mosedale of *City Pages*, for proposing the book; Penny Petersen, for sharing the results of her extensive researches in Minneapolis history; Alan Woolworth, Minnesota Historical Society, for sharing his Carver's Cave files; and my exploratory friends over the years, including Andy, Dave, Gabe, Jana, Jason, John, Mark, Mike, and Tim. And, of course, my loving Cindy, who was so supportive of her Cave Man.

INTRODUCTION

MANY CITIES AROUND THE WORLD are famous for their subterranean features and legends. Sewer tourists have a respectable lineage, going back to the ancient poets who explored the Cloaca Maxima, the famous sewer that drained ancient Rome. Paris, of course, has its catacombs and sewers and a long literary tradition that began before Jean Valjean was chased through the sewers in Victor Hugo's *Les Misérables* (1862). London's subterranean spaces have been explored in Stephen Smith's *Underground London* (2004) and by others going back before John Hollingshead's classic Victorian offering, *Underground London* (1862). Judging from the burgeoning bookshelves, it seems that New York City's underground gets rediscovered about once every decade or two, the latest offering being Julia Solis's delightful *New York Underground* (2004). Before that was Jennifer Toth's *The Mole People: Life in the Tunnels beneath New York City* (1993), Pamela Jones's *Under the City Streets: A History of Subterranean New York* (1978), and Henry Granick's *Underneath New York* (1947). Closer to home, Chicago's freight railroad tunnels in Bruce Moffat's *The Chicago Tunnel Story* (2002) and St. Louis's lost caves in Charlotte and Hubert Rother's *Lost Caves of St. Louis* (1996) have been the focus of book-length works.

The Twin Cities of Minneapolis and St. Paul also have a remarkable and growing subterranean tradition. As early as the 1890s, the Twin Cities had a national reputation among engineers because of the ease of excavation in its underlying St. Peter Sandstone, allowing the creation of myriad utility tunnels. The underground has served numerous uses in the development of the Twin Cities: tourist attractions beginning in the mid-nineteenth century; industrial sites for the production of silica, beer, mushrooms, and blue cheese; and the location for the vast network of utilities and sewer lines that allow the Twin Cities to function each day. In recent years that reputation has grown exponentially among urban explorers, attracting them from as far away as

Alaska and Australia. Sadly, the underground has also been the site for tragic accidents involving young people who were unaware of or unprepared for the dangers.

This is the first book to attempt to comprehensively document the subterranean Twin Cities, as seen through the eyes of a geologist and avocational historian who participated in much of the early exploration. My very earliest recollections of a serious interest in the urban underground date to my student days on the streets of London in 1981. I recall being puzzled by the Serpentine, a famous pond in Hyde Park. Water flowed into it, but there was no surface stream draining out. Taking up the challenge, I worked out the path of its subterranean drainage below the city. I thereafter began to study geology, ultimately receiving an advanced degree in the subject from the University of Connecticut. I worked as a professional geologist at several different environmental and geotechnical consulting firms around the United States, and in each location I sampled the fare that the local cities had to offer in terms of urban exploration. While living on the East Coast, I used to wander through the subway and train tunnels under New York City with an artist friend, looking for the fabled Mole People, homeless men and women who made a place for themselves underground. I have fond memories from my days in graduate school when I explored the brownstone labyrinth below Hartford, Connecticut, with its well-known sewer eels, and the barnacled outfalls of the Boston waterfront, where you had to time your expeditions to the ebb and flow of the tide. One time, after emerging from the sewers, I went to a fast-food restaurant where a stranger offered to pay for my meal. Being used to walking around like the Creature from the Black Lagoon, I hadn't realized what an object of charity I must have appeared to be. While a resident of St. Louis, Missouri, I enjoyed visits to Cherokee Cave, a famous bone cave under the streets of that city. I did not actively explore aboveground structures, such as abandoned mill buildings and so forth, although I have a keen interest in industrial archaeology to this day, and I belong to the Society for Industrial Archeology.

I began exploring Minnesota caves in 1988 as a member of the Minnesota Speleological Survey (MSS), a local chapter of the National Speleological Society (NSS). The MSS is a welcoming organization that has been exploring local caves since its founding in 1963. From them I learned the basics of caving, a background that I think would benefit many urban explorers today, many of whom do not seem to be aware of the significant safety risks that face them or of what can be done to minimize those risks.

Most of the exploration conducted by the MSS takes place in the southeastern corner of the state, especially in Fillmore County, which has more natural caves than the rest of the state combined. Not many MSS cavers were interested in exploring caves in the Twin Cities, even though many members lived there and the monthly meetings were held there, so to some extent I had the field to myself for a while. I began maintaining my own files of cave information, which have steadily grown over the years. I combed through all the old MSS files, decades' worth of accumulated documents stored in many boxes, for information about the subterranean Twin Cities. At the Minnesota History Center, surrounded predominantly by genealogical researchers, I felt somewhat out of place, being more interested in the ancestry of caves and tunnels than of people. I was invited to write a series, St. Paul Underground, which began appearing in *Ramsey County History* magazine in 1995 and detailed my extensive historical research of the urban underground in local archives.

My most enlightening experience was the summer I spent in 1994 as a researcher at the St. Paul Public Works Department, where I acquired an intimate familiarity with the underground of that city. My favorite files were the old aperture cards of sewer structures and the P. H. file; the initials stamped on the documents stood for "Pigeon Hole." I found many items of great historical value among them, including the earliest complete map of Fountain Cave. After a while, longtime employees of St. Paul Public Works began asking *me* where to find various records. I recall how the sewer maintenance workers told me of jobs they had been on, places where they had seen caves in the sewers, and interesting places that I might want to explore. I carried out similar, though less extensive, investigations in the Minneapolis Public Works Department, which was organized very differently. I loved the old engineering sketches I found there. Some of them were real works of art, with the details of geological layers painted in watercolors.

After several years of subterranean exploration in the Twin Cities, I began publishing some of my geological observations in the technical literature, giving presentations on them at national caving conventions, and describing them in my geology lectures at local colleges. I discovered the existence of a new category of cave in the St. Peter Sandstone, the maze cave. Tubular caves, such as Fountain Cave, had long been known, but Minneapolis's Schieks Cave was a hitherto unrecognized example of a maze cave in this layer, which underlies much of the Upper Midwest. More fundamentally, I formally recognized a third category of caves in the world. Natural and artificial caves have been recognized since the dawn of history, but Schieks Cave belonged to an intermediate class, which for lack of a better word I called "anthropogenic." They are not natural caves, but they are not truly artificial. They developed inadvertently as a result of human activities such as sewer construction. This kind of cave seems to be especially characteristic of the St. Peter Sandstone. I was also the first to point out the thermal anomaly existing in the groundwater under downtown Minneapolis, based on my thermometric survey of the caves there. Over the years I have provided information to Minnesota Department of Natural Resources personnel about significant bat hibernacula under the cities, one of which I discovered. On the national level, I became the editor of a scholarly cave history publication, the *Journal of Spelean History*, first established in 1968, and in 2005 I was given the Peter M. Hauer Spelean History Award by the NSS for my cave history research over the years. In 2004, Trails Media published my first book, *Iowa Underground*, a 223-page guidebook to publicly accessible caves, mines, and tunnels of the Hawkeye State. In 2005 I appeared on the History Channel in a feature about St. Paul caves.

I've studied the subterranean Twin Cities for more than two decades, and I've noticed some disturbing trends in urban exploration in recent years. There's been a rise of shadowy groups who operate almost like SWAT teams, with advanced skills in the use of ropes and night-vision goggles, swooping down in the middle of the night on vaguely important "missions." Another involves Web sites. A high-quality artistic, historical, or scientific Web site is welcome and useful, but too many of them began giving away hitherto secret details of how to get into various places, or at least providing enough circumstantial detail for others to be able to easily deduce the remainder. In the past, every local explorer knew the caves and tunnels in his own backyard, of course, but not what was in the next—unless he was sufficiently dedicated to spend years at the task. This weeded out the less-committed souls. But suddenly, every would-be explorer could connect the dots using the Internet and set up his or her own Web site in turn. The result was predictable: the subterranean venues, hitherto silent and inviolate, were overrun. While some explorers simply enjoyed experiencing unique urban spaces or worked creatively in photography, others clearly did not belong. Some of the explorers, becoming jaded, went further, glorying in acts of trespass and vandalism. The authorities, of course, soon learned of the Web sites and how explorers were getting into places, and thus they were able to better secure them. I believe that many urban exploration Web sites are ultimately self-defeating, unwittingly destroying access for fellow explorers.

Another significant change in attitudes was the response to 9/11. The easy familiarity, indeed, collaboration, which I enjoyed with public works departments belongs to an earlier era. I can't imagine that any public works personnel today would dream of suggesting a good tunnel for an outside researcher to explore. The threat of terrorism has caused officials to rethink the advisability of letting anyone know too much about the urban infrastructure even though, in the final analysis, it's all basically public information.

At the same time that attitudes toward urban exploration were changing, a long-term physical change in the Twin Cities underground was manifesting itself. The great sewer separation projects of both cities, which began decades ago and aimed to separate storm water from sanitary sewage, severed many classic, well-traveled subterranean routes. Many of the places discussed in this book are now inaccessible.

Given how radically the environment for urban exploration has changed over the years, my advice for the would-be explorer is to join a recognized caving club, such as the Minnesota Speleological Survey (http://www.mss-caving.org). Not only will they teach you safe caving techniques, but occasionally they will have officially sanctioned trips to some of the locations described in this book. Risking a misdemeanor on your record and a blemished future is not necessary. In order to discourage unauthorized urban exploration, I do not reveal specific locations in this book.

In 2004, I served on a consultation committee to assist Mayor Randy Kelly of St. Paul to decide on a permanent solution to the problem of the deaths and injuries occurring in the caves of that city. I implore readers not to attempt to visit these places. I no longer visit these caves myself.

The following book is a strictly armchair tour of the subterranean Twin Cities. It is certainly not meant as a guidebook, and to that end, no contemporary maps are provided. I have undergone some perils in collecting this information, and I did an immense amount of research in local archives over the years. I hope my experiences will provide the reader with a unique perspective on the internationally famous subterranean Twin Cities. While I've also spent a lot of time over the years investigating the extensive caves and tunnels under other cities in Minnesota, these are not discussed except in passing.

I do not use last names in this book except where the people involved have already made themselves public. Many friends have accompanied me over the years, and I could not possibly have visited the places I did without their help, for which I am immensely grateful. In granting them some degree of anonymity, I'm simply respecting their wishes, not trying to steal the spotlight from them or pretending that this was a one-person show.

This book is organized in roughly chronological order. An initial introductory chapter, "The Geology of the Sewers," will familiarize readers with names and terminology that will be used throughout the book. In Part I, "The Early Caves," I begin with the simplest under-ground voids, the tube-like natural caves found along the Mississippi River such as Carver's and Fountain caves—the latter considered the womb of St. Paul in a historical sense. These caves, sacred to Native Americans, were frequently used during the pioneer period of Minne-sota history. Surface streams, in the early days, that were later made to run in tunnels are the topic of Part II, "Buried Rivers," especially Trout Brook in St. Paul and Bassett Creek in Minneapolis, as well as several other less-well-known streams. Part III, "The Great Sandbox," brings the reader into the late nineteenth and early twentieth centuries. Numerous industries in the Twin Cities created underground spaces in the sandstone that were essential to their businesses of brewing, mushroom farming, cheese ripening, and silica mining. In Part IV, "The Milling District," I explore the former Minneapolis flour-milling district, a veritable subterranean Venice, with the densest clustering of tunnels in the Twin Cities. Chute's Cave as well as Nicollet Island are included. Part V, "Utilities," investigates the most highly evolved, most complex underground spaces. The thirty-mile long Fort Road Labyrinth of St. Paul is featured, as well as multilevel utility spaces, such as the tunnels for water, electric, and gas, under the downtowns of both cities. Part VI, "Pluto's Kingdom," delves into the remotest urban caves of all, the "lost world" of Schieks Cave, located seventy-five feet below street level in downtown Minneapolis, and the great

Channel Rock Cavern, large enough to hold several volleyball courts. "Sources and Further Reading" lists the more important sources used in writing this book, as well as books about other cities and topics that have been referenced in the text, including a selection of articles that I have published on the subject.

THE GEOLOGY OF THE SEWERS

Sewers have been fruitful in furnishing antiquarian and geological discoveries.

JOHN HOLLINGSHEAD, *UNDERGROUND LONDON*

WHILE THERE ARE SEVERAL GOOD ACCOUNTS of the geology of the Twin Cities, I will focus here only on those aspects most relevant to subterranean places—geology from a caver's perspective. I picked up quite a lot of geology just by grubbing about in the caves and sewers of the metropolis over the years.

Let's take an imaginary journey downward through the geological layers of Minnesota by way of a sewer. Not all of Minnesota's geology is visible in any one city or particular location. This will be a composite trip, and in that sense, the trip is even more purely imaginary. Furthermore, since bedrock is only occasionally exposed, in unlined sewers, let's say that the sewer walls are transparent—similar to one of those transparent plastic tubes you find in a child's playland.

Popping a manhole lid on a street in downtown Minneapolis or St. Paul, the first layer we would see—if we could see through the walls—would be the glacial deposits (often called glacial drift) laid down during the last ice age, which ended ten thousand years ago. Since these deposits are usually loose materials containing gravel, sand, silt, and clay, tunnels that pass through this layer are almost always lined, most often with brick or concrete. While glacial drift can be several hundred feet thick in buried river valleys, in most parts of the Twin Cities it's usually much thinner, no more than several tens of feet.

In some sewers, actual glacial deposits have found their way into the system or have been left behind by construction workers. For example, in an old sewer under Dayton's Bluff I found glacial erratics—granite boulders about the size of medicine balls and larger—sitting in the laterals, or small side branches, which had been carved

1

out of the solid bedrock and left unlined. Doubtless the boulders were encountered during excavation and it was easier for the contractor to just leave them there than to haul them out, as long as they weren't getting in anyone's way. Likewise, a large amount of glacial material can be seen in the ceilings of sandstone passages under the West Seventh Street neighborhood of St. Paul. It's as if the old-time contractors, in digging these bedrock tunnels, grazed the underside of the glacial deposits and left them precariously exposed in the ceilings.

While a few tunnels have been constructed wholly in the glacial layer—most notably the Bassett Creek tunnel in Minneapolis—glacial times are more important to cavers in that the melt waters from the great ice sheet, blocked by the ice from draining to the north, formed an enormous lake, called Glacial Lake Agassiz, which eventually cut the present river gorge through the Twin Cities. This left a lowered base level—a lower place for water to drain to—which was important for the development of both natural caves and the subsequent man-made drainage systems. In fact, despite the excellent tunneling properties of the St. Peter Sandstone, few tunnels could have been constructed in this layer had there not been a lower level for the water to drain to.

Going deeper, immediately below the glacial deposits we encounter bedrock, but there's an enormous geological time gap between these two layers. The missing layers in between either were not laid down in Minnesota to begin with or, if they were, they were completely removed by erosion over a vast span of time. This uppermost bedrock layer was laid down in Ordovician times (500 to 440 million years ago, in round numbers).

In the old brickyards of Lilydale, near West St. Paul, you can see the Galena Limestone exposed at the very tops of the cliffs. No caves are found in this layer in the Twin Cities, but in southeastern Minnesota, especially Fillmore County, which has been called the heart of Minnesota cave country, all the big caves, like Mystery and Niagara and several hundred others, are found in this layer. This rock forma-

A cross section of the geological layers along the Mississippi River at Robert Street, St. Paul, looking upstream.

FROM SCHWARTZ AND THIEL, *MINNESOTA'S ROCKS AND WATERS*. REPRINTED COURTESY OF THE MINNESOTA GEOLOGICAL SURVEY.

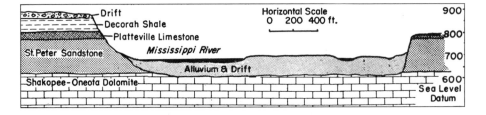

tion was named for exposures in Galena, Illinois; there and in adjacent states, it contains lead veins. The Illinois place-name derives from galena (lead sulfide), an important ore of lead.

The Decorah Shale, named for its outcrops in Decorah, Iowa, is very well exposed just below the Galena Limestone. This thick, green shale layer is a happy hunting ground for local fossil collectors. Since the shale provided the clay content for the former brick-making operation, the brickyards are also known as clay pits. Owing to the imperviousness of this clay, there are abundant springs in the clay pits where the shale has intercepted descending groundwater, forcing it sideways to the exposed rock face. In winter, the spring water freezes, leading to the growth of gigantic ice columns, stout as oak trees, that last well into the spring season. Not surprisingly, the clay pits are a favorite ice-climbing locale in the Twin Cities. The floors of the clay pits, equally impervious, are lined with cattail marshes. All in all, it's a unique postindustrial landscape.

Below the Decorah Shale is the Platteville Limestone, formed in the warm shallow seas of about 450 million years ago, an environment frequently compared to the Bahamas of today. The presence of fossil green algae indicates that the Platteville seas must have been fairly shallow, around 150 feet or so, for the light to have been able to penetrate the water. The largest fossil in the Platteville layer is the well-known giant ice-cream-cone-shaped mollusk *Endoceras*, as long

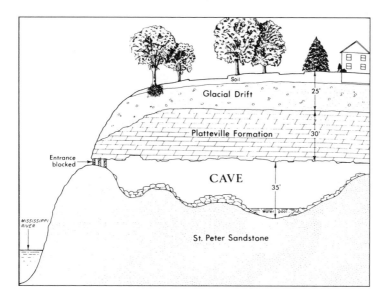

A geological section through a typical Twin Cities sandstone cave.

FROM R. K. HOGBERG, *ENVIRONMENTAL GEOLOGY OF THE TWIN CITIES METROPOLITAN AREA.* REPRINTED COURTESY OF THE MINNESOTA GEOLOGICAL SURVEY.

as thirteen feet, which you occasionally find in the Mississippi gorge, where they have been confused with petrified logs. The Platteville also contains volcanic ash layers derived from ancient former volcanoes in what are now the Appalachians. Many species of invertebrates living in the Platteville seas became extinct when this ash fell, as if from atomic fallout. The ash layers are impervious to water; some of the most famous springs in Minneapolis, such as Chalybeate Springs, owe their existence to them. This limestone layer, named for rock exposures in Platteville, Wisconsin, frequently makes up waterfall ledges, for example, at St. Anthony Falls and Minnehaha Falls.

The Platteville Limestone was a favored building stone in the early days. One of the early Minneapolis city halls was built of it. The historic Pillsbury A Mill in Minneapolis, the first architect-built flour mill, six stories high, is made wholly of Platteville Limestone and is still standing; it has recently been converted into lofts. Because the shaley layers form planes of weakness in the rock, the Platteville is no longer used as cut and shaped stone blocks except perhaps as rubble masonry in building foundations and park structures. Many small abandoned Platteville quarries, used by the Civilian Conservation Corps for park structures in the 1930s and now overgrown by vegetation, can be found along the banks of the Mississippi. Another use of the Platteville was in the walls of the great classic sewers of the Twin Cities, such as Bassett Creek in Minneapolis and Trout Brook in St. Paul. Today, this limestone is often crushed for aggregate—to be incorporated into concrete or for gravel roads—or powdered for agricultural lime.

Man-made openings in the Platteville Limestone usually take the form of shafts, rather than tunnels, owing to the hardness of this limestone as compared to the softer layers above and below it. When you need to cross this layer, you want to get through it in as short a line as possible, minimizing the amount of hard rock that has to be excavated, and that means going directly downward. Indeed, since the Platteville Limestone is usually thirty feet thick under the Twin Cities, I made the rope ladders that I constructed for exploration purposes thirty feet long, matching the most frequent shaft depths.

Twin Cities caves are often below the layer of Platteville Limestone, which serves as their ceilings, as in Chute's Cave. Crawlway Cave, in southern Minnesota, is very much the exception: its entire two-thousand-foot length was formed completely within the Platteville Limestone.

Having climbed down our imaginary Platteville shaft, we find ourselves in the most important layer of all, the St. Peter Sandstone. There
is a thin intermediate layer, usually two or three feet thick, known
as the Glenwood Shale, between the Platteville Limestone and the
St. Peter, but no tunnels are wholly within this layer. Almost always,
the Glenwood, where visible, forms the ceilings of unlined sewer tunnels in the St. Peter. Where it collapses, it is responsible for much of
the "grody" appearance of sewer spaces. It's a crumbly green rock
full of tiny fossils known as conodonts, which resemble microscopic
saw blades.

The St. Peter Sandstone, often called sandrock by city engineers,
is the most important layer in terms of subterranean exploration;
owing to its ease of excavation, it has the most tunnels and caves.
The pioneer geologist David Dale Owen officially named this rock in
1852 for outcrops near Fort Snelling, along the St. Peter River—now
the Minnesota River. The St. Peter layer has an average thickness of
about 100 feet regionally. However, it's about 150 feet thick at its type
section at Fort Snelling, and it ranges up to 500 feet thick at Joliet,
Illinois, as determined from drilling records. That leaves plenty of
three-dimensional volume for caves and tunnels. While this layer is
quite uniform, there are subtle ways of telling approximately where
you are inside it, vertically speaking, when you are walking through
unlined tunnels that pass through it. If, for example, you see wild red
swirls of iron pigment—technically called Liesegang bands—left by
groundwater, you know that you are somewhere near the top of the
layer, at least in the Twin Cities. Near the bottom of the St. Peter layer,
the sandstone is much siltier.

The St. Peter is very extensive for a single formation, covering
nearly a quarter million square miles in the Midwest. St. Paul was
known to the Dakota Indians as White Rocks because of this glaringly
white layer exposed in its river bluffs. Crystal City, near St. Louis, Missouri, was named for the fact that the Pittsburgh Plate Glass Company
used the St. Peter sand that outcropped there for making glass, as was
also done at Ottawa, Illinois, and Clayton, Iowa, among other places.
Locally, the sand was also used for glass making, as at the Ford sand
mines under St. Paul, with its miles of tunnels. To the south, the layer
extends into Arkansas, Oklahoma, and Tennessee, and as far east as
Ohio and Kentucky, where it sometimes contains oil and gas.

The St. Peter has an almost saintly purity throughout most of this
range, suggesting that it has been recycled from older sandstones,

geologically winnowed of its impurities. The St. Peter is called a sheet sand, meaning that it was laid down flat, like a sheet, over large areas by a warm shallow sea that invaded the continent from the south. It was the last major sandstone layer to be deposited in the Upper Mississippi Valley. The most prominent fossils in this otherwise almost barren layer include the scolithus, a U-shaped worm burrow, and molds of some of the earliest known clams. In unlined sewer tunnels you can sometimes see cross-bedding in the walls, representing the old sand dunes of the shoreline beaches.

Most important, the St. Peter Sandstone, in the Minnesota part of its range, lacks natural cementation, hence it is friable and easily excavated. Historically, it was often compared to loaf sugar, a commodity rarely seen nowadays. In other locations, however, the St. Peter has plenty of cement holding the grains together, as at Starved Rock State Park in central Illinois, where this sandstone stands proud as high cliffs.

The St. Peter Sandstone was so easy to excavate that it actually led to more tunneling than was really necessary, to the delight of later generations of cavers. It may be fairly said that St. Paul's, and to a lesser degree Minneapolis's, sister city is Paris, France—under the skin at least—owing to the extensive, catacomb-like excavations. How different this is from the schist under Manhattan or the limestone under St. Louis, where you have to blast through hard rocks to make tunnels!

Another important characteristic of the St. Peter Sandstone in the Twin Cities is that it is near the surface. Even though the St. Peter layer is present below the city of St. Louis, for example, it is so deep there that it does not serve any practical purpose except as an aquifer.

Natural caves are formed in the St. Peter Sandstone by a process known as piping, a form of erosion caused by flowing groundwater. The term was borrowed from civil engineering practice in the late 1940s. It was used originally to refer to the pipe-shaped voids formed by water seepage around failing dams. One particular layer within the St. Peter, called the Cave Unit by the geologist Robert Sloan, is more susceptible to piping and thus more favorable to cave formation than the others. Piping forms two different kinds of cave in the St. Peter: tubular caves, best exemplified by Fountain Cave in St. Paul, and maze caves, best seen in Schieks Cave under downtown Minneapolis. Note that while the rocks themselves are old, the caves found in them are usually much younger, no older than the carving of the river gorge to which they presently drain.

Channel Rock Cavern, on the Mississippi River in Minneapolis, is an example of how a cave might have formed after carving of the river gorge. When St. Anthony Falls, in postglacial time, retreated upstream past what is now Thirty-fourth Street, water on the adjacent river terrace found a shortcut by diverting through a sinkhole, following rock joints that it enlarged by piping, and spilling out into the gorge below. The cave exit sealed itself naturally with slope debris by the time of European settlement, so the cave was only discovered during sewer construction in 1935.

Apart from completely natural and explicitly man-made excavations in the St. Peter, a third category of cave, also best exemplified in the Twin Cities, is the anthropogenic cave. It's where human activities have unintentionally created caves, as by leakage from wells or sewers. The best example is Schieks Cave in Minneapolis.

In order to continue our imaginary journey downward through the geological layers, we leave the Twin Cities and go to the city of Hastings, in southeast Minnesota, where we find the Prairie du Chien (PDC) layer, which is largely dolomite, a magnesium-rich limestone. Although this layer is actually found deep under the Twin Cities, no tunnels run through it. Instead, coupled hydrologically with the underlying Jordan Sandstone, it serves as Minnesota's most prolific aquifer, supplying up to three thousand gallons of water per minute to wells drilled into it. The high discharge is possible partly due to the fact that this layer has large water-filled voids, which, if they were drained, would be considered caves.

At Hastings, the PDC layer is warped upward enough to be exposed at the surface, thus its caves are available for human exploration, such as Lee Mill Cave, overlooking scenic Spring Lake, and Miles Cave, below the falls of the Vermilion River. Most of the best caves in Wabasha, Winona, and Houston counties of Minnesota and some of adjoining Wisconsin's best-known caves are found in this layer. Most known PDC caves are maze caves. The rock is quite vuggy, interspersed with small cavities like Swiss cheese. Most of its fossils were altered beyond recognition in the change from limestone to dolomite.

We go farther down through progressively older layers. Cambrian period (545–500 million years ago) rocks are below the Ordovician. Under the city of Red Wing, Minnesota, there is a veritable labyrinth of tunnels in the greenish Franconia Sandstone, containing beautiful formations.

Nearly nine-tenths of all Earth's history falls under the domain of Precambrian time—when the Earth's crust was formed and life originated. To see tunnels in rocks of this age, you have to go north of the Twin Cities. Probably the oldest sewers in Minnesota, or rather the sewers running through the oldest rock, are found in Duluth. The intriguing Chester Creek tunnel, for example, passes through lava flows 1.1 billion years old. Higher segments of the tunnel, far up the slopes, make it seem as though you were exploring tunnels in the sky.

But while rocks of Precambrian age are not exposed in the Twin Cities per se, the Precambrian still makes itself felt because such rocks form Minnesota's basement. More than a billion years ago, North America was nearly cleft in half by plate tectonic action, and lava flows oozed out from the resulting rift—flows that can still be seen along the North Shore of Lake Superior and, closer to home, in the Dalles of the St. Croix River at Taylor's Falls. This defunct rift runs like a giant scar from Minnesota south to Kansas, where it is located far underground. The rifting stopped for some unknown reason, but it left a depression that filled with sediments over time. This was the origin of the Twin Cities Basin, a thousand-square-mile geologic saucer that formed the foundation for all the layers to follow—including the familiar layers seen locally in the Mississippi River gorge that I explore in the chapters that follow.

PART I

THE EARLY CAVES

QUEST FOR THE INNER SANCTUM
CARVER'S CAVE AT MIDNIGHT

A remarkable cave of amazing depth

JONATHAN CARVER, *TRAVELS*

AS THE MILLENNIAL YEAR 2000 APPROACHED, everyone began making plans for what they would do at the fateful moment when computer systems were expected to malfunction. One of the jokes among local cavers at the time was that at the stroke of midnight the computers at the municipal sewage plant would suddenly begin pumping sewage in the opposite direction—back into people's homes! My own Y2K plan was simple. I was going to spend midnight in St. Paul's most famous cave, Carver's Cave, with more than a hundred feet of good, solid rock over my head in case the world should end. I really didn't believe in the Y2K problem as such, but I thought it would be a fun thing to do.

Fortunately for my resolution, it was a warm winter's night. Shortly before midnight I drove to Mounds Park, atop Dayton's Bluff, with its twinkling panorama of downtown St. Paul (perhaps soon to plunge into chaos—where better to watch the spectacle?) and began to climb down the steep river bluff. Even though it was pitch dark, I knew every hand- and foothold by long practice as I descended the heavily eroded sandstone badlands below the cave's historical marker. I knew where to turn about to face the rock, where to stretch out my leg, where to jump down a bit.

Walking now in the shadows among the dirt mounds at the foot of the bluff, I made my way through a wilderness of buckthorns and busted toilet bowls, a sort of no-man's-land between the park and the rail yards, finally reaching a small triangular lake of my own creation. I squeezed through a small opening into Carver's Cave, sat down on the sandy beach of a subterranean lake, and removed my pack.

My solitary vigil that night in Carver's Cave was full of melancholy brooding. For more than a decade I had made efforts to drain the subterranean lake so that I could enter the mysterious inner sanctum of rooms that supposedly existed at the back end of the cave, but they remained flooded. It seemed as if Unktahe, the Dakota god of water and the underworld, who was said to inhabit the lake, had laughingly thwarted my efforts.

The first I ever heard of Unktahe (there are many variant spellings of the word) was in the late 1990s, during the final days of the decades-long Highway 55 (Hiawatha Avenue) "war" in Minneapolis. The reconstruction of the highway through a corner of Minnehaha Park was opposed by Native Americans on the grounds that it would entail the removal of sacred oaks. As a hydrogeologist at an environmental consulting firm at the time, my overlooked contribution was to push the spring diminution argument. Basically, I argued that the new highway could impact the flow of the nearby Camp Coldwater spring and filed a brief on behalf of the Native American cause. Changes were later made to the highway design that helped mitigate the problem.

Historically, the Camp Coldwater spring was associated with Unktahe, who was often visualized as a fish or serpent. Mary Henderson Eastman wrote in 1849, "Unktehi, the god of the waters, is much reverenced by the Dahcotahs. Morgan's bluff [present site of the Veterans Hospital], near Fort Snelling, is called 'God's house' by the Dahcotahs; they say it is the residence of Unktehi, and under the hill is a subterranean passage, through which they say the water-god passes when he enters the St. Peter's [Minnesota River]. He is said to be as large as a white man's house."

Unktahe was also associated with Carver's Cave by some elders. Gary Cavender, who identified himself as "the spiritual leader of the Prior Lake Shakopee Dakota band," said that he was warned by his grandfather never to go deep into Carver's Cave because Unktahe resides in the lake that fills the cave. Or maybe in those flooded rooms at the back?

I had first become interested in Carver's Cave because of such rich history. Jonathan Carver gave the first published account of a cave in the Upper Midwest after visiting it in 1766 and 1767. It was written up in his *Travels through the Interior Parts of North America*, first published in London in 1778 and in the United States in 1784, with many editions to follow, and became a best seller and a standard source of information about the region for many years. Carver's Cave is the baptismal font of Minnesota caving.

Jonathan Carver (1710–1780), born in Massachusetts, served as a captain in the British army during the campaigns of the French and Indian Wars, narrowly escaping the treacherous ambush that followed the surrender of Fort William Henry in upstate New York in 1757. Casting about for something to do afterward, he became acquainted with Robert Rogers, the famous colonial ranger. Rogers visited the English court and petitioned for resources to lead an expedition to explore the King's newly won dominions in North America—an endeavor that foreshadowed what Lewis and Clark would do forty years later for the U.S. government. Rogers even promised to find the long-sought Northwest Passage to the Orient in the bargain. When the huge expedition was turned down, Rogers commissioned Carver to follow through on the plan. Departing from Boston, Carver went to the Hudson Bay Company's fur-trading post on Mackinac Island, the uttermost British fort in the Old Northwest, and from there, left for the wild interior of the continent in 1765, at the age of fifty-five. You've got to admire someone for that sort of thing.

Arriving at Prairie du Chien by way of the Green Bay–Fox River portage, Carver ascended the Mississippi, reaching what is now St. Paul. On November 14, 1766, he explored what he called "the Great Cave" and what others have called Carver's Cave. Native Americans prefer to call it Wakan Tipi, the house of the Great Spirit. The most heavily quoted passage from Carver's best-selling *Travels* describes the scene:

About thirty miles below the Falls of St. Anthony, at which I arrived the tenth day after I left Lake Pepin, is a remarkable cave of an amazing depth. The Indians term it Wakon-teebe, that is, the Dwelling of the Great Spirit. The entrance into it is about ten feet wide, the height of it five feet. The arch within is near fifteen feet high and about thirty feet broad. The bottom of it consists of fine clear sand. About twenty feet from the entrance begins a lake, the water of which is transparent, and extends to an unsearchable distance; for the darkness of the cave prevents all attempts to acquire a knowledge of it. I threw a small pebble towards the interior parts of it with my utmost strength: I could hear that it fell into the water, and notwithstanding it was of so small a size, it caused an astonishing and horrible noise that reverberated through all those gloomy regions. I found in this cave many Indian hieroglyphicks, which appeared very ancient, for time had nearly covered them with moss, so that it was with difficulty I could trace them. They were cut in a rude manner upon the inside of the walls, which were composed of a stone so extremely soft that it might be easily penetrated with a knife: a stone every where to be found near the Mississippi. The cave is only accessible by ascending a narrow, steep passage that lies near the brink of the river.

Carver carved the arms of the king of England in among the petroglyphs in the cave. He thereafter visited St. Anthony Falls and ascended the Minnesota River, spending the winter with the Dakota in a bark house. The following spring he returned to the cave and on May 1, 1767, while attending "a grand council," was made an honorary chief, supposedly receiving from the Dakota a grant of ten thousand square miles, stretching from Minneapolis to Eau Claire, Wisconsin. Carver never made the claim himself; it surfaced after his death and took many years to play out. One of the promoters of the story was the bizarre Reverend Samuel Peters, who wanted to establish a colony known as Petersylvania with a capital near present-day Fountain, Wisconsin. U.S. Chief Justice John Marshall disposed of the claim in an 1823 decision.

Carver prophesied the emergence of "kingdoms" in what is now the Midwest, one of which I guess became our very own metropolitan area. Not finding the promised supplies to continue on to Oregon—a name he popularized—Carver returned by way of the north shore of Lake Superior to Boston in 1768, having traveled about seven thousand miles. He left the following year for London.

One of the unusual creatures mentioned in Carver's manuscript was the buffalo snake, which reads like another manifestation of Unktahe. The tale grew more bizarre with each telling. The following version appeared in the *Pittsburgh Gazette*, May 19, 1818:

Returning from the Indian hunting ground situated near the mouth of the St. Peter's, I had occasion to go ashore at a rock which forms the cave, mentioned by Carver. Our attention was attracted by a noise, resembling the bellowing of a Buffaloe; we immediately proceeded in search of the object, and at the mouth of the cave, encountered a serpent of prodigious appearance, probably fifteen feet long, and proportionately thick, with four short legs, resembling the alligator; his head was disproportionately large, with glossy eyes, situated towards the back of the head; the back was of a shining black, covered with strong, and apparently impenetrable scales; the belly variegated with different colours; its tail, on perceiving it, was coiled on its back, except when it beat the ground, which was also accompanied by bellowing. The whole party stood with muskets cocked, transfixed with terror, until it quietly glided into the cave.

As if that wasn't bad enough, Carver's account, so long taken for granted by most readers, was roundly attacked as plagiarism by the Yale scholar Edward G. Bourne in 1906. It is now thought that extracts from Charlevoix, Lahontan, and other early travel writers were inserted into his manuscript by unscrupulous editors.

After Carver's visit, the cave had an annoying habit of periodically sealing itself by landslides from the bluffs above, and it had to be dug open again about once each generation. Lieutenant Zebulon Pike, U.S. Army, on his way up the Mississippi in 1805 and the first traveler to search for the cave, found that loose rock above the entrance had fallen, and it was inaccessible. Major Stephen Long, U.S. Corps of Topographical Engineers, stopped to explore what he was the first to call Carver's Cave, in 1817. To enter the small cave opening he found, one had to be "completely prostrate." The cave, in shape resembling "a baker's oven," contained "a stagnant pool." Henry Schoolcraft, in 1820, visited Fountain Cave by mistake, which understandably led to some head scratching on his part. By 1837, when the cartographer Joseph Nicollet arrived, the cave was closed by debris, and it took several days of digging to reopen it. By the summer of 1849, when the writer E. S. Seymour arrived, the cave entrance was again blocked. In 1851, Lyman Dayton (for whom Dayton's Bluff was named), dug it open again.

With the founding of St. Paul in 1841, Carver's Cave received more visitors. James Goodhue, the editor of the *St. Paul Pioneer Press*, explored the cave in 1851 but was rather dismissive: "We found the remnants of a bark canoe in the cave. Carver's cave looks about like the roof of a man's mouth seen through a magnifying glass." Daniel Curtiss, in his *Western Portraiture and Emigrants Guide* (1852), reported that "Carver's Cave is one of some note; but it can rarely ever be explored, as the entrance to it is constantly changing and being obstructed by sliding rocks and earth, which frequently fill up the orifice, so that there is no access for several days, till the little stream issuing from it bursts out again, leaving a passage, sometimes, through which a man can enter and explore, though it is a hazardous experiment, not often attempted."

In 1867, the Minnesota Historical Society held a "Carver Centenary" in the cave, and local druggist Robert O. Sweeny drew the first-ever depictions of the cave from several perspectives. The famed rattlesnake petroglyphs were admired by torchlight while the guests rode in a boat. The rattlesnakes may have symbolized the underworld generally or may have been intended to represent one of the many snakes found on the sunny, southwestern aspect of Dayton's Bluff. Other petroglyphs, as sketched by the antiquarian Theodore Lewis in 1878, represented men, birds, fishes, turtles, lizards, and so forth.

A boat was usually left in Carver's Cave for the convenience of tourists, according to a guidebook of the day. A former coal miner, more adventurous, claimed to have floated for a mile into the 113-foot-long cave, finding a connection with Phalen's Creek.

Railroad tracks were soon laid in front of Carver's Cave, and the cliff was shaved back to accommodate them. Many of the petroglyphs had been located near the entrance and were destroyed. The railroads pumped water from the cave. In 1870, the cave was dammed, and a hydraulic ram was installed to lift water to "the old pop factory," a nearby bottling concern. In 1876, a dozen thieves were apprehended in the cave at gunpoint and marched off to jail. In 1886, Thomas Newson, in his *Pen Pictures of St. Paul*, wrote, "The entrance to the cave is at present blocked by a railroad track. Its capacious chamber is filled with beer barrels. Its pearly stream has ceased to flow. It is slowly dying of civilization."

John H. Colwell and his team at the reopening of Carver's Cave, November 1913.

COURTESY OF THE MINNESOTA HISTORICAL SOCIETY.

The most dramatic reopening of Carver's Cave, and the one that most directly inspired my own efforts, occurred in 1913. John H. Colwell, president of the Mounds Park Improvement Association, was appointed to the "exploration committee" of the Association of Commerce and promptly set out to relocate Carver's Cave. To learn its whereabouts, Colwell first "talked with A. L. Larpenteur, St. Paul's oldest pioneer, about the cave." John W. Armstrong, Ramsey County surveyor, showed Colwell where to dig to reopen the cave, which had been "lost thirty years" owing to the accumulation of talus at the foot of the bluff. Shortly after, Boy Scouts were set to begin digging open the sealed cave—a role they have played up to the present day in many other Minnesota caves.

Digging was suspended during the summer of 1913, but the work was resumed near the end of the year, on October 27. No Boy Scouts proffered their help this time, so Colwell resorted to a horse-drawn scraper and a team of men. On November 5, they reopened Carver's Cave to the rays of the setting sun. Colwell's goal was to commercialize the cave, stringing lights and building a flight of stairs down the bluffs from Short Street. A gaudy electric sign on the bluffs would be visible from the downtown area, attracting even more visitors.

First Colwell had to drain the twelve-foot-deep lake inside Carver's Cave and explore it to the very end. But it was not that simple. While the lake water drained away, more was pouring into the rear of the cave from hidden sources. In addition, it was necessary to drain the water to a spot lower than the nearby railroad tracks so they would not be inundated.

On November 11, a newspaper reported a nearly fatal accident connected with the drainage project. Frank Koalaska, foreman of the men assisting Colwell, built a raft from "logs and railroad ties," intending to pole to the rear of the cave "to find out whether the water had receded enough to allow passage into the second chamber." "Owing to the danger of explosive gases, they were unable to light a torch and progress through the darkness was slow. His son, along for the ride, was knocked unconscious when the raft banged him into the low ceiling. The boy slid into the lake, and his father thought he was playing until, receiving no response, he plunged in and rescued the boy.

Strange visitors from the dark, mysterious interior of the cave began to show themselves. On November 13, a newspaper reported, "Blind crayfish have been found in Carver's cave. Several have floated from the subterranean lake or beyond from the unexplored chambers that lie past the narrow opening of the first cavern." It added that the "lake [is] about half drained."

On November 16, Blackfeet Indians, traveling from Glacier National Park in Montana aboard an excursion train, stopped at Carver's Cave for a staged photo opportunity. One of them informed his audience, "It was while hiding in the cave that the chief decided to bury his treasure to lighten his heavy burden. Placing a curse on whoever dared to touch it, he left it to return for it later." In another variation of the treasure story, the mayor of St. Paul received a strange letter stating, "A dying man had confided to him that he was a member of a band of outlaws that had hid treasure in the cave. He said that he had a chart showing the location of the treasure."

The next day Carver's Cave was given a "clean bill of health," that is, its identity was confirmed by local experts (no trivial matter even today). A crowd of two thousand people gathered, resembling "an old settlers' reunion," according to one journalist. Led by Judge Edmund W. Bazille, seven of them made up the crew of "a light skiff," armed with "a powerful electric searchlight." Viewing hundreds of names and initials carved on the cave's wall years earlier, among them their own, the judge announced that "the whole gang's here." They reminisced how the cave had been their local swimming hole—a little hard to believe considering that the water is unbearably cold even on the hottest summer day, as I found for myself. Even more dubiously, they asserted, "A large chest could be discerned under the water, at a depth of about nine feet, just inside the entrance of the second cavern. Much speculation is rife concerning the contents of this chest. It will be impossible to get at it for a week, and until that time its contents will be a mystery."

Carver's Cave seemed to be fairly awash in treasure chests. The unfortunate remark, perhaps made in jest, was reported in the papers. "The news that there is a chest deep in the cave has brought no end of curious crowds to the cave," it was said. Colwell posted a "special policeman" and placed an iron gate at the entrance to prevent effacement of the petroglyphs. The second room was soon thereafter entered.

On December 3, 1913, the following article appeared in the *St. Paul Dispatch*. It's the earliest document I've seen regarding the mysterious inner sanctum of Carver's Cave, and it's also where the story takes a new twist. After the cave was reopened by Colwell, Armstrong entered into a prolonged contest with him for control of the cave. Each party placed their own locks on the gate, delivering ultimatums to the other. Armstrong, emboldened by the "defection" of Colwell's foreman Koalaska, tried to score points by finding a new room in the cave. The clipping makes it sound as though Colwell had passed up a major discovery through sheer incompetence.

NEW INNER ROOM IN CARVER'S CAVE

"Blind" Passageway Leads Explorers to Third Great Chamber.

NEVER ENTERED BY MAN

Frank Koalaska Makes Discovery After Removing Intervening Rock—Proud of Achievement.

A third chamber in Carver's cave, one which was never known to have been entered by man, was discovered yesterday by J. H. Armstrong, county surveyor, and Frank Koalaska, foreman in charge of the work of restoring the cave.

"I do not believe that anybody else ever has entered this chamber," said Mr. Armstrong today. "There are no marks or hieroglyphics on the walls and from the way we discovered it, I believe that Mr. Koalaska and myself were the first men to ever visit it.

"About 25 feet from the orifice of the cave, there is a passageway about 8 feet wide and about 20 feet long. This was hitherto believed to be a 'blind passage-way.'"

Rock Is Removed.

In draining the water out of the cave, Mr. Koalaska and his men have been dredging dirt out of the bottom of the lake so as to make a deeper ditch. While the men were working at the end of this passageway, yesterday a huge rock was removed and a small hole was discovered leading farther into the wall. A rod ten feet long was pushed into this hole and it was found that no further wall was struck.

Koalaska telephoned to Mr. Armstrong and with picks and axes they chopped away much of the sandstone, making a hole about 3 feet high. When they had penetrated about 8 feet of the wall, another cavern, 75 feet long and 25 feet wide with a ceiling 10 feet high was discovered.

Walls Not Smoke-stained.

Taking a lantern, Armstrong and Koalaska crawled through the new tunnel and made an investigation of the cavern. No markings were discernible on the walls, which were not stained by smoke as are the other caverns. Nothing but sand drifted in with the water was on the floor of the cave. The farther end of the cave also was filled with water and sand. Mr. Armstrong believes that this leads to another cavern.

"I do not believe that anybody else has ever been in this cavern," said Mr. Armstrong. "None of the older settlers have ever heard of it and if the Indians had used it as a council chamber or dwelling place it is almost certain that we would have found some of their markings or relics. I believe that we were the first two men that ever penetrated the cave."

The water is still too high in the farther end of the main cavern to penetrate any farther into the other covern [sic] which is just beyond.

"I feel proud of discovering this new cavern," said Mr. Koalaska. "To think that thousands have passed it year after year without ever knowing of its existence, and that we have added one of the biggest attractions to Carver's cave seems worth almost any effort. We will keep right on with the work at the other chamber, and I feel that even a bigger thing will result."

On December 15, Koalaska claimed to have made an even greater find, dubbed the "4th Carver's Cave." "The innermost chamber is 50 feet high at one place," a newspaper reported. "The roots of trees growing on the bluff penetrate the walls, and there is a 20-foot fall of pure water in it. A piece of clay pottery bearing Indian hieroglyphic inscriptions was found underneath the sand on the floor of the cavern." The room was dubbed "the most beautiful of any so far discovered." After this outrageous claim, the foes became even more embittered, with Colwell setting off loud blasts of stolen dynamite in the cave, until a nearby landowner threatened "to fill the cave up" unless he desisted. Journalists, producing reams of column, began characterizing the dispute in mock-heroic martial terms, describing it as a "War for Fame," until a "truce" was declared on January 7, 1914.

Perhaps because of this bitter feud, Colwell's original plans never came to fruition. A decade later, Colwell authored a series of eight articles, "The Story of Dayton's Bluff," which appeared in the *Minneapolis Tribune* in late 1924. His articles, sandwiched in among glowing advertisements for "Lydia E. Pinkham's Vegetable Compound," make no mention of further plans to commercialize the cave. "Carver's cave," he concluded somewhat mysteriously, given all the media hoopla, "has never been officially explored."

A journalist, Charles T. Burnley, drafted a conjectural map of the alleged discoveries in 1913, and in his crude cartography Carver's Cave resembled a diagram of the stomach of a cow, with all its various chambers. But the Burnley map, silly though it was, would be the starting point for my own efforts many years later. Getting into those rooms—especially that elusive and spectacular waterfall room, at the very back, was quite a draw.

While I suspected the third and fourth rooms might be fictional—conjured into existence to discomfit Colwell—the second room (labeled C on Burnley's map), at least, seemed real enough, as I could thrust probes into it while standing at the back end of the first room (labeled A and B), just as Colwell had done. In fact, at many times during my quest for Carver's Cave, I got a sort of déjà vu feeling, encountering exactly the same sorts of conditions as the bold warriors of 1913.

Exploration fever having subsided during World War I, Carver's Cave took on a more mundane role during the Great Depression. W. C. Fuller prepared a WPA manuscript, now at the Minnesota Historical Society, in which he reported, "Mr. James Nankivell and the writer of this article made a trip to the [Carver] cave in January, 1936. There were three shacks occupied by jobless men in the entrance. A narrow passage way between two of the shacks led to the lake." James Nankivell, the "veteran spelunker," was associated with Carver's Cave in one way or another for the first half of the twentieth century. His laundry business had bankrolled Colwell's 1913 opening of the cave, and he was associated with several subsequent reopenings before his death in 1963.

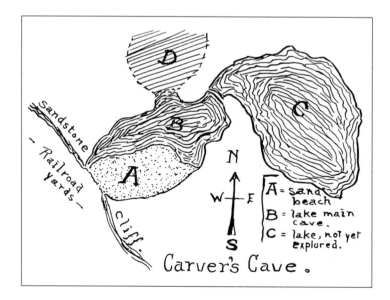

Charles T. Burnley's map of Carver's Cave from 1913, showing conjectured rooms at the back (marked C and D) that remain underwater to this day.

About 1938, Carver's Cave was reopened, again by Boy Scouts, who paddled around the lake in a boat. The cave promptly resealed itself. The journalist Will Reeves undertook the task of relocating the cave as part of the 1949 Minnesota Territorial Centennial celebration. Yet another Boy Scout troop performed the necessary drudgery. The cave had reacquired its fabled length, being supposedly seven miles long—perhaps it was a way to motivate the kids to work. The cave was opened on November 15, 1948, and soon lost again.

A St. Paul diver, Gene Betz, took over the quest in the late 1950s, establishing the Carver's Cave Foundation. He drafted legal forms, hired equipment to dig out the buried entrance, and even dickered with the Chicago, Burlington & Quincy Railroad to remove surplus soil on flatcars. Tragically, he was not able to get into the cave before dying of cancer a short time later.

On September 16, 1977, Carver's Cave was again found and opened with a backhoe as part of an official city bicentennial project, and Native Americans visited it the next day. Double steel doors were erected, which in the coming decades were themselves buried by a debris fan of material sloughing off the bluffs above.

In 1991, a California photographer, inspired by local historical novelist Steve Thayer, author of *St. Mudd*, which includes a scene involving a chase through Carver's Cave, explored the first chamber with scuba gear but claimed that his bulky air tanks prevented him from getting through the small aperture into the rooms beyond.

During the time I have known Carver's Cave, since the 1980s, the entrance has been open, but it has always seemed on the verge of sealing itself again with debris from the bluffs above. The concave morphology of the bluff immediately above the cave funnels the falling debris in front of the entrance, in the same way that an alpine couloir funnels avalanches.

My first visit to Carver's Cave came one warm summer night in 1988 under the guidance of my cave photographer friend Jason. We parked in the lot at the Carver's Cave historical marker on top of the bluffs. On the way down the bluffs to the cave, we climbed over the Sand Castle, as the locals call it. Quarrying the overlying limestone caprock left the sandstone beneath unprotected, and erosion formed a miniature badlands resembling a castle, complete with turrets and windows. A few hundred feet upriver, a tramp had set up housekeeping in the abandoned North Star Brewery cave, and we could hear his barking dogs. We made our way through the willow grove that back then surrounded the entrance to Carver's Cave. Fumbling with flashlights in the gloom, shining them over the lake inside the cave, it now seems in golden memory like one historian's description of it as "a small sylvan lake of crystal waters, resembling the Brazen Sea in Solomon's Temple."

The really distinct thing I recall from that night was seeing the scuds (tiny freshwater shrimp) in the cave lake by the light of a flashlight. Years later I mailed some of them in a test tube to a national expert, thinking they might be rare, but they turned out to be a species commonly found in cold spring waters *(Gammarus pseudolimnaeus)*. In my later investigations of the cave biota, I also found a planarian (flatworm) and a snail—forming the so-called triad that biologists have noted in springs elsewhere. The Carver's Cave ecosystem, lacking photosynthetic inputs, depends on the dead leaves that blow into the cave through the space over the steel doors to sustain these creatures.

About this time a local crank, whom we cavers referred to as Mr. W., stated, in his best perverse mode, that what is now commonly accepted as Carver's Cave really wasn't. Understanding his twisted psychology, we knew he was just trying to get a rise out of us, so we ignored him. We learned later that he was hunting for the old Indian treasure chest, which seemed entirely in character for him. Based on a map that Sweeny drew in 1867, we concluded that we had had the right cave all along; the passages tallied perfectly with the old description. Using the bedding plane seen in the sandstone at the base of the bluff just at the level of the cave ceiling as a marker, and comparing where that marker stood in old photos, it was apparent that the cave was far more capacious in the past. This suggested to me the possibility of digging down and draining the lake, as Colwell had done in 1913, thus exposing the inner sanctum, which had lain unseen for generations, like an aquatic Tutankhamen.

Trips into Carver's Cave required a wetsuit, owing to the intense chill of the springwater that supplies the lake. Even in the dog days of summer, when almost any degree of coolness should be welcome, the cave water, at 48 degrees Fahrenheit, feels painfully cold. In winter, in subzero temperatures, the water by contrast seems almost warm, and if you go down there on a cold winter's day, the cave actually seems to be blowing out steam. Unktahe's breath, I called it.

Going farther back into the lake, beyond the entrance debris, the water rapidly deepened. There was often a saliva-like skin on the surface of the cave lake, and every step stirred up bubbles, as if I were walking through a lake of soda water. The cave passage curved to the left slightly and entered total darkness. The water came up to my chin, while the cave ceiling pressed against the top of my head, and my toes could no longer touch the floor. I progressed awkwardly, twisting my head sideways. The shelving walls of the cave gurgled with every slap of the waves. Ahead, the ceiling met the water line.

To keep the water clear, I had to float on my back like a river otter so as not to stir up clouds of floor silt. I could see the opening to the second chamber below the surface and crudely felt out its dimensions with a stick. I could thrust a long pole through, so it seemed there was a room back there, but after ducking down into the chilly water, it became apparent that the hole was rather small. I considered holding my breath long enough to squeeze myself through into the room beyond (where there was hopefully an air pocket) but I didn't feel good about doing that sort of thing in such icy water when I was alone. The whole lake would have to be drained first.

My first big dig at Carver's Cave took place in 1995, during one of my infrequent respites from graduate work at the University of Connecticut. I trenched through the debris fan outside the cave, which had been accumulating since 1977, and tapped off about eighteen inches of the lake. Still the sump refused to crack. I purchased a hundred feet of flexible plastic pipe and brought it down to the cave. Entering by myself one evening at sunset, wearing a wetsuit, I wrestled with the hose, trying to fill it up with water to begin siphoning and drain the lake. The hissing of leaks in the hose, which I futilely attempted to seal with duct tape, and the way it writhed about, made it seem as if I were wrestling a live anaconda—or perhaps Unktahe himself, who sometimes appeared as a serpent in the old tales.

On another occasion something really *was* in Carver's Cave with me. I heard a splash far back in the lake that fills the cave. I assumed it was a rockfall. When I heard a second splash, I thought there must be a person back there. After the third splash, I glimpsed an irritated beaver swimming about. While I would encounter beavers even in abandoned St. Paul sewers in the coming years, this one was quite a jolt. On a subsequent visit, I found a pile of chewed sticks resting on the sand beach just inside the steel door that partially seals the cave's entrance.

My next idea was to drain the cave lake with a gasoline-powered trash pump, otherwise used to drain construction sites. I rented the pump and went down to the cave one cold night with a friend, planning to let it run all night and enter the back rooms before sunrise. But after the heavy pump was off-loaded from a pickup truck at the parking lot on the top of the bluff and we had wrestled it halfway down, a searchlight suddenly began sweeping the Sand Castle. Perhaps there had been a wild party in the park the night before, and official vigilance had increased. We had obviously been spotted, and if they were thinking we were manhandling a heavy keg down the bluffs, then maybe they were just trying to scare us off. We laid low for a while, then scrambled back up the cliffs with the heavy pump and drove off. I concluded later that even if we had gotten the pump to the cave, the short intake hose could not have reached the lake unless the pump was placed inside the cave, which would have created deadly fumes in the unventilated space—not an option.

One summer, I drove down to Carver's Cave almost every morning, stripping off my shirt and working doggedly at digging a great drainage canal outside the cave, about four feet deep. If nothing else, the dig was a great way to achieve perfect abdominal definition. A friend once told me that he had been roughed up by a teenage gang down at the cave, so I felt I had to watch my back all the time, my tools able to do double duty if the need arose. Finally, I struck a peat layer with a sulfide odor—the original wetland surface, which had been smothered by cliff debris.

After the sun peeked over the top of Dayton's Bluff, it became insufferably hot most days, and I'd switch to my other project, hunting for Dayton's Cave, where the bluff remained in the shadows somewhat longer. This cave was said to be located four hundred feet upriver from Carver's Cave, so I wheeled off the distance with an odometer, which brought me to the approximate location. I then utilized Colwell's old method of locating hidden caves—looking for seepage at the foot of the bluff and tracing it back to its source. Dayton's Cave is supposedly the Sistine Chapel of St. Paul in terms of its petroglyphs, but unlike Carver's Cave, it remains unknown to this day beneath the shifting sands of the Bruce Vento Nature Sanctuary.

I was never able to make much headway on either of these projects due to lack of help. One person can shovel only so much dirt. Here, as elsewhere, many "explorers" prefer glamorous projects with quick payoffs. Any suggestion that actual work is involved—anything more than tapping a beer keg—is often the kiss of death for a project.

Later that year, I breached the dam that had been holding back the cave water, lowering the lake about twelve inches—still not enough to expose the opening to the rooms at the back of the cave. Ominously, a large pool of drainage water began forming outside the cave and eventually spilled over a low spot and created a second pool. The first pool, triangular in shape, was the cold pool, as it was water direct from the cave, and the second was the warm pool, filled with water that had warmed up to ambient temperatures. I gave a sigh of relief when the rapidly enlarging pools finally stopped growing. In the aftermath, fishes and frogs worked their way up the drainage system and entered the cave, devouring the tasty scuds. A friend named the pools after me. It was my contribution to the geography of St. Paul.

The drainage canal required maintenance. From the moment it was dug, it began filling with cliff debris. Another problem was that visitors to Carver's Cave didn't like the canal, as it meant they got their shoes wet in getting to their favorite party spot, so they threw in logs, which blocked the stream flow, causing sediment deposition. Every few weeks I had to go down to the cave and clear out the canal.

I frequently found John "Caveman" Knowles down at Carver's Cave during these trips, where he sat with his guitar, composing music and practicing, often with other members of his band, Cave Music. Knowles played at the Turf Club ("Best Remnant of the 40's") in St. Paul for many years. The band wore caving helmets during their performances. One of his albums, *Banjo from Hell*, had a photo of a burning banjo on the cover; it was actually a banjo that he sacrificed down at the cave one night, he confided. Once when I went down to the cave, the whole band was there, complete with drums and all their other instruments. I took my shovel and cleared the drainage canals while listening to the jam session.

Within a year or so the painstakingly dug canal had vanished, and except for the pools outside the cave, I couldn't even tell it had been there. Water levels in the cave rose higher than ever, and Unktahe had the last laugh. The entrance would have to be trenched down at least six feet to expose the opening to the second cave, I estimated, and that really wasn't possible with the steel doors in place, so I finally shelved the project.

In 2005, Carver's Cave became the centerpiece of the new Bruce

Vento Nature Sanctuary, named for the congressman who had represented the East Side of St. Paul for many years. An EPA grant for
$400,000 had been secured for the twenty-seven-acre Lower Phalen
Creek Project to clean up the contaminated railroad soil. Over fifty
tons of trash were removed by volunteers. I recall seeing roll-off trash
dumpsters filled to the brim with stolen bikes that had been flung over
the bluffs during many years. The countless invasive buckthorns that
clothed the bluffs were also removed, and native trees were planted.
Within a few months the old rail yards were landscaped with a chain
of pools connected by stone-lined canals, fed by the drainage from
Carver's Cave and other cave springs. The post-1977 debris fan in front
of the cave, where I had spent whole summers and met such interesting characters, was scooped away in a few seconds by the landscapers.
After listening to the testimony of Native Americans regarding Wakan
Tipi and learning what it still meant to them today, I regretted my
whole project.

Epilogue—or prologue? With nothing to do but await the millennium, I smoked one cigar after another inside Carver's Cave. Time
ticked blank and busy on my wrist. The old millennium was fading
fast now. Just at twelve, the St. Paul Cathedral bells burst into song.
Moments later, several airplanes in succession took off from Holman
Field just across the river. (One Y2K rumor was that airplanes would
crash if they were caught in the air at midnight, so why take any
chances?) When the sky failed to rift on cue, which really didn't surprise me, I drove back home, sick to my stomach from smoking too
many cigars. Welcome to the new millennium.

A WILD GOOSE CHASE THROUGH THE SEWERS
THE HUNT FOR FOUNTAIN CAVE

Many such subterranean palaces are said to be found in Minnesota.

FREDRIKA BREMER, *HOMES OF THE NEW WORLD*

I LAY ON MY BACK in the grave-like void deep under the dry bed of a former glacial river. I dug into the loose sand beside me with a stubby trenching shovel, knowing that the ceiling above, which appeared to be little more than a jumble of loose boulders, could collapse at any time, burying me alive. The candle that I had brought along for lighting—a candle that would also warn of bad air—created flickering phantoms on the surrounding sandbanks. The sewer breathed out, then in, an unending and unpleasant alternation of sickly warm sewer air and cold river air, sucked up through the outfall. Beads of sweat covered my brow, mixing with the other grime. Welcome to K, as the old sewer map called it. An abstract point on the map that could become a deadly tomb—or perhaps a backdoor to the celebrated Fountain Cave.

Fountain Cave dates to the waning of the last ice age. The meltwater from the ice sheet to the north pooled up to form the enormous Glacial Lake Agassiz, with more water than all the present Great Lakes combined, and the spillover from this lake formed Glacial River Warren, an ancestor of the present Mississippi. A waterfall on this glacial river, thought to have been grander than Niagara Falls, chewed its way upstream from downtown St. Paul, carving the present gorge and exposing the St. Peter Sandstone. The sandstone aquifer, thus uncorked, drained laterally along preexisting rock joints. The flowing water enlarged the joints into a cave.

On July 16, 1817, on his way up the Mississippi River from Prairie du Chien to reconnoiter the Falls of St. Anthony, and again the following day on his way back down, Major Stephen H. Long, of the newly created U.S. Corps of Topographical Engineers, disembarked from his "six-oared skiff" in what is now St. Paul to explore something mysterious that perhaps the local Dakota bands had told him about.

A few miles below the confluence of the St. Peter and Mississippi rivers, there was a gap in the bluffs where a small stream, later dubbed Fountain Creek, met the great Father of Waters. Disembarking, Long and his men ascended the ravine for more than a hundred yards. They came to a natural amphitheater of snow-white sandstone whose walls, forty feet high, formed three-fourths of a circle, making it seem as though they were standing at the bottom of a gigantic pit. Swallows darted from innumerable holes in the cliffs. The creek issued from a Gothic-shaped cave entrance sixteen feet high and about as many wide.

They passed through the cave's pearly-white gates and entered a large winding hall about 150 feet long. The sharp drop in temperature came as a welcome relief on this hot summer day. At the far end of the room they crawled through a narrow passage that opened into "a most beautiful circular room" about 50 feet in diameter, where their candles flickered against the walls.

"The lonesome dark retreat," Long later wrote in his journal, was cheered by the "enlivening murmurs" of the "chrystal stream." Wading in icy-cold water up to their knees, the soldiers continued along the meandering passage, encountering more rooms of circular form and penetrating about two hundred yards before their candles went out. They halted and began to grope their way back in stygian darkness. The U.S. Army, in the persons of Major Long and his men, had just discovered what was thereupon named Fountain Cave. I share Long's opinion that Fountain Cave is "far more curious & interesting" than the nearby Carver's Cave, which he had also just visited.

Other explorers soon followed. In 1820, by the terms of Colonel Leavenworth's treaty with local Dakota bands, Fountain Cave became one of the boundary markers for the newly established Fort Snelling Military Reservation. Leavenworth was soon joined by a party of U.S. soldiers, who had just completed the first known overland traverse by white men of what is now the state of Iowa. Captain Stephen Watts Kearny, for whom Fort Kearny, Nebraska, was later named, accompanied this trek and kept a journal that was published in 1908. Leaving

Fort Snelling, returning down the Mississippi on a flatboat, Kearny stopped at Fountain Cave on July 29, 1820. He penetrated an estimated four hundred yards into the cave—twice Long's distance—noting that in some places the water was so deep that he could not touch the bottom. Kearny remarked on "the roaring of the waters from within, like distant Thunder."

Henry Rowe Schoolcraft visited Fountain Cave less than a week later, on August 2, 1820, recording his observations in his *Narrative Journal of Travels*, published the following year. Mistakenly assuming that he had found Carver's Cave, Schoolcraft was understandably puzzled by the bizarre metamorphosis the cave seemed to have undergone in the half century since Carver had explored it. Even though Fountain Cave was supposedly located in a "howling wilderness" at the time, Schoolcraft was able to comment on "the number of names found upon the walls." Nothing loath, he and Governor Cass added their own.

Schoolcraft was at this time mineralogist to Governor Lewis Cass's expedition to the headwaters of the Mississippi. He reported that Fountain Cave contained "small pebbles of so intensely black a colour as to create a pleasing contrast [with the white sand], when viewed through the medium of a clear stream." This was the first suggestion of an upstream entrance to the cave somewhere.

On July 5, 1831, in belated celebration of Independence Day, Joseph R. Brown and others brought a cannon downriver from Fort Snelling and discharged it from within the mouth of Fountain Cave, nearly collapsing the arch. They explored the cave "for a distance of nearly one mile, when they reached a precipitous water fall. Here their candle burnt out." They had another, but no means of lighting it. "After long retrogression," the writer continued, they regained "the light of the sun." Minnehaha Falls originally was known as Brown's Falls, after this man who had first reported a waterfall in Fountain Cave.

Joseph N. Nicollet, the French émigré scientist who drafted the so-called mother map of Minnesota, visited Fountain Cave in 1837. It is marked New Cave on his famous 1843 map, *Hydrographic Basin of the Upper Mississippi River*. In the report that accompanied the map, he stated that "the cave now referred to is of recent formation. The aged Sioux say that it did not exist formerly." This went beyond even the statement of Long in 1817 that "the Indians formerly living in its neighbourhood knew nothing of it till within six years past." The idea of recent formation apparently influenced the Native American name for Fountain Cave, "the new stone house," as transliterated and recorded by James Duane Doty in the official journal of Cass's expedition, not published until 1895. It may be that Nicollet's name for the cave was nothing more than an abbreviated form of the aboriginal designation.

It is more likely, however, that Fountain Cave was not newly formed at this time, merely newly opened. The cave entrance may have been concealed by collapse debris and flushed open again by Fountain Creek in 1811. But Nicollet was right on the mark when he described *how* the cave had formed. The disturbed geology of the Fountain Cave site is nowhere better described than in his posthumous papers, which were included in Schoolcraft's massive volumes on the Indian tribes of the United States. Briefly, Nicollet noted that the cave had managed to divert a surface stream (Fountain Creek) into itself, which helped to flush out and enlarge the sandstone passage. In 1932, St. Paul landscape architect George L. Nason added the finishing touch to our present understanding of the cave when he described how the ravine at the cave's entrance—"the beautiful little valley," as he lovingly called it—was "formed by the caving in of the roof at various times."

Fountain Cave inspired legends. When Canadian visitor Peter Garrioch explored it on November 16, 1837, he recorded in his diary a story he had heard about how "a soldier and two Indians formerly penetrated so far into this cave that they were never heard of any more." It was something that Garrioch himself could relate to. While deep in the cave his torch had gone out—in the best Fountain Cave tradition—and it was with some anxiety that he escaped from "the gloomy and direful abode of spectres, hobgoblins, and other sweet and tender creatures of fancy."

By the time the famous Pierre "Pig's Eye" Parrant—depicted with his pirate-style eye patch on countless beer cans in our own day—arrived on the scene, also in 1837, Fountain Cave already had a respectable written history. The 1837 treaty with the Ojibway opened for settlement the triangle of land between the St. Croix and Mississippi rivers. Parrant staked a claim at this cave because it was the nearest point to Fort Snelling that was not actually on the military reservation, thus shortening the distance for the soldiers to whom he sold whiskey. There was also a convenient river crossing to the fur-trading post at Mendota.

Parrant was a French-Canadian voyageur. He built a log cabin, often loosely described as a saloon, at the mouth of the secluded gorge so that potential customers could see it from the river. Some squatters at Camp Coldwater, near Fort Snelling, soon moved downriver to join Parrant, and cabins began to sprout like mushrooms at the cave. Much of his historical importance rests in the fact that his cabin, erected on or about June 1, 1838, was one of the first buildings on the site of what is now part of St. Paul. But the platting of the city of St. Paul in 1849 actually began in what is now the downtown area, not at Fountain Cave, so the traditional claim that Parrant founded the city is untenable.

Parrant soon lost his claim through a mortgage foreclosure of sorts, and from this transaction we learn that Fountain Cave was worth $90. His fellow settlers were evicted in 1840 when the Fort Snelling Military Reservation was resurveyed and expanded.

Strange things were reported of Fountain Cave about this time. "In later years," a 1920 newspaper clipping claimed, "children of the settlers playing within its chambers heard shrieks of the dying Indians, just as they had occurred hundreds of years before when put to death by their enemies, and saw white-robed spectres floating from chamber to chamber, it is said. Even now, after one has found his way down the tortuous sides of the river bank to the spot where a few fishermen's cottages still stand, children of the neighborhood will tell of the strange happenings that go on in the ravine at the mouth of the cave."

The pioneer Midwestern geologist David Dale Owen visited Fountain Cave in 1848. Educated in Switzerland, Owen poetically compared the snowy whiteness of this sandstone cave to a glacier cave. Owen coined the term St. Peter Sandstone based on his study of rock outcroppings along the St. Peter River—now the Minnesota River—at Fort Snelling.

The years from 1850 to 1880 were Fountain Cave's golden age. It became a fashionable Victorian cave—the first commercial cave in the Upper Midwest. A correspondent in the *Minnesota Pioneer*, December 12, 1849, described the steamboat *Dr. Franklin* loading barrels of cranberries at Fountain Cave, at the entrance to "a fairy little dell," and one of the rooms in the cave as being "more beautiful than could be made with all the wealth of Astor." The *Minnesota Democrat*, June 16, 1852, called it "a delightful Retreat," going on to say:

The celebrated cave on the river, about two miles above the American House, is one of the greatest curiosities and wonders of the West. It is one of the most beautiful spots in this beautiful Territory. On the other side of the Mississippi there is a handsome lake, full of fish—just the place for a summer resort.—Seeing this, Messrs. Tracy & Cave have rented the ground from H. M. Rice, Esq., and are now erecting there a sans souci *summer retreat, where visitors will find such refreshments as ice cream, lemonade, soda, mead, cakes, confectionary; strawberries and cream, oysters, &c., all served up in the most approved style. If you want to try your luck at fishing, the proprietors will furnish boats, rowers, lines, &c., send you over to the lake, bring you back, eat and drink you, fish you, bathe you—for they are building bathing houses—and send you back to St. Paul, all for a trifle. This establishment, if properly conducted, of which there is no doubt, is sure to prosper. We need many such in the Territory, for the accommodation of our liberal friends of the South. An omnibus will be constantly running day and evening, between St. Paul and the cave.*

Minnesota governor Alexander Ramsey himself went spelunking there in the following year, as related in Elizabeth Ellet's *Summer Rambles in the West*, published in 1853. "A rustic pavilion stands in the woods," she wrote, "where lights can be procured to enter the cave." A footbridge over the ravine also had been constructed. She compared Fountain Cave, which she called Spring Cave, to "a marble temple," and its stream to "a shower of diamonds." Fredrika Bremer, in her *Homes of the New World* (1853), described Fountain Cave as "a subterranean cavern with many passages and halls, similar probably to the celebrated Mammoth Cave of Kentucky. Many such subterranean palaces are said to be found in Minnesota." A letter to the *Boston Congregationalist*, September 19, 1856, described a visit to the cave, mentioning "the torch of birch-bark which your guide manufactures for the occasion."

The most elaborate account of Fountain Cave at this time was presented by the Galena, Illinois, journalist E. S. Seymour in his *Sketches of Minnesota, the New England of the West*, published in 1850—a version that was to be reprinted and plagiarized more than any other in the coming years. Seymour's description establishes that the cave was basically an unbranched tube, wholly in the sandstone layer. Apart from widenings of this passage, called rooms, much of the passage was crawlway. There were four rooms, successively decreasing in size upstream, and he gave the dimensions. The third room back was the only named feature in the cave, called Cascade Parlor because it contained a waterfall two feet high; he suggested planking over the stream here to make it more accessible to visitors. He did not go beyond the fourth room, having penetrated an estimated distance of sixty rods (990 feet), but stated that he could hear a second waterfall in the distance.

The oldest known graphic depiction of a Minnesota cave is a pencil and watercolor of Fountain Cave by an unknown artist, looking into the entrance, about 1850. Adolph Hoeffler, a German landscape artist, responded with a view looking out, a small woodcut in his "Sketches on the Upper Mississippi," published in *Harper's New Monthly Magazine*, July 1853.

The German landscape artist Henry Lewis painted scenes along the Mississippi River from St. Anthony to the Gulf of Mexico, and he has a separate entry for Fountain Cave in his book *Views of the Mississippi*, originally published in German in 1854. Much of his information about the cave appears to have been borrowed from others. Lewis calls the local bluffs the Cornice Cliffs, perhaps an allusion to how erosion has sculpted them into pseudoarchitectural forms. He notes, paradoxically, that as the cave diminished in size upstream, the stream inside it deepened.

Another German, the prolific geographer Johann Georg Kohl, visited Fountain Cave in 1855. "It is called Crystal Cave," he wrote, "because the small stream that bubbles out of it is clear as crystal.

Fountain Cave. Pencil and watercolor by an unknown artist, ca. 1850. This is the oldest known graphic depiction of a Minnesota cave.

COURTESY OF THE MINNESOTA HISTORICAL SOCIETY.

The entrance is a true painter's dream." But "sand has other uses," he continued mundanely, "and a glass factory will soon be built here." "The cave twists deep underground," he added. "In its depths can be heard a hissing and boiling as in a kettle, said to come from subterranean falls of the stream that exits the cave."

In 1857, during the fever of real estate speculation that smote early St. Paul, the present Grotto Street was platted. It was said to have been named after Fountain Cave, because if the street were extended it would supposedly strike the river at the cave. In fact, it would miss by a half mile. A plan by the Junior Pioneer Association of St. Paul to construct a "fine boulevard approach" to the site in 1920 would have been more deserving of the name, but nothing came of it.

An article in the *Knickerbocker*, or *New-York Monthly Magazine*, October 1857, offers a more jaundiced view of the commercial heyday of Fountain Cave:

In its primitive simplicity it was doubtless a beautiful place, opening as it does in a deep glen near the Mississippi, and surrounded with luxuriant verdure. But

Exterior and interior
views of Fountain Cave
from the 1870s.

PHOTOGRAPH OF CAVE
INTERIOR BY WILLIAM
HENRY ILLINGWORTH;
PHOTOGRAPH OF CAVE
EXTERIOR BY JOHN
CARBUTT. COURTESY OF THE
MINNESOTA HISTORICAL
SOCIETY.

that rapacity which exhibits itself in all the walks of life, has made its appearance
here; and the spot, being "private property," now rejoices in a little seven-by-nine
shanty, where, "for a consideration," you may obtain a "guide" and a tallow
candle, and upon returning from your explorations, for another "consideration"
some fiery brandy and a rank segar. Aside from that, the place has lost much of
its old charm, for during the summer months it is thronged with visitors daily; the
paths leading to it are dusty and travel-worn, and the soft, white sand-stone walls
are marred all over with the names of the Joneses and Browns who have honored
"the Cave" in the "grand rounds." Why is it, by-the-way, that so many Americans
seem to think it an imperative duty when they visit a place of any note, to leave
behind them, for the edification of after-comers, through the instrumentality of
the omnipresent jack-knife, their common-place names, and in the most staring
capitals possible?

By the end of the American Civil War, the less desirable tourist trappings of Fountain Cave had melted away. A Danish visitor, Robert Watt, reported in 1871, "Fortunately nothing has been done in the way of artificial embellishment, no obtrusive guide presents himself

for service, and a person can enjoy peacefully and quietly the sight of this mysterious opening in the earth." He thought that he might "penetrate a couple of miles beneath the surface either by canoe or by picking his way along the narrow white sand edges of the stream." Most photographs of Fountain Cave are stereoscopic souvenir views from about this time. Those by William H. Illingworth are classics, giving you a good feel for the roominess of the original cave.

A tourist guidebook by James Davenport, published in 1872, reveals that directions to Fountain Cave from downtown St. Paul were surprisingly uncomplicated, "the route being out Fort Street to the outskirts of the city, and then by turning to the left down to the river bank." In 1879, Fountain Cave was featured in *Tourists' Guide to the Health and Pleasure Resorts of the Golden Northwest*, published by the Milwaukee Road; one of the engravings shows elegantly dressed cave visitors, complete with top hats and walking sticks. In 1881, William H. Dunne published *The Picturesque St. Croix and Other Northwest Sketches Illustrated*, one of the last travel guides to suggest a trip into Fountain Cave. An accompanying engraving, depicting boats inside the cave, was actually a purloined depiction of the Cave of the Dark Waters in the Wisconsin Dells.

In 1887, Captain Willard Glazier published *Down the Great River*, in which he attempted to redefine the true source of the Mississippi in his own favor—Lake Glazier—and his book contains a rather late reference to the popularity of Fountain Cave, "This cave is a favorite resort in the summer." In Glazier's secondhand account, the two-foot waterfall inside the cave had mysteriously grown to a height of fifteen feet.

As the years rolled past, local memory of Fountain Cave grew very hazy, approaching sheer fantasy. In 1945, for example, in his "Forgotten Facts about St. Paul" column for the *St. Paul Shopper*, Mark Fitzpatrick wrote: "In early times one entering the grotesque lunar shape mouth of the cave beheld a magic island with a natural fountain playing dreamingly with its hazy spray and misty prismatic rays. On all sides of the main entrance were labyrinth chambers deep in size and overhung with drooping stalagmites of a unique conception." Beautiful imagery to be sure, but never mind that stalagmites grow from the floor, not the ceiling.

In 1960, the original, natural entrance to Fountain Cave, the one used by so many famous explorers, was sealed by the highway department. The construction of Shepard Road along the river bluffs, begun years earlier, was intended to create a fast route downtown from the Minneapolis–St. Paul Airport. Unfortunately, the cave ravine lay directly in the path of the new highway. Moreover, the engineers were looking for a good place to dump "25,000 [cubic] yards of dirt." Anticipating the grading crews, Mayor Joseph Dillon of St. Paul and the city engineer, the eponymous George M. Shepard, went searching for the cave on June 16, 1959. "Historic Saloon Eludes Officials" was the *Pioneer Press* headline the next day. "The place was hidden deep behind wild trees, grape vines, nettles, old tires, rotting boards and myriad wild mosquitoes.... Dillon and Shepard could find no sign of that cave," it was reported. "Shepard said that quite likely falling rock, sand and debris have hidden the mouth."

Since I wanted to explore Fountain Cave, I began to wonder whether there was another entrance. In 1880, the newly formed Chicago, St. Paul, Minneapolis, and Omaha Railroad (called the Omaha) began building a roundhouse and repair shops in the triangle of land bounded by Randolph, Drake, and the river. The oldest and only complete map of Fountain Cave known to exist dates to the 1880s and shows this facility already in place. For convenience I'll refer to this as the A-41 map, in keeping with the stamp on it. The map was a serendipitous find at St. Paul Public Works while I was trolling for other subterranean information, and it was to play a big role in my hunt for the cave. Judging from the A-41 map, Fountain Cave is the longest (but not the largest, in terms of volume) natural sandstone cave in Minnesota, about 1,100 feet, and this alone made the cave a prize worthy of exploration.

The pioneer Minnesota geologist Newton Horace Winchell stated in 1878, "The water that issues at Fountain Cave, St. Paul, is that of a creek which disappears in the ground about half a mile distant." Winchell provided the key to understanding the A-41 map. At the top of the map, Fountain Creek, flowing on the surface, is shown entering a sinkhole near the Omaha Railroad shops. It flows through the cave as a dashed line and reemerges in the ravine, flowing to the Mississippi. Other early maps indicated that the ultimate source of Fountain Creek was the old Fort Road wetlands to the west, long since paved over.

I was able to pinpoint the exact location of the sinkhole using old real estate plats. In 1923, however, a railroad spur servicing the Ford Motor Company plant in Highland Park was built right over the spot, meaning that the "upper entrance" to the cave, if ever humanly enterable, was now sealed. Once the Fort Road wetlands and the sinkhole were built over, the water supply to the cave was cut off, and cliff debris began to accumulate at its entrance—debris that ordinarily would have been flushed away by the cave stream. This explains why Dillon and Shepard "could find no sign of that cave" in 1959.

In 1920, a newspaper reported that Fountain Cave "is surrounded by desolation and is used as a part of the sewage system of the Omaha railroad shops." While unfortunate for the cave, and making it less of a prize to explore, it suggested that I might be able to enter the cave through the sewer system somewhere.

The Minnesota Historical Society had erected a historical marker for Fountain Cave, a sort of tombstone, in 1963. The bronze plaque stated, in raised, gilded lettering, that Fountain Creek joined the Mississippi "downstream from this marker." The author of this plaque didn't realize what a wild goose chase his wording was going to inspire a generation later. Going to the spot, I saw an RCP (reinforced concrete pipe) forty-two inches in diameter projecting from the weed-covered embankment. Could this somehow be the same cave drainage water that Major Long had seen, nearly two centuries earlier?

I climbed into the pipe and began to trace the water on hands and knees. Following the old course of Fountain Creek, the pipe snaked its way through the buried ravine toward the cave, and my hopes began to rise. There was a strong petroleum odor in the pipe, which the Minnesota Pollution Control Agency attributes to massive spills at the nearby former Clark Oil tank farm in the 1960s. Cars roared along the highway overhead, kerplunking the manhole lids as they passed. After crawling four hundred feet through the pipe, it suddenly opened into a Gothic-shaped space in the sandstone. The air was close and fetid. High and wide enough to stand in, this place was much frequented by raccoons, judging from the abundant scats.

By now the rumble of cars had died away and nothing could be heard but the dripping of water. I pointed my flashlight into the darkness and continued to follow the silver thread of water, hoping it would lead me to Fountain Cave. At intervals, I saw niches in the smoke-blackened walls, looking as though they were meant to hold candles. Several hundred feet later, the narrow passage expanded into an oval room in the sandrock. Was this Fountain Cave, I wondered?

I soon realized that the Gothic space was not Fountain Cave but a large, antique sewer very close to where the cave ought to be. In map view, this sewer was Y-shaped, with a thousand feet of passages, and I examined its remotest recesses like a good proctologist. It was dubbed the Omaha tunnel in a surveyor's field book, so that's the name I adopted for it. I found no big, obvious windows into the cave proper.

A railroad engineer named Strother prepared a map of the Omaha tunnel in 1939, identifying various features with the letters of the alphabet. The most unusual place in the tunnel was labeled K on his map. For a while, I felt sure that this irregular void, accessed via a short crawlway from the main tunnel, was natural in origin. The void had a lot of loose, dry sand, which I naively interpreted as a deposit of Glacial River Warren at the time, because it appeared to exhibit cross-bedding and other classic sedimentary features, which I had just learned about in my geology courses. I spent a lot of time digging about in that nasty hole, to no avail.

The possibility of finding an open connection to Fountain Cave from the sewer not panning out, I minutely examined the unlined bedrock walls of the sewer tunnel for natural weaknesses—rock joints—where perhaps I could make some headway if I chose to dig. But calculating from known elevation benchmarks, the elevation of river level, the thickness of various rock layers, and the known size of the cave, I found it hard to place the cave either above, below, or next to the Omaha tunnel. There just didn't seem to be enough space to fit the cave into the picture.

For prospective trips into the Omaha tunnel, I usually checked the Corps of Engineers Web site to access real-time data on the current river level. Knowing the elevation of the outfall, I could tell whether it would be flooded with river water, thus avoiding a wasted trip. The Omaha tunnel was completely inaccessible in springtime due to flooding, so I never even bothered at that time of year.

One day, going through the Omaha tunnel with some friends, I had a double scare. Despite the usual precautions with regard to the weather, I misjudged the situation, and it began to rain outside. The ominous sound of rushing water began to thunder through the tunnel even before the torrent hit us. We had to exit at once. In our haste to escape, we used an exit new to us, marked "Special Manhole No. 24" on the sewer maps. When we threw the lid up, we found ourselves in the gravel lot of the overlying grain elevator. Before we could get our bearings, a truck came to a sudden stop in front of us. The bewildered driver stared at us and asked if we were OK. We said yes and tried to joke it off. The gal with us on that trip received such a shock that she never came back.

Another point on Strother's map, labeled D, was a manhole that appeared to give direct access to Fountain Cave. Manhole D, it turned out, was quite historic. The travel writer Dunne spoke of "the shaft of the railroad company" during his "gymnastic" exploration of Fountain Cave in 1880. It dawned on me that this was the shaft through which sewage had entered the cave from the Omaha shops. And once sewage began flowing through the cave, after 1880, the place lost its pristine, fashionable air. This is when the top-hatted Victorian tourism ended and the cave's dark ages began.

Manhole D, unfortunately, was located smack-dab in a high-security railroad loading zone. A chain-link fence, laced with barbed wire, surrounded it. Enlisting the help of my friends at Public Works, who brought along a metal detector and some official access, we found that Manhole D had been paved over. It was an enormous disappointment; we were prepared to enter the great cave that very day.

On Strother's map, where all the tunnel features were labeled with letters, the search for Fountain Cave became a sort of subterranean algebra game. Walking through the Omaha tunnel years later, I found several places where people had attempted to dig through the walls of the sewer and left their initials or some other message. None of the graffiti had been there during our project in the early 1990s. So the old game was still in play! Fountain Cave retains its secrets, despite the many urban explorers who followed in our footsteps.

PART II

BURIED RIVERS

THE URBAN NILE
THE SUBTERRANEAN STREAMS
OF ST. PAUL

*Going up that river was like travelling back to the earliest begin-
nings of the world.*

JOSEPH CONRAD, *HEART OF DARKNESS*

INDUSTRIAL MESOPOTAMIA:
THE TROUT BROOK—PHALEN CREEK SYSTEM

While strolling along the St. Paul waterfront in the late 1980s, I came
across a manhole lid on which the words "Trout Brook" had been
crudely spray-painted in fluorescent orange letters. Scanning the riverbanks below, I spied a cavernous sewer outfall, more than garage-
sized, disgorging a multihued stream of water to the Mississippi River.
I scrambled down for a closer look.

The outgoing stream had the appearance of strong green tea, swirling in arabesques where it met the powerful brown river current. A
meaty sulfide aroma wafted over the water to my nostrils. An unlikely
place for trout, I remember thinking. Many people would have been
revolted by this spectacle, but I was strangely fascinated. Here was a
stream flowing through the very heart of St. Paul, and I had never seen
it before. Psychologically speaking, it was as remote as one of Joseph
Conrad's literary rivers. Poking a convenient stick into the water at the
outfall to check its depth, I resolved to get a flashlight and do a bit of
exploring. This was one of my earliest ventures into the urban underworld. Little did I realize at the time that it would also be a voyage into
St. Paul's past and times even more remote. Reaching the headwater
lakes of the Trout Brook system was analogous, in a very minor way,
to the Victorian explorers reaching the lakes at the headwaters of the
Nile. This was a sort of subterranean Nile, with many little Egyptian
motifs in the way of sewer architecture to spur interest.

Surface streams get buried and "lost" for a variety of reasons. Sometimes a stream is deliberately hidden to cover what has become an eyesore or channeled to alleviate flooding. Sometimes the land on which the stream flows is needed for other purposes. Or sometimes, as in the case of Trout Brook, the adjacent street grade just grew upward around it over the years.

In a very real sense, of course, the former surface streams are not lost since they are still flowing as lustily as ever. Indeed, it would take a very expensive feat of engineering to get rid of them completely. To truly eliminate a stream you have to fill the drainage basin, eliminating the topographic focus of the drainage, which could involve shifting many cubic miles of soil.

Some cavers think you can tell the difference between a boring old storm drain and a more exciting true underground stream by some special markings on the manhole lid, but the obscure art of interpreting the heraldry of manhole lids, alas, leaves much to be desired. What you really need is some good solid historical research, and tracing the pedigree of a pipe can be difficult.

One of the most salient topographic features of downtown St. Paul is the mile-wide gap in the white crescent of sandstone cliffs along the Mississippi River. City Hall stands on a full thickness of bedrock, but the sandstone thins out where Kellogg Boulevard goes downhill, vanishing from sight altogether before reappearing in all its glory at Dayton's Bluff. Lowertown occupies the resulting gap.

Geologists surmised that this gap was carved by a preglacial precursor of the Mississippi, flowing down from the north. The Mississippi has changed course several times in the past million years or so and has only lately carved its present gorge. The topographic depression left by a precursor became the focus of postglacial drainage. Phalen Creek now runs through the gap, together with its largest tributary, Trout Brook.

The Mississippi floodplain is a muddy place and was even more so before engineers tamed the river. Imagine a stream of water from the surrounding uplands directed down on top of all that mud, and you get an idea of what the early Trout Brook–Phalen Creek delta was like. No wonder it was described as "a bottomless bog" in Josiah B. Chaney's classic *Early Bridges and Changes of the Land and Water Surface in the City of St. Paul*. Published in 1908, this book is a wonderful reference for descriptions of the vanished streams and lakes of old St. Paul.

Just trying to throw a road across this wetland was a Herculean task, as may be gleaned from the old city council minutes. Grading East Seventh Street across the morass was first proposed in 1860, but it wasn't until 1873 that the job actually got done. Bridging the streams required expensive stone-arch culverts; the culvert for Phalen Creek cost twice as much as that for the smaller Trout Brook. These streams are represented in early, but now defunct, street names: Culvert Street was named after Phalen Creek, Brook Street after Trout Brook, and Canal Street for the combined stream below the confluence.

But something had to be done about the Lowertown wetland as a whole. In one of the most dramatic cut-and-fill jobs in municipal history, Baptist Hill, a mound of glacial debris fifty feet high, formerly located where Mears Park is today, was carted eastward after the Civil War under the direction of city engineer David L. Curtice and dumped into the wetland. In the process, Phalen Creek and Trout Brook were left at their original, lower level—already well on their way to becoming subterranean.

While the Trout Brook–Phalen Creek valley was a curse to roads, it was a blessing for the railroads. On June 26, 1862, the steamboat *Key City* unloaded the first locomotive in Minnesota, the *William Crooks*, at St. Paul. How would you get this locomotive out of the deep river gorge and to the town of St. Anthony, its destination? Perhaps hoist it up the sheer eighty-foot cliffs with a crane? Such heroic remedies proved unnecessary because of the stream's gap in the sandstone bluffs. The train steamed up through the gap and rolled into St. Anthony, ten miles away, less than half an hour later.

Railroads have so dominated this valley ever since that the land between Phalen Creek and Trout Brook came to be known as Railroad Island, a sort of industrial Mesopotamia. Three roundhouses were built in the valley, and a large railroad machine shop existed where the Pennsylvania Avenue exit of Interstate 35E is now located. So consistently did the railroad engineers favor the old streambeds to lay their tracks, to achieve the lowest possible gradient (rerouting the streams to tunnels below) that one caver joked that "Soo Line" was all but synonymous with "sewer line."

Moreover, at a place called Westminster Junction you will find tunnels for the trains themselves. The Westminster tunnel, with the date of 1885 carved into its keystone arch, is the classic railway tunnel of the Twin Cities, 1,100 feet long. Shady characters often hung around in these railroad tunnels, so I actually felt much safer walking through the storm drains under the Trout Brook valley rather than along the tracks.

In 1893, city engineer George Wilson undertook the task of formally burying the lower reaches of the two streams, though several short segments had been roofed over years earlier. It was officially dubbed the Canal Street sewer. We learn that the supposedly bottomless bog actually did have a bottom: "The length of piles below cut-off varied from 15 to 28 ft., at which point a hard gravel bed is struck." With commendable thoroughness, the location of every one of those piles is noted in the old surveyor's leather-bound field books, stored in the Public Works vaults to this day.

Wilson's magnum opus still exists and is easily distinguished by its innovative steel-beam ceiling, Platteville Limestone rubble-masonry walls, and granite floor. The most endearing details by far are the "gargoyles"—curiously wrought iron spouts that vomit water into the tunnel. Wilson was so proud of his handiwork that in 1894 he published an article about it in *Engineering News*, and one of the accompanying figures became incorporated into sewer textbooks (though at least one of the textbooks misattributes it to Minneapolis). Wilson's annual reports for these years contain classic photos of the project.

Wilson's tunnels are large enough to drive a truck through, and something like that actually happened in August 1983. During a heavy rainstorm, Lowertown flooded and a T-Bird was swept into the open

Two views of the junction point for the Trout Brook and Phalen Creek sewers in St. Paul. From the 1894 annual report of the Saint Paul City Engineer's Office.

channel segment along East Fourth Street. The car ended up in the Mississippi, where for some days after gawkers could get a glimpse of it resting peacefully on the bottom.

The Canal Street sewer, usually filled with waist-deep, stagnant water, is essentially a roofed-over bayou of the Mississippi, filled with the river's backwater. Walking upstream from the river wearing a poor man's wetsuit (street clothes), I could easily tell where the storm drainage met the actual river water by where my feet got tangled in the antler-pronged driftwood that spun about in the gloom. This was a convergence zone in the sewers—a place where two bodies of water, with different temperatures, mingled together, creating tunnel fogs.

By the time I came to explore it, the Canal Street sewer, already a century old, was showing its age. The underlying mud had pushed up the granite floor into slippery "whalebacks" that later split open, allowing the mud to wash out, leaving large, eroded cavities in the floor. At other places, especially under leaks in the tunnel ceiling, there were petrified sandbars, where lime minerals dissolved from the concrete above had been redeposited by the dripping water onto loose sediments, cementing them firmly together into a solid, durable mass.

Phalen Creek was named after Edward Phelan, whom some call St. Paul's first murderer. Discharged from Fort Snelling, the former soldier built a cabin near downtown St. Paul, circa 1840. We first

read of Phalen Creek in an early deed, dated September 2, 1844, from Edward Phelan to William Dugas, of "160 acres on Faylin's Creek and Falls." Dugas built St. Paul's first sawmill here. The creek also went by other names back then. On one of the earliest maps of St. Paul, it is shown as McCloud Creek. In 1852, William Gates Le Duc, later to become President Hayes's commissioner of agriculture, provided yet another name when he wrote, "At the mouth of Mill Creek, pike from one foot to eighteen inches long may be taken by the hook and line at any favorable time." People still fish at the gaping Paleolithic sewer outfall here—but not for pike.

There was good reason to call it Mill Creek. The geologist Newton Horace Winchell gave a list of the mills on Phalen Creek in 1877, adding that "since the railroads have encroached on the natural course of Phalen's creek and the city water works have diminished its volume, some of them have been abandoned." Winchell's remark refers to St. Paul's first waterworks, built by Charles Gilfillan, which drew water from Lake Phalen through a sixteen-inch pipe. Originally, the plan had been to draw water from the creek itself, but the mill owners objected.

Above the junction with Trout Brook, Phalen Creek flowed through Swede Hollow. This deep ravine protected residents from the blasts of winter and kept them cool in summer. Originally taking its name from the Swedes, the hollow became a focal point for subsequent immigrant groups as well, such as Irish, Italians, Poles, and finally Mexicans. Many of them worked for the St. Paul & Duluth Railroad, whose tracks ran alongside the ravine. Once they learned English, they usually left the hollow for other neighborhoods.

Living conditions there were often unsanitary, with outhouses built on stilts over Phalen Creek. Nels M. Hokanson, a former resident of Swede Hollow, recalled Wilson's tunnel from his childhood: "Residents instituted cleanup days.... Women and boys raked the garbage-strewn alleys. Later ... the boys waded in the creek to keep the mass of refuse in the center until it disappeared in the tunnel. When the day was over, Swede Hollow was neater and cleaner than it had been in a long time." But apparently not clean enough from the City's standpoint. In 1956, the St. Paul Health Department condemned the community, ordering the residents to vacate, after which the fire department torched the hollow in a mighty conflagration. There was little left to see afterward except for the entrances to the abandoned

Drewery Caves, formerly used for storing ale and porter. Even those were sealed in 1964, after some tragic cave deaths.

By this time, however, the Phalen Creek tunnel had been extended under Swede Hollow itself. Here there was a side branch, the eighty-four-inch Tar Pipe, a steel culvert internally coated with bitumen. This tenebrous tunnel lining seemed to suck up light like a black sponge whenever I explored it, and someone once called it the "stealth tunnel" for this reason. After paralleling the main trunk for a while, the pipe struck out on its own, zigzagging north and heading under Edgerton Street, where there were some strange sewer chambers, suggestive of the boiler room of the *Titanic*.

Above Swede Hollow and upstream from the historical Hamm's (and later Stroh's) Brewery, now vacant, through which it flowed, Phalen Creek was encased in what seemed to me the finest example under the Twin Cities of a large circular brick sewer. Upstream from this point, according to all the old maps, Phalen Creek should connect with Lake Phalen, where it originated. That's not what I found. At Ocean Street, the Phalen Creek tunnel ended abruptly and unexpectedly at a brick wall.

This hydrological enigma bothered me. If most of the water seen flowing through the Phalen Creek tunnel is just local street runoff, then where did Lake Phalen drain to? There were large inlets at the south end of the lake, taking water, but the sewer maps I had did not provide much insight about where it was all going. What had happened to the *real* Phalen Creek? I found the surprising answer to this question while investigating the Trout Brook tunnel.

The aforementioned Edward Phelan, lately acquitted of murder only for lack of evidence, and wanting to get out of town, sold his claim, which included Phalen Creek and also one of its hitherto unnamed tributaries, to Edmund Rice for $400 in gold. Rice built a mansion, called Trout Brook, on the tributary, which gave the stream its name. Back then, the stream was not only good enough to support trout, it was good enough to drink. In 1953 a descendant of Rice, Maria Dawson, in her *Letter about Trout Brook*, wrote:

The house was situated on a hill in the center of a forty-five acre tract ... This land was bounded on the west by Mississippi Street, on the north by York Street, on the east by the Arlington Hill district and on the south were railroad tracks. By damming the brook Father made an artificial lake covering nearly an acre, on the shore of which was a boat house.... Bonfires would be built around the lake and it was all very beautiful.... A plum orchard near the brook was a perfect fairy land in the spring when in blossom.... In order to have running water in the house, we had an enormous cistern in the cellar which was kept filled with water hauled from the lake. This was pumped up to the attic filling a tank and from there it was distributed through the house by pipes.

The Northern Pacific Railroad purchased the Trout Brook mansion in 1883 and razed it to make way for its tracks.

In the 1920s, a new city engineer appeared on the scene, George Shepard (in whose honor Shepard Road was later named). Shepard was one of the great architects of underground St. Paul, ranking right up there with Joseph Sewall, father of the Fort Road Labyrinth (see "A Lonely Day under the Mortuary"). In 1926–27, Shepard extended the Trout Brook tunnel quite some distance. Later, the tunnel was extended again, running under Maryland Avenue all the way to Como Lake, reducing the original Trout Brook, which today plunges underground near Arlington and Jackson, to a mere side passage. Shepard's tunnel is ferroconcrete horseshoe over much of its length, meaning that it is a steel-reinforced concrete tunnel with a horseshoe-shaped cross section. Its most distinctive features are the square access shafts (cleanouts) that jut from the ground like the conning towers of a land-going submarine. You can see the cleanouts today along the various railroad tracks that thread the Trout Brook valley.

During especially heavy rains, Lowertown used to flood very badly. The problem was focused at the meeting of the waters, the junction of Trout Brook with Phalen Creek. Water couldn't get through the tunnels fast enough and backed up into the adjacent streets. I got a sense of the power of these floods when, strolling through these tunnels in dry weather—tunnels large enough to drive a truck through—I saw ragged bits of trash snagged on projections near the ceiling. To further alleviate flooding in Lowertown, the decision was made in the 1980s to decouple Trout Brook from the Phalen Creek tunnel, giving them separate outfalls, thus effectively doubling the discharge capacity of the system.

The new Trout Brook outfall, a double-box section, is located five hundred feet upriver from the old Canal Street outfall. The resulting tunnel is too deep to wade through and too long to swim through. At one point the crown of the tunnel is just inches from the water, too close to get a boat through. I used a wetsuit and flippers during one trip, paddling on my back like a river otter. After a thousand feet, it connected to the old Trout Brook tunnel by a steep flume segment, and I could walk the remaining five miles to Como Lake.

A six-hour wetsuit trip into the flooded Trout Brook tunnel that I took with some friends was particularly scary. To plan the trip, I laid out the photocopied 1:100 sewer maps in my house, and they filled the whole living room. Arriving down at the Mississippi for the trip, we put on wetsuits and paddled up the pipe, braving the occasional wake sent churning up the tunnel from the outside by passing boats. After getting past the deep tunnel water to a place where we could finally walk, we removed our wetsuits to avoid overheating. We explored the foggy junction rooms where hot and cold waters mix and saw new forms of tunnel life. We explored the subterranean Spaghetti Junction, a veritable tangle of tunnels not all that far from the real traffic tangle of that name in downtown St. Paul. After gratifying our curiosity, we returned to the deep water, put our wetsuits back on, and began swimming out. But something was amiss. We noticed right away that our heads scraped against the tunnel ceiling much more than on the way in. The pipe was filling up! We got out of there as fast as possible, and indeed it was raining as we emerged from the outfall.

At several places, before they were sealed off, there used to be little holes where I could exit from Trout Brook to rest a bit or eat lunch among the cattails on the banks of a storm water detention pond. Crayfish, frogs, and turtles entered the sewers at these points along with human explorers. One such place was the now-vanished Williams Hill, one of the legendary seven hills of St. Paul, where I pondered the story of the hermit Chester who lived inside the hill for fifteen years. Newspaper columnist Don Boxmeyer told the story very feelingly in a piece for the *Pioneer Press* (May 26, 2001). Chester lived in the abandoned cistern of a demolished rooming house known as Swede Castle, which once sat atop the hill, but the hill was gradually nibbled away for its sand and gravel, and the elderly hermit, a Korean War veteran, was eventually sent to the hospital.

The construction of the Great Northern sewer, a tributary of the Trout Brook tunnel, through the heart of Williams Hill, was an epic story. An 1889 newspaper article by Frederic N. Van Duzee, "Underground Highway," referred to "St. Paul's Monster Sewer," nine feet in diameter. The "monster tube" was built of "Chaska brick" and ran for

1.5 miles, tunneling through hills and under Oakland Cemetery. At the time it was constructed it was probably St. Paul's largest sewer; it predated Wilson's masterwork, to which it is now merely a tributary. Problems with quicksand and underground springs are described in the article, and "the dirt machine," an excavator, is pictured. Putting the best face on the matter, Van Duzee claimed that all the water spurting into the tunnel—suggestive of shoddy construction and known to modern engineers as I/I (infiltration and inflow)—helped to cleanse the great bore. "A great city is like a sieve," he blustered.

I once paid a visit to the "monster tube," which was located at the top of a very steep, slippery sewer slide. True to its name, the tunnel was large, constructed of limestone rubble-masonry walls with a floor of granite pavers. Every once and a while a train would thunder overhead, and since the tunnel ran right under the tracks it would sound like a flood of water approaching. As if that wasn't unnerving enough, the tunnel would then fill up with gagging diesel fumes. I recall a light-hearted moment in the monster tube when a video-toting friend slid down the Devil's Slide that had been so much trouble getting up. With cameras rolling, he cut loose and went rocketing down the steep passage, hydroplaning on the storm water but shredding his waders in the process.

Upstream from where the monster tube entered, there was a series of jogs and rapids in the Trout Brook system, eventually leading to a well-lit room that was barred from the outside world like a jail cell. Upstream from this point, the passage changed from a square to a horseshoe shape and got very dark and boring for a great distance. I found this stretch unusual in being virtually devoid of sandbars, or anything else for that matter. Shepard had calculated his flushing gradients to the last decimal.

The next feature of interest was the small waterfall where Trout Brook, the surface stream, entered the tunnel, some distance after leaving its headwaters at Lake McCarron, and received additional wastewater from the city water utility. There was a fast-food restaurant here, a favorite waypoint because I could grab a bite to eat before heading down the hatch again and continuing my journey.

A thousand feet or so upstream from the active Trout Brook inlet there was a parallel but defunct Trout Brook inlet, a dead-end passage hundreds of feet long but only five feet high. The passage was filled with peculiar sediments, like a giant clogged artery. Originally built under a wetland, the overlying mud had oozed through the gaps between the tunnel segments over the years, forming red mud sta-lactites and filling the passage with red, gooey sediments that oozed upward into the waist-deep water with every footstep, exactly like the amoebal blobs inside lava lamps. The air was oppressively warm and stagnant, a bad sign.

The main trunk line turned west and ran under Maryland Avenue toward Como Lake. Near Loeb Lake, there was a wall blocking further advance. Water poured from an eighteen-inch opening at the base of the wall. I lay down on my back, held my breath, and squeezed through the aperture, with the filthy tunnel water pouring over my face. Some-times a dam of sticks, dead leaves, and trash built up behind the con-striction, and it had to be painstakingly cleared by reaching through the opening and pulling the bits and pieces out before I could get through. Finally, I came to Como Lake. When conditions were favor-able, after exiting the tunnel I could catch a glimpse of the whirlpool, just offshore, marking the submerged "bathtub drain" for the lake.

Based on topographic maps, Como Lake has an elevation of 882 feet above sea level (ASL), whereas the pool elevation of the Missis-sippi River where the water discharges is 687 feet ASL. That's a descent of 195 feet in five miles, as the bat flies, the longest "door-to-door" tunnel trip in the Twin Cities. In later years a steel-bar grating was built over the Como inlet, preventing access.

I surmised that when Como Lake was plugged into the original Trout Brook watershed, a new difficulty must have been created: a much greater volume of water was channeled into Lowertown during rainstorms. To compensate, Lake Phalen was unplugged from its natu-ral watershed by walling off the old tunnel at Ocean Street, and Phalen Creek was made to drain into a wholly new tunnel, the Belt Line tunnel, which runs mostly under Johnson Parkway and discharges to the Mississippi River near the former St. Paul Fish Hatchery.

The Belt Line tunnel, constructed in the 1920s to drain the East Side, is about four miles long. It was named after the Twin City Belt Railway, an interurban line. I found a way into the tunnel and walked its length, exploring the various branches along the way. There was a lengthy horseshoe-shaped side passage to Beaver Lake, in the north-eastern corner of St. Paul, for example, badly decayed when I saw it years ago. A crack ran the whole length of the tunnel at shoulder height, and reddish groundwater continually oozed from this wound into the tunnel. Ames Creek, which flowed on the surface until vanishing into a storm sewer in Sackett Memorial Park (named after the tragically slain police officer), near Phalen Shopping Center, formed another branch.

The design discharge for the Belt Line tunnel is 2,000 cubic feet per second (cfs), which is amazing when you consider that the Mississippi River itself averages 6,000 cfs at Minneapolis. At the downstream end of the Belt Line there was a steep flume, with a 10 percent gradient, and at the bottom of that there was a blow-off manhole for storm water, which resembled a concrete volcano. That's exactly what happened after one horrific rainstorm years ago—I found the manhole lid had been blown off by the force of the water, which must have been under very high pressure indeed with such a steep gradient.

Below the flume, the Belt Line continued under what were then the fish hatchery grounds. Touring the tunnel late one night with a large exploratory herd, not my usual practice, I saw fish from the hatchery making good their escape into the storm drain and ultimately the river. As we approached the river itself, the water got deeper, and unfortunately we discovered, from all the panicky noises, that we had a non-swimmer among us. It was difficult to coax this fearful lad through the final stretch of tunnel. After exiting to the river, we scrambled up the wooden bargeboards along the docks, finding ourselves in a salt yard and swept by bright searchlights. We were eager to "surrender" until we realized that it was just a barge coming up the river and shining its light around looking for landmarks.

THE DIVERTING STORY OF CASCADE CREEK

Several miles away from the Trout Brook–Phalen Creek system, and unrelated to it in any way, St. Paul had another, very different, subterranean stream. Modern maps no longer show Cascade Creek, which was located in the West Seventh Street neighborhood. One of the few historical maps that does is the one accompanying Winchell's 1877 report, *The Geology of Ramsey County*. Originating in a wetland near what is today Cretin–Derham Hall, the stream flowed eastward and down the ravine now occupied by Ayd Mill Road, continued along the line of Jefferson Avenue, and joined the Mississippi River near the foot of Western Avenue.

In the early days, Cascade Creek was famous as a millstream. In

1860, John Ayd built the first and only gristmill in Reserve Township along its course. The creek was dammed to form a millpond, which a subsequent owner stocked with trout. The Milwaukee Road later ran its "Shortline," connecting Minneapolis and St. Paul, through the ravine, obliterating these early features.

The name Cascade Creek first appears on a real estate plat dated 1856. There was a Cascade Street (now part of Palace Avenue) in the vicinity as early as 1854. The name fascinated me, as it suggested the presence of a defunct waterfall (cascade) somewhere.

I was delighted to find more references to the waterfall in the old literature. The Galena journalist E. S. Seymour, after visiting Fountain Cave in 1849, wrote, "A short distance below the cave there is a little creek or rivulet, that leaps over a succession of cascades, making, in all a fall of about eighty feet." The most elaborate description was by Elizabeth Ellet, who in 1853 wrote, "A miniature waterfall flashes through the depths of a narrow dell, making thirteen successive shoots in a winding course, each falling into a lovely basin several feet in depth, which serves for a bathing place, curtained by a drapery of woods. This little cascade is closely embowered in foliage of vivid green, and its picturesque beauty makes up for the want of grandeur. It is a lovely spot to spend a summer morning or afternoon." This may be the waterfall that local residents knew in later years as Buttermilk Falls.

I was able to pick up the obscure thread of Cascade Creek in other old records. The 1885 *Sanborn Insurance Atlas*, for example, showed a pronounced indentation in the river bluffs near Cascade Street— perhaps the waterfall itself? In 1923, the Milwaukee Road spanned the ravine with a wooden trestle, and it became a general dump for the neighborhood.

Having exhausted the surface history, my investigation of Cascade Creek took a subterranean turn. If rainfall patterns hadn't changed much since the last century, where could the little creek have gone? Most likely, the rainfall runoff was flowing into a storm drain some-where. If I could identify that sewer, I might be able to follow the modern course of the creek underground.

I first tried to find a sewer outfall at the location where Cascade Creek should have joined the Mississippi according to the old maps. I ventured into the wilds of Ross Island, covered with silver-maple floodplain forest, which harbored a homeless tent colony. After some bushwhacking I came across a likely outfall where the stagnant water was pooled up waist deep and coated with an oily green scum, which I presently lowered myself into.

Arched over with limestone rubble masonry, this tunnel was a colorful place. Iron, nature's favorite pigment, had stained the walls yellow, orange, and red, like some sort of Paleolithic art gallery. My flashlight illuminated a beautiful transparent water mold in a pool in the rocks. The tunnel veered one way, then another, with smaller passages branching off to either side. I realized that I had entered the distinctive, nineteenth-century sandrock labyrinth that honeycombs the West Seventh Street area. I was not following anything that could be called Cascade Creek. The whereabouts of the stream remained a mystery. Little did I realize at the time how far back in history I would have to go to solve this one.

Norman Kittson was a famous fur trader in the early history of Minnesota. He built a huge mansion on the site where the St. Paul Cathedral now stands. After retiring from business, he built horse stables in the Midway area of St. Paul and in Erdenheim, Pennsylvania. The St. Paul stables were known as Kittsondale.

Midway, as a place-name, made its appearance at least as early as 1885, when Midway Heights was platted—midway between the Minneapolis and St. Paul downtowns. The same symmetry came into play when the sewer drainage of the area was laid out. Although there had been small-diameter sewers in the area for years, it was not until the late 1920s and early 1930s that the large-bore Kittsondale tunnels, as they are called in Public Works documents, were built. Basically, two mirror-image tunnels, draining sewage in opposite directions, were dug. Kittsondale East drained sewage from Midway toward the east; Kittsondale West drained to the west.

I wondered right away if the two tunnels connected somewhere under the Midway, providing a continuous pathway such that an intrepid sewer explorer might walk clear under the city and emerge at the opposite side. This turned out to be a mere pipe dream, however, as the tunnels diminish in diameter upstream and nowhere connect.

The Kittsondale tunnels are distinguished from all other tunnels under the Twin Cities by their curious architecture. Rather than simply slanting downward, the water is directed along vast subterranean stairways that descend more than a hundred feet into the earth.

These stairways, or flight sewers as engineers call them, are occa-

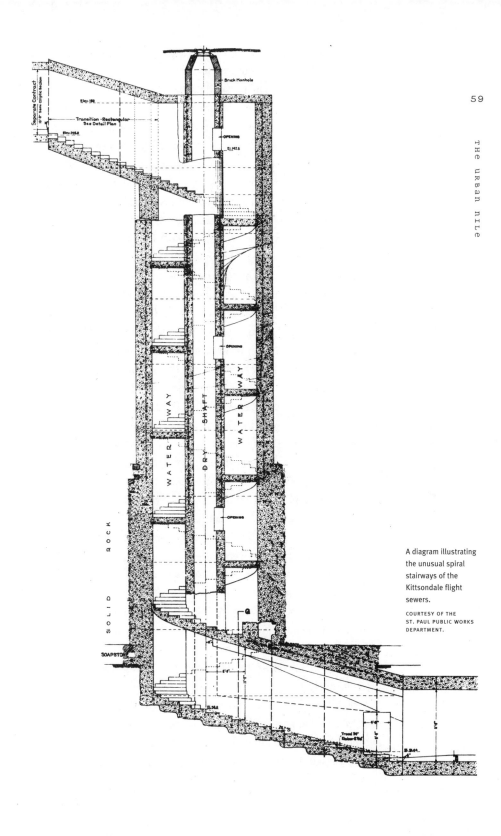

A diagram illustrating the unusual spiral stairways of the Kittsondale flight sewers.

COURTESY OF THE ST. PAUL PUBLIC WORKS DEPARTMENT.

sionally used where a sharp drop is necessary. Ordinary shafts can also serve this function but are plagued with problems of waterfall erosion at the bottom. The Kittsondale stairways served to convey large volumes of water from the highlands of St. Paul down to the level of the Mississippi. Nowadays, an impact dissipater—which looks sort of like a hunk of steel Swiss cheese, complete with holes—would be built at the bottom of a shaft if such a situation arose, or in recent years there has been a trend toward using a simple steel plate laid flat on the bottom of the shaft to absorb the falling water's impact.

While flight sewers are not uncommon, even in the Twin Cities, the Kittsondales contain *spiral* stairways. I had long known of such, but it had not occurred to me that one of them was located directly under the former surface course of Cascade Creek. In other words, the elusive creek, or the water from its watershed, was now draining to the East Kittsondale tunnel. A spiral stairway—a man-made cascade of sorts—had replaced the old, natural waterfall at the river bluffs. The diverted Cascade Creek now joins the Mississippi upstream from Ross Island, where I had originally looked based on the old maps.

Blueprints of the Ayd Mill spiral suggest a subterranean Tower of Pisa. The spiral is more than a hundred feet high and is twenty feet in diameter. Together with the outfall tunnel to the river, the structure cost more than a half million dollars when it was built in 1929. The spiral consists of seven whorls of stairs wrapping around a hollow core. There are twenty-four steps to each turn of the spiral, and I always got dizzy going up or down, even at a normal walking pace. The spiral is now more than three-quarters of a century old—time enough for the growth of mineral formations mimicking those found in natural limestone caves: the stairs were coated with a thick, orange flowstone, from the lime minerals that were dissolved from the upstream concrete and redeposited here.

The hollow core of the spiral is topped with a spiderweb-pattern manhole lid. When going on long trips through the Kittsondale system, I always used to stop here to check whether I could see a reassuring ray of sunlight streaming through the grate at the top, far above, rather than storm clouds.

Following the tunnel upstream beyond the spiral was a three-mile hike. Some parts of this tunnel were heavy with solvent vapors at times, enough that I feared lighting a match. Eventually, where the tunnel passed under Interstate 94 near Concordia College, I crawled through a framework that resembled the ribs of a whale and up the manhole. The "ribs" were all that remained of a previous tunnel structure that had rotted away in the warm sewer gas, leaving only the skeleton on this grim sewer beach.

The West Kittsondale tunnel, built in 1931, on the opposite side of St. Paul, is not associated with any known historical stream, nor does it have thick mineral deposits; however, it has *three* spiral stairways. Its main spiral, located under the intersection of University and Fairview avenues, resembles the Ayd Mill spiral; the other two are small-diameter redbrick spirals situated at points where branches join the tunnel. An interesting difference between the small- and large-diameter spirals is that they coil in opposite directions. It became a point of humorous contention as to which direction of spiral followed the supposed toilet-flush direction for the Northern Hemisphere. The unique West Kittsondale tunnel was a favorite of one of the Twin Cities' first subterranean artists, the photographer David Gericke, who was profiled in the *Minneapolis Star and Tribune* in 1987.

Because of its three spirals, I gave West Kittsondale the name Triple Helix tunnel, which was adopted by the on-line sewering community. I was thereafter contacted by Jason Chapman, creator of the Australian Web site www.urbanadventure.org, which had an astronomical number of hits. He was planning another one of his world tours and wanted to visit the Twin Cities based on what he had read of us on local Web sites. Although I had been contacted by other Aussies in the past, this was the first guy to actually follow through.

Chapman, after describing the Dungeon, the largest storm drain in Melbourne—so large that he drove a car through it—said that it was because of the Triple Helix tunnel that he had included Minnesota on his globetrotting itinerary. I was mystified why he was so enthusiastic about it. Later it dawned on me this was one of my own schemes that had come back to bite me. Years earlier, seeing the proliferation of urban Web sites, I had puffed the Triple Helix in purple prose to attract visitors there and to divert them away from sensitive caves that needed to be protected. Now someone had crossed the earth to view the red herring up close.

With Chapman in tow, I descended the Mississippi River cliffs to the West Kittsondale outfall. A stiff breeze was blowing out of the heavily spray-painted opening. As with many other tunnels, the major graffiti dies away quickly as you get farther from the entrance.

At this point, I became aware of major differences in our experiences, a sort of subterranean culture shock. During the trip, the Aussie exhibited an extreme fear of getting his feet wet, hopping the sewer stream like a kangaroo from Down Under. I thought this was bizarre for such a veteran drain explorer. Then I considered the aridity of Australia. When you walk through drains in Minnesota, water is just part of the picture. In Australia, all these fine exploits I had been told about were conducted in huge, dry concrete tubes. This also explained his reluctance to enter any tunnel where you had to stoop because of a low ceiling. And why was the Aussie hydrophobe following me so closely? He had left his "torch" back at the motel and needed to walk in my pool of light. The giant Australian drains apparently have plenty of skylights, so you don't need to bring your own lights.

After exploring the Kittsondale side-spirals, we walked to the end of the main tunnel, more than one mile, viewing a couple of powerful "fire hose" springs jetting from the walls. Arriving at the main spiral, we walked upward. At the top, we continued on for some distance through the ever-diminishing pipe to a place where we could peep out at the Snelling Avenue street scene, a sort of sewer voyeurism. Here, as elsewhere, it was useful to have a "periscope," which consisted of a dental mirror that could be pushed up through the ventilation holes on a manhole lid and slowly rotated, offering a 360-degree view of the surface above. When not in use, the dental mirror was stowed away in a plastic toothbrush case. On the way out, we encountered the familiar Kittsondale tunnel phantom, a mist of water from a shaft in the ceiling, which from a distance resembles a human being walking toward you because of its constantly changing form. I bade Chapman farewell, wishing him well on his next adventure, which was in Edmonton, Alberta.

FIGHTING THE WATER AT BATTLE CREEK

The last great subterranean stream I tackled under St. Paul was Battle Creek, named after a battle between local Indian tribes that took place in 1842. Much of its course is now contained within Battle Creek Park, noted for the dozen shallow sandstone caves—partly natural and partly artificial—found in the scenic lower coulee along U.S. Highway 61. In 1975 a really bad flood shut the park down. The neglected park became an illicit party spot until a young woman was killed in a cave collapse in 1988. Before the park was officially reopened in 1992, several of the caves were destroyed, leaving the shallow rock shelters seen today—which you are still forbidden to enter. For me there was another, greater subterranean attraction, quite invisible to the casual visitor—the great Battle Creek flume.

Battle Creek begins at Battle Creek Lake in Woodbury. Tracing the stream on foot beginning at McKnight Avenue, near 3M's world headquarters, I found that it soon entered a deep ravine and then plunged underground at the huge caged inlet near Upper Afton Road. The stream reemerged on the west side of Highway 61, joining the Mississippi via Pig's Eye Lake.

Entering, with a friend, the safer downstream end of the flume, we found ourselves in a reinforced concrete pipe, eight feet in diameter.

A view of Battle Creek, ca. 1925. The sandstone caves along this stretch were destroyed in the 1980s. Photograph by *St. Paul Daily News.*

COURTESY OF THE MINNESOTA HISTORICAL SOCIETY.

We began wading upstream, against the flume's fast-moving water. Far in the distance there was a roaring sound—presumably where the gradient increased. Would we be able to ascend the steep tube? Dammed back by our feet at every step, the water showered up around us in sheets, soaking us. We passed under half a dozen well-lighted "conning towers," shafts that stuck up above the Battle Creek pocket wetlands above, for which the tunnel obviously served as an overflow. Looking up, I saw an overcast sky, which gave me concern as I envisioned how fast a tunnel like this could fill up when the rain began to pour. But then I noticed something peculiar. At several places in this roaring flume, there were one-foot-long, delicate soda-straw stalactites, obviously derived from the lime minerals of the concrete. This suggested that the tunnel rarely floods to the ceiling.

After going a third of a mile we came to a waterfall drop shaft. That was it—no long slide down from Upper Afton Road was possible. Disappointed, we ascended one of the conning towers, pushing off the lid at the top, into a sudden burst of sunshine. I had come to the end of St. Paul's boisterous subterranean streams.

AMONG THE SPICE ISLANDS
MINNEAPOLIS'S UNDERGROUND RIVERS

Bassett's Creek is the most talked of water-course within our borders at the present time, as well as the most annoying and puzzling, a creator of no end of disturbance in our quiet and peaceable municipality.

FRANK O'BRIEN, *MINNESOTA PIONEER SKETCHES*

IN THE SUMMER OF 1991 I got a call from my friend Jason who told me that he had seen a "big white sugar pile" in the midst of the Warehouse District of Minneapolis. It meant that a big dig of some sort was well underway, as the crews were piling up mountains of snow-white sand from a deep tunneling project in the St. Peter Sandstone under the city. We went down for a closer look after dark.

After snooping about, we found a huge construction pit fifty feet wide and eighty feet deep. We readily descended the scaffolding that ribbed the pit. We explored the enormous, cathedral-shaped concrete tunnel passage, thirteen feet high, leading off from the pit. We came across a drowsy woodchuck, which I prodded with a stick; he had probably gotten into the system by mistake and could not find his way out. Eventually we encountered deep water in the tunnel, which extended as far as our lights would go. By following a branch tunnel we eventually located a distant manhole lid along the side of Interstate 94, which allowed for less conspicuous ingress and egress during future trips. We decided to return again, properly equipped, to check out the exciting tunnel lake we had discovered that night. What would we find on its far shores?

On our second trip, Jason brought a small inflatable raft, and I brought a tombstone-shaped polyurethane kickboard and waders. I thought it would allow me easier access to tight spots and save the time spent pumping up and deflating a bulbous raft, but it was a disas-trous choice. After hiking up the tunnel we came to the flooded seg-ment, where the floor dropped away into deep water. It looked as green as the Chicago River on St. Patrick's Day, or as if laced with antifreeze, and it was speckled with Styrofoam flotsam. As we got our gear ready, we were somewhat unnerved by a distant, low roaring noise about every ten minutes or so, followed soon after by the water sloshing in the tunnel lake as if a tide were crashing ashore. The Styrofoam par-ticles bobbed up and down jauntily. We had no idea what was going on at first and joked nervously about the "heartbeat of Minneapolis." I wasn't looking forward to getting into that cold, green water, but as on so many other occasions, I hadn't come this far only to turn back. I often depended on that factor to get me through trips like this.

Jason put his raft in the water and paddled into the void without a hitch. His headlamp created pools of light on the cathedral-vaulted concrete passages, and he soon vanished around a corner. He kept yell-ing back to me, but with all the echoes it was impossible to make out what he was saying. I entered the water myself, very tentatively, and sort of hopscotched my way along a chain of submerged sandbars—sand brought down by storm events and deposited in this stagnant deep. The farther I went, the deeper the sandbars, until I could barely touch the last one, like an aquatic ballerina, on tiptoes.

I pushed off into cold deep water with my kickboard and began kicking vigorously. I heard the oncoming tunnel "tide" rushing toward me and braced myself. It wasn't all that bad; out in the open water I was buoyed upward a foot or so and then let back down gently an equal distance as the water subsided again. The tide thereafter lost its terrors, and I even looked forward to it as a diversion from the drudg-ery of the endless green soup. All the while, the mysterious glub-dub "heartbeat" grew louder and piqued my curiosity. Would I be able to pass through the great beating heart of Minneapolis—whatever the hell it was—as in the movie *Fantastic Voyage*?

It was abundantly obvious by now that my gear was hopelessly inappropriate. The waders ripped at the crotch and the cold water spilled through the hole, soaking my pants. The rip rapidly enlarged until the waders dangled in shreds behind me, like seaweed festoon-ing a dugong. I made very little progress with the kickboard because I didn't have flippers on my booted feet—something else I hadn't thought through very well. I stopped every few minutes to rest, hanging in the water at an awkward angle. Occasionally the kickboard wrenched about, and I got a good swig of green tunnel water, which I hastened to expel by vigorous spitting. Now I began to worry that I was going to get sick, too.

It wasn't long before the cold water got to me in a more serious fashion. I was becoming hypothermic. That's when I really began to worry. Jason was well out of earshot and there was no end in sight ahead, so I turned around and began to slowly kick my way back through the hundreds of feet of tunnel that had been so painfully gained. I was feeling so numb that regaining the chain of submerged sandbars would have seemed like entering paradise. Finally, Jason rounded the distant elbow in the flooded tunnel and was soon abreast of me, hoisting me into his already overloaded small raft, which now nearly swamped. I don't know how much longer I would have lasted in the water.

Jason told me that after he had paddled around the corner, he arrived at a place where the ceiling came down to the waterline, and it appeared that he could see out to the Mississippi River, but there were only a few inches of airspace—not enough to get through on his raft. My misguided kickboard concept might actually have worked there if I could have made it that far. Years later, another sewer explorer nearly drowned in that same stretch of tunnel when his canoe overturned.

BASSETT CREEK:
MINNEAPOLIS'S OTHER CREEK

We subsequently learned that the great tunnel we had been paddling through was the new, lower level of our dear old friend, the venerable Bassett Creek tunnel. The waters of Bassett Creek were diverted into this deep tunnel, eighty feet below street level. The old tunnel spilled into the Mississippi River above the St. Anthony Falls Lock and Dam; this new tunnel, below the dam. To understand why this was done, a digression into the history of Bassett Creek is necessary.

While Minnehaha Creek plays the role of a respectable bourgeois surface stream today, Bassett Creek is sometimes called Minneapolis's "other" stream. Originating at Medicine Lake in Plymouth, Bassett Creek collects water from forty square miles in nine municipalities and from springs along its banks such as the famous Glenwood-Inglewood Springs before entering a conduit and flowing underground 1.5 miles to the Mississippi River. The stream, a dozen miles long, follows a depression left by a forerunner of the present Mississippi, marked by the present Minneapolis chain of lakes. In deep sewer excavations in this valley, I'm always amazed to view "the slippery blue clay below the peat," as city engineer Andrew Rinker described it in 1910, which marks this buried river valley.

Bassett Creek was named after Joel Bean Bassett, who settled along the banks of this stream in the 1850s and built a sawmill there in 1870. Railroads soon overwhelmed the area, and it rapidly deteriorated. In 1883, the famous landscape architect Horace W. S. Cleveland, father of Twin Cities parks, who devised our present Grand Rounds, referred to "the risk of malaria" in the Bassett Creek valley. In 1904, historian Frank G. O'Brien described the heavy pollution of the creek. The Near North area of Minneapolis, as it came to be called, was prone to flooding, sometimes to the extent of isolating houses on little islands. Sometimes the flooding was caused by backflooding of the creek from the Mississippi itself. To alleviate the problem, Rinker set about digging the North Minneapolis Tunnel in 1889, hoping to tap off the superfluous waters of inundation and drain them to a point below the falls. He successfully emptied Hoag's Lake and a number of others, but problems continued. In 1906, fed up, he proposed to the city council that

Two views of Bassett Creek from 1936.
Above: Trash was routinely set on fire at the Cedar Lake Road dump.
Next page: Under the concrete bridge at North Sixth Street by the Great Northern tracks.

PHOTOGRAPHS FROM THE *MINNEAPOLIS TIMES*. COURTESY OF THE MINNEAPOLIS CENTRAL LIBRARY, JAMES K. HOSMER SPECIAL COLLECTIONS, MINNEAPOLIS COLLECTION.

Bassett Creek be diverted southward into the chain of lakes. Rinker noted that the discharge of the stream varied from an average of 10 cubic feet per second (cfs) to 1,000 during flood stage—a whopping hundred-fold difference. His plan was not adopted.

After the great Bassett Creek flood of 1913 it was decided that something really had to be done. In 1914 a project was begun to box the creek. Beginning at Sixth Avenue North and Dupont, a flat-topped conduit, ten feet high by twenty feet wide, was constructed. After one year the work had reached Lyndale, nearly a mile away, but progress was thereafter slowed because of World War I. Work resumed and was completed in 1923, at a cost of $280,000. In the late 1930s, the sprawling Sumner Fields public housing project was built atop the conduit.

Bassett Creek originally meandered through a series of wetlands that were eventually tamed and melded into Theodore Wirth Park in the 1930s. Downstream from there, things remained blighted except for the stretch near Glenwood-Inglewood Springs and Fruen's Mill. The Warden Oil Company located on its banks, contaminating the area so badly that it was later declared a Superfund site. In 1934, a gang, the Bassett Creek Scorpions, infested the area, using a subterranean rendezvous—perhaps dry parts of the tunnel itself—to hide themselves until the police learned of it and literally burned them out.

Perhaps even more bizarre, the nearby Bryn Mawr Meadows, which drains to Bassett Creek, is the site of a supposed underground train. A locomotive ran off the track, the story goes, sank in the muck, and was never recovered.

In 1969 the Bassett Creek Watershed Management Commission was established. They asked the Corps of Engineers for help, and in 1976 the Corps recommended that the stream be diverted into a deep-level tunnel from Glenwood and Colfax and out to the Mississippi below the falls. In 1987 an unusually heavy rainfall drove home once again the need for the project. Work began in 1988, creating the big pit already described. The project was finished in 1992 at a cost of $28 million—a hundred times what the original conduit had cost.

Many people over the years have canoed into the yawning mouth of the Bassett Creek tunnel from the Mississippi River out of idle curiosity. In the early 1980s, however, a crew of determined cavers explored the Bassett Creek tunnel on a twelve-foot inflatable raft powered by a 3.5-horsepower motor. They were in search of Smuggler's Cave, a mythical Minneapolis cave that has lured explorers for many years. Smuggler's Cave was supposedly used during Prohibition to smuggle liquor from river craft to dispensaries in the Loop. They didn't find Smuggler's Cave, but they did make significant discoveries along the way, including Bassett Creek, and wrote their adventures up in the monthly newsletter of the Minnesota Speleological Survey.

Motoring upstream, the cavers came to an elevated dry area, which they dubbed the Beach, giving them access, through a trapdoor, into the basement of a building. Later, when they got upstream to the point where Bassett Creek shallows out, they deflated the raft and pulled it up through a manhole—to the bewilderment of onlookers.

It was about this time that Raleigh's Ribs, a restaurant in a building above the Bassett Creek Tunnel, installed a glass-covered opening in the floor so that you could view the sewer tunnel while savoring your tasty food. I suppose it all depends on what floats past. The viewing portal was paved over years ago, its location still marked by a peculiar pattern in the floor at that spot. The building is now occupied by Open U, among other tenants.

In 1990, before the deep diversion project was complete, Jason and I decided to canoe Bassett Creek through the entire length of the tunnel, starting at the upstream end. I rented a canoe at Midwest Mountaineering and mounted it atop my Camaro, giving the appearance of some bizarre metallic rhino charging down the city canyons. We put into the creek and were embarrassed when some guy, who was sitting over the inlet, asked us smilingly whether we were going paddling in the sewer. We answered sheepishly, weighing anchor as fast as we could.

Floating through the first stretch of the Bassett Creek tunnel, which runs under Dupont Avenue, we encountered obstacles almost immediately. The tunnel was blocked by enormous dams of driftwood brought in by floods that had collected behind projecting manholes. The manhole lids sat atop stubby brick towers about three feet high. The dams backed up the stream into waist-deep pools of filthy, stinking water. We portaged six of these dams, each one successively smaller than the last. We speculated, tongue in cheek, about the race of giant subterranean beavers that must have constructed them.

At the sixth and largest Dupont teakettle, where the tunnel swerves under the Olson Memorial Highway, I was amazed to see a pinhole camera effect created by light streaming through ventilation holes in the street above. Most amazingly, I could actually see images of aircraft, about an inch long, passing in the skies above, crossing over the top of the manhole lid. I dubbed this lid the Wizard's Table. While I have seen this effect in other sewers over the years, this one was by far the most striking.

Once we got the canoe into the clear beyond the dams, my greatest fear was plunging over waterfalls inside the Bassett Creek tunnel. Every time I heard rushing water ahead of us, I stared apprehensively into the fog bank and prepared to jab an oar downward. It usually turned out to be only a small pipe dumping a minor amount of water into the tunnel. In retrospect, it was almost ludicrous because the water through most of the tunnel is only ankle deep, at least until we got near the river itself, where it became chest deep. In fact, the gradient isn't much at all: in more than eight thousand feet of tunnel, the vertical drop is only nine feet.

When not watching ahead for waterfalls, my eyes were riveted on the tunnel sediments, looking for shiny coins and other trumpery, and thus occupied I would sometimes crack my skull on an overhead water main, to the amusement of my fellow paddler. The tunnel alluvium was a continual source of fascination to me, and I fancied myself a sort of Craig Blacklock of the sewer sediments as I photographed them. I was bemused by the dozens of shopping carts that had been swept into the tunnel during floods, where they got incorporated into the sandbars. Occasionally I jerked back suddenly, having mistaken one of them for a projecting human rib cage.

As we paddled along, I observed that the Bassett Creek tunnel was not monolithic in construction like so many other tunnels but rather a rich, harlequin patchwork of different styles and materials. Most commonly, concrete box sections alternated with Platteville Limestone rubble masonry, and again with red or yellow brickwork. Until I came to recognize these various landmarks better, I could read our progress through the tunnel from the street names spray-painted on the walls by sewer workers.

The Bassett Creek tunnel is not straight; it curls under the city of Minneapolis in the shape of a huge question mark. The curve is known as Winchell's Angle, after the pioneer state geologist who depicted the stream in his reports. Winchell's Angle is architecturally distinctive, characterized by squinch (angled) arches; the streets passed overhead obliquely here rather than perpendicularly as elsewhere. At one point along this stretch, we beached our canoe to explore a side gallery. Washed-in seeds germinated in the half-light, forming a meadow of ghostly sprouts on the sandbar. Clusters of mushrooms sprang from jagged fissures in the walls, looking like the ghostly white fingers of a hand thrust upward in supplication from another dimension. The spiders of these subterranean gardens seemed large, strange, almost tropical. In another spot, I glimpsed a pool of goldfish, an incident that was described by author Jack El-Hai in one of his Lost Minnesota columns for *Architecture Minnesota* magazine in 2003.

A little farther along was the great Lyndale sandbar, largest in the tunnel. We dubbed this whole chain of sandbars, which usually occurred along the inside of tunnel bends, where water flows more sluggishly, the Spice Islands, for obvious olfactory reasons.

About midway through the tunnel, the single large passage was divided into two smaller parallel passages by a partition, which had been added to support Interstate 94, above our heads. The passage on one side of the partition was filled with dry sand deposits corrugated with mega-ripples indicating violent storm flows, while the other side contained the diminutive, dry-weather stream.

Finally, nearing the downstream exit, we arrived at the largest open space in the Bassett Creek tunnel, supported by concrete mushroom columns. The water was deeper here, with large carp nosing about like submarines. This chamber was dense with fog, as the cold stream mixed with the warm river. Ceiling spouts vomited water into the tunnel from above, and these could be heard more easily than seen; we advanced slowly through the fog to avoid getting drenched by them. We tied up our canoe at a sort of subterranean dock, climbed up a convenient ladder, and explored an interesting subbasement accessed through a trap door. After gratifying our curiosity, we paddled under the old patch in the ceiling marking Raleigh's Ribs, past a Romanesque arch where bats roosted in the chinks, and finally out into the Mississippi River.

It was more interesting exploring the Bassett Creek tunnel in the early days because the odd side passages, some of them with classic, nineteenth-century egg-shaped cross sections, had not yet been sealed off by the overzealous separation engineers. At one point a subterranean spring had left a large, jellyfish-shaped deposit of calcareous minerals several feet across. These formations occur commonly in caves, where they are called medusas. It was the largest "cave" formation in the whole tunnel, much larger than the boring, red sewer rusticles (rust stalactites) that drooped from the ceiling everywhere. The medusa was removed during the separation project.

On subsequent trips, we dispensed with canoes entirely, parking our cars upstream near the Glendale Church. We joked darkly that that is where you say your last prayers before entering the Bassett Creek tunnel. A car parked at the downstream end brought us back at the end of the day. In 1993, after the new deep diversion was fully established, I wondered what they had done to the old tunnel and decided to tour the whole thing again. I took elaborate notes, recording all my distances using a Rolatape odometer, noting every little change in rock type and shape of the tunnel, the locations of side passages, the directions of air and water currents—even the locations of the more persistent odors. It took the better part of a day, but I was able to produce a large-scale map of the tunnel that I referred to for years afterward. By this time the old upstream canoe entrance was gone, replaced by steel bars, and so too were the driftwood dams. In recent years, there have been several studies that have looked at daylighting this and other streams, that is, removing the roofs and making them surface streams again.

In 1999, a photographer for *National Geographic Adventure* magazine flew into the Twin Cities to get some photos of us for an article on urban exploration that was under preparation. We met up with him late one summer night and entered the deep Bassett Creek system. We hiked the considerable distance down to Niagara Falls, the place in the diversion where the whole stream pours over the waterfall to the deep level. This waterfall descends what had originally been the open construction pit I described at the beginning of this chapter, now under the parking lot behind Déjà Vu Nightclub, where you can hear it thundering below the huge iron trapdoor.

The subterranean waterfall was very noisy, and approaching it from downstream was difficult owing to the strong currents and slippery floor, especially after several days of heavy rains. One fellow's glasses got so foggy that he had to retreat, which motivated him to get Lasik eye surgery so he would no longer need to wear glasses on deep sewer expeditions. I slowly inched my way up to the magnificent sight of the subterranean Niagara and then walked behind the curling sheet of water, a breezy space where there was plenty of standing room.

During a trip through the Bassett Creek tunnel in 2000, I mapped out the sediments with the aim of investigating the layering and what that might say about storm events. Several DNR personnel came along to count bats. I found the sewer stratigraphy fairly trivial, but the horizontal distribution of sediments was especially interesting. Basically, sediments of large-grain size (sand and gravel) were located near the active water inputs to the tunnel, but as I progressed downstream from these inputs, the grain size decreased, reflecting a transport process where the heavier sediments drop out first. Eventually, beyond the belts of sand, silt, and finally mud, I encountered bare tunnel floor, which would last until the next input, where the sandbars started again.

BRIDAL VEIL CREEK: MISTRESS OF BOTH CITIES

While the Old Bassett Creek, with its Spice Islands, and the New Bassett Creek, with its Niagara Falls, are the best examples of subterranean streams in Minneapolis, there are others. Bridal Veil Creek gets its name from Bridal Veil Falls, where it pours out of its concrete pipe and plunges over a ledge in the shadow of the Franklin Avenue Bridge, on the east side of the Mississippi River. Waterfalls with the bridal veil moniker (for example, the more famous one in Yosemite National

Park) fall from such great heights that their waters dissipate in a "veil" of mist before reaching the bottom.

In 1862, the St. Paul & Pacific Railroad, the first railway in Minnesota, ran track over the ten miles of prairie between St. Paul and St. Anthony, making use of the Bridal Veil Creek valley over part of the course. The old Eustis farm, for which Eustis Street was later named, used to occupy much of this land, but it was eventually swallowed up

BRIDAL VEIL FALLS, MINNEAPOLIS.

A postcard view of Bridal Veil Falls, ca. 1908.

COURTESY OF THE MINNESOTA HISTORICAL SOCIETY.

in the SEMI (South East Minneapolis Industrial) area. In my years as an environmental consultant I became very familiar with this part of Minneapolis, the so-called Valley of the Drums. Its PCB-tinged soil was so heavily contaminated that no landfill in Minnesota would accept it, so it was loaded onto railcars and hauled to Utah for final burial. I spent many latex-gloved summer days in thistles over my head collecting soil samples during that project, often conversing with the melancholy but good-natured hobos who wandered about the valley. They had set up elaborate camps in the dense buckthorn thickets, where they could detect intruders well in advance.

An odd historical fact about Bridal Veil Falls is that it was once a mineral spa of sorts. Famous under the alternative name of Meeker's Creek, it had iron and sulfur springs, and in 1869 it was actually described as a "new watering place." An old newspaper clipping referred to the stream by still another name, Oil Creek, probably because groundwater seepage often resembles oil slicks. By 1911 the creek was boxed, put underground.

Ironically, Bridal Veil Creek remains an informal spa of sorts. I saw men ostentatiously bathing themselves in the shower of water in the secluded glen below. They didn't seem to realize that the water meandered among several coal-tar rich Superfund sites before reaching the waterfall. Later, the MPCA ordered this segment of the stream put into a pipe, thus isolating it from the underlying contaminated soil, so park goers can now bathe with more assurance.

My introduction to the Bridal Veil tunnel involved hiking up the pipe from the waterfall end. Just getting to the waterfall ledge where the tunnel entrance was located required some nerves, as the rocks were crumbly and slick with algae. It would have been all too easy to slip and fall sixty feet into the glen below. The tunnel itself was easy to traverse but soon hunkered down to Quasimodo dimensions. I came across a forlorn crayfish making its unwilling way through the pipe toward the deadly waterfall, and I examined a fawning frat pledge hastily scribbled on the walls. That's where the easy stuff ended. I had to pass through a small waterfall of sorts inside the tunnel, getting myself drenched in the process. Eventually, reduced to all fours and utterly bedraggled, I arrived under University Avenue, where the pipe became too small to follow. At the time, I thought that was the upstream end of the stream, but I was quite mistaken.

Bridal Veil Creek is one of the few streams to cross the city line, flowing from St. Paul to Minneapolis. The stream has three distinct underground segments, strung together by surface reaches, and I had as yet seen only the downstream one. The upstream segment, originating at hillside springs on the Les Bolstad Golf Course, collects itself and flows under the adjoining University of Minnesota St. Paul campus, following the boundary with the State Fairgrounds, until it empties into the Sarita Wetland. In 1909, the State Fair Board, seeking a new attraction, excavated the wetland in their efforts to create a lagoon and canal that would carry passenger boats. Overflow from the wetland now drains to the Eustis Street tunnel and disgorges to the Mississippi River just above the Lake Street Bridge.

I used a somewhat ratlike maneuver to enter the midstream Bridal Veil tunnel. I laid down full length in a street gutter along Como Avenue and then rolled sideways through the slotlike opening in the curb into the leafy catch basin below—something I wouldn't be able to do today for reasons I won't mention. Paradoxically, or through some optical illusion, the tunnel appeared to decrease in diameter as I followed it downstream, and the water became ever sudsier as I approached the dreaded Superfund sites. There, I saw minnows spinning head over fin in the vile soup, obviously having been carried downstream from a cleaner headwater pond and stunned by the deadly toxins in the water—toxins that were also bathing my own skin, since I was wearing jeans rather than waders.

After traversing the midstream segment, Bridal Veil Creek re-emerged at Bridal Veil Pond, along Energy Park Drive. There was a notorious bird kill there in the early 1990s; I saw Canada geese floating belly-up in the toxic soup. Another link in this chain of interconnected wetlands is Kasota Pond, fed by historic Skonard's Spring, whose water was once potable and much used by the local residents.

THE GEYSER DRAIN:
SPOUTING OFF ON THE INTERSTATES

The largest and longest storm sewer under Minneapolis is the great Geyser Drain, a drainage tunnel dug under Interstate Highway 35W in the early 1960s with hydraulic lances at a cost of $4.8 million. Properly speaking, it wasn't an underground river at all in that it didn't carry a former surface stream, as did the other tunnels already discussed in this chapter. But when it rained heavily, a veritable river did indeed spill from the cavernous outfall into the Mississippi River. The out-fall, despite its immense size, is nearly invisible, tucked in among the hydraulic folds of the St. Anthony Falls area.

The giant tunnel is nearly five miles long and arranged like the letter Y. Starting out fourteen feet in diameter, the passage splits after one and a half miles, with the smaller, right-hand branch, nine feet in diameter, running three-quarters of a mile to Loring Park, where there is a drop shaft. The other branch runs south under Interstate 35W, telescoping downward from a dozen feet to smaller diameters as it goes, finally ending near Minnehaha Creek, a distance of two and one-third miles.

The Geyser Drain does not usually impinge on the public con-sciousness unless it rains very intensely, and that's where it got its nickname. At such times, even though the tunnel is a good 120 feet below the surface, so much water is trying to enter the system all at once that it backs up through shafts and geysers out in great fountains from large vents located along the median of the interstate highway. When this happens, it usually makes the evening news and sometimes YouTube. It should also suggest to potential explorers that the tunnel is a very dangerous place.

Because of its geysering potential, John and I would have preferred to tackle this tunnel in winter, when there would be no possibility of a downpour incommoding our expedition. I also dreamed of seeing 120-foot long icicles in the soaring drop shafts. Those mythical icicles fascinated me. However, there was also the chilling possibility of hypo-thermia. The tunnel held cold, flowing water and strong convectional air currents at all times of the year, and if we expended all our energy slogging to its remotest extremities in the dead of winter, we might not be able to make it back alive. There were some places in the tunnel, which we knew about from preliminary reconnaissance, where power-ful garden-hose-size springs in the walls showered everything below, so you couldn't escape getting soaked, even in winter.

Taking all this into account, we opted for a trip late enough in the year that the flood hazard was negligible but before the really deep cold set in. Since the stream of water was much too shallow for canoes, and the tunnel was too long for walking, we decided to mountain bike to its extremities. It was a logical but poor choice.

Late one moonlit evening near Thanksgiving, we began setting up our ropes and ladders. The outfall could not be entered by foot from the river end, where the water was too deep. To get into it from above, we had to lower our bicycles with ropes. Unfortunately, the special, lightweight mini-ladder that I had constructed for this trip failed miserably, leaving me with a nearly dislocated shoulder, but I decided to continue since we had come this far. Sound familiar?

Our mountain bikes had some modifications for their subterranean mission. We added headlights and fenders because when you bike through puddles the tires throw curling loops of water onto your back. We also protected ourselves with rain suits.

Standing at the entrance to the tunnel that night, it was apparent that the winter updrafts had already begun. Concealing our dangling ropes and ladders as best we could, we set out. We picked up speed on the bikes and congratulated ourselves on our cleverness for escaping the mind-numbing drudgery of hiking for mile after mile through the vast, boring concrete tube. One annoyance was the circularity of the tunnel, which forced us to keep our tires within a very narrow range, even though the tunnel was a full fourteen feet in diameter. Another annoyance was the need to avoid striking driftwood.

After riding several blocks up the big bore, we began to encounter waterlogged sandbars. Our tires sank in, making for laborious peddling. If we kept up enough speed, we could plow through the isolated sandbars easily enough, but as we advanced farther upstream they became more abundant. At the same time, the water in the tunnel got deeper—not by much, just enough so that our feet dipped into the chilling stream with every turn of a pedal, causing a lot of extra drag and fatigue. I began to have doubts.

The sandbars multiplied and finally merged into a continuum of sand, so we stopped to rest and evaluate the situation. It was agreed that we should continue to the big Loring Junction, where hopefully the sand deposits would end. Perhaps the sand came from the Loring branch of the tunnel, in which case we would ride to glory in the other branch. Failing that, perhaps we could stow our bikes and continue south on foot, at least to the first geyser vent along the interstate highway, which we could view from below—along with those wonderful icicles!

When we arrived at the Loring Junction, however, we were dismayed to see that the sandbars stretched southward to infinity beyond the reach of our light beams. The sand deposits apparently derived from the sanding of the highways in winter, and so there would be no end of them. We propped our bikes against the wall, safe from the tunnel currents, and began to hike south, but we sank into the waterlogged sand whether we were on bike or afoot. The latter was no less fatiguing.

We contented ourselves with some idle speculations about the origin of the frogs we found in the Loring Park branch. Had they fallen down the deep drop shaft from the ponds in that park, far above our heads? If so, they were pretty sturdy little critters. One of the streams draining the Loring ponds, known historically as Lost Brook, was a tributary of Bassett Creek, but after the construction of the interstate highway tunnel, excess water was redirected our way, perhaps carrying the woebegone frogs with it. Or perhaps the frogs had ascended wearily from the distant river—as certain other fools had just done. I had seen drop shaft frogs in other tunnels, however, and I made a good argument for that alternative.

Nudged by Jack Frost, we turned our bikes toward the distant outfall and grimly began the lengthy return trip. I was so exhausted by this time that when I needed a rest from the sandbars I dismounted and simply portaged over them instead of trying to ram through. I called this bar hopping. After leaving the tunnel, what seemed like an eternity later, I never slept so soundly. I later wrote a chastened trip report about the whole affair, "Bar Hopping Down Under."

OTHER DRAINS IN PASSING

Another peculiar little drainage area is near the Minneapolis–St. Paul International Airport, a place you wouldn't dream of exploring nowadays, in our post-9/11 world, especially since even back then it was monitored with security cameras. When I lived in St. Louis, Missouri, I explored Coldwater Creek, which ran through a tunnel directly under the main airport, Lambert Field. So when I observed a large concrete bowl just off to the side of the freeway near our own airport, I decided to check it out. Before it was entirely reconstructed in recent years, there were two outfalls draining into this bowl, which I dubbed Airport Creek and Cemetery Creek, respectively. Whether they were in fact natural surface streams at one time is unclear. In any case, I traced Airport Creek underground for some distance, noting the reddish sediments and sulfurous odor emanating from the marshy Mother Lake in the northwest corner of the airport. As I advanced farther, I was temporarily overcome by dread as a horrifically loud blast of sound advanced toward me inside the dark tunnel—an airplane taking off! Further progress was obstructed by a subterranean waterfall. I was glad to get out of there. Cemetery Creek, by contrast, was fairly ordinary, running around the perimeter of Fort Snelling National Cemetery and then alongside Interstate 94. No floating coffins were seen, although I was hoping to eventually pop up under Camp Snoopy at the Mall of America, if only I could get that far.

PART III

THE GREAT SANDBOX

THE CAVE UNDER THE CASTLE
BREWERY CAVES

Anyone who knew anything about those caves is long dead.

JOSEPHINE MARCOTTY

IN YEARS PAST, many people who had a casual interest in visiting the St. Paul underworld—perhaps to party wildly away from the prying eyes of parents or from public scrutiny generally—chose to do so in the abandoned brewery caves below the city's various neighborhoods. I thought it an interesting twist that the very caves that were used to produce beer back in the late nineteenth century became a place of its consumption in the twentieth. The abandoned lagering caves were among the first that I explored, even though I never partied in them. There was one cave, Stahlmann's Cellars, that was larger and remoter than any of the rest and the last one I was to get to. But first the story of the "easy" brewery caves, which became a sort of training ground for the tougher ones.

Between the mid-1840s and 1870, German immigrants to the United States brought with them their traditional fondness for beer, which had not previously been of great importance in this country, where hard liquor was usually preferred. Ironically, this beer invasion was facilitated not only by the burgeoning German population but also by temperance agitation, which originally focused largely on "ardent spirits," leading many Americans to choose the less potent beverage.

Prior to 1840, there were no breweries in America producing the German-style lager beer. Lager beer differed from the prevalent English and American beers, such as ale, in that the lager yeast fermented at the bottom of the vat rather than the top, and the beer required lagering, or storage, for several months at lower temperatures. In the old days, lager beer was only brewed during the winter months, when cellar temperatures were sufficiently low. But in northern states, such as Minnesota, natural ice was readily available and ice cakes could be harvested from nearby lakes and rivers in winter and stacked in caves so brewing could continue year-round to meet the growing demand.

YOERG'S BREWERY

Minnesota's first brewery, which produced lager beer, was established in 1848 by Anthony Yoerg in St. Paul. Yoerg, like many St. Paul brewers to come, was a native of Bavaria, the cradle of the German brewing industry. In 1871 Yoerg moved to the location that was to be so closely associated with his name, on the west side of the Mississippi River.

The brewery was built in a snug little cove along Ohio Street, an idyllic spot once referred to as the City of the Birds because of all the holes that cliff swallows had dug in the sandstone bluffs. The St. Paul historian Edward Duffield Neill was able to report in 1881 that Yoerg "has five cellars excavated in the bluffs." The brewery prospered mightily until Prohibition came along, when it eked out a meager

An interior view of the lagering cavern operated by Yoerg's Brewery. Yoerg's was one of the last breweries to use caves in this way following Prohibition.

COURTESY OF THE RAMSEY COUNTY HISTORICAL SOCIETY.

existence as the Yoerg Milk Company in the face of stiff competition from existing milk companies.

Many of Yoerg's newspaper advertisements after Prohibition featured Rip Van Winkle awaking from his slumbers and elves rolling kegs out of the cave. Longer than other breweries, Yoerg used its cave for lagering, producing its "Cave Aged Beer," as proudly advertised on its cone-top cans. The brewery closed in 1952.

The property was rented to the Charles Harris Plumbing & Heating Company, which used the cave for storage. Reminders of this era, in the form of busted toilet fragments, are still visible in several passages in the cave. After a fire tore through their warehouse in 1958, Harris left. The charred shell of the building remained until it was demolished in 1970. A friend told me that as late as the 1980s you could still see actual toilet bowls stacked up to the ceiling in the cave passages. Vandals have found them irresistible targets; the average size of the toilet fragments has been diminishing ever since, as visitors seem to need to have something to bust.

In 2004, Yoerg's Cave again entered public consciousness—with a bang. Several teenagers digging in the cave, which had always been readily accessible, found old boxes and burlap sacks containing 1,100 pounds of gunpowder from the 1950s. The St. Paul Bomb Squad removed it. Shortly thereafter, the kids went back and dug up more; the bomb squad made a repeat visit. Other publicity-seeking youths sent a video to a local TV station, showing themselves lobbing Molotov cocktails inside the cave, nearly hitting each other—in the same room where the gunpowder was later found. I recall watching the evening news in dismay, seeing a fireball illuminate the cave I knew so well. Sometime later, a teenager was arrested for making terroristic threats on his Web site involving use of this gunpowder. To add to the problems, three teenagers died in nearby Fandell's Cave, just a few hundred feet down the bluff, right after this gunpowder plot had played itself out. The city's caves seemed to be under siege. I decided it was time that I resurveyed Yoerg's Cave; I hadn't visited it for many years. Several others accompanied me.

Yoerg's Cave is thousands of feet long with most of the passages on one level. Using the 1962 Civil Defense map as a basis for comparison, I found that half the passages in the cave were unmapped. It was unlikely that these unmapped passages had been carved since 1962; rather, the defense mappers only needed to show the major passages in which people could find protection from fallout after a nuclear attack.

The largest unmapped area was an upper level of Gothic-shaped stoopways, which could be reached only by precariously balancing rusted fifty-five-gallon steel drums atop one another and then climbing the pile. Another passage at a still higher level was accessed by means of a knotted gym rope hanging down into one of the rooms. One of the athletic bucks in our party agreed to climb it. One of the motivations for exploring such high passages was the usual long-standing rumor of a secret tunnel connecting the lagering cave to the brewmaster's house on the bluffs above. No such connection was found.

Under the floors of the main level there was an unmapped plexus of tight sandrock tubes through which I crawled, but the presence of segmented clay pipes in these passages indicated they were intended for sewers—a unique drainage arrangement found in no other brewery cave that I'm familiar with.

In the gunpowder room, the ordinarily white sandy floor was stained black from the powder, and the walls were blackened from the roaring Molotov fires. A strange, rubbery odor pervaded the air. I tested the remaining gunpowder by touching a lit match to a small sample of it. It was with great difficulty that it could be made to burn, giving off an acrid, ghostly blue flame that stank of sulfur. The gunpowder had obviously degraded over the years, with the soluble saltpeter component leached out, and stood no chance of igniting, even if a Molotov had struck it directly. I filled sample jars with leftover gunpowder for further tests, but it was already evident that all the media hype about the possibility of devastating explosions was overwrought.

That wasn't the only weird thing we found in the gunpowder room. Piles of rusted paint cans, rusted steel drums with dried resins and weird smells, and a big green wooden box, neatly stenciled "Property of United States Maritime Commission, Vancouver, Washington," containing numbered steel tubes of unknown use, littered the floor. Before I could undertake further investigation, the city plugged the remaining entrances to Yoerg's Cave by pouring concrete over them.

BANHOLZER BREWERY

The West Seventh Street neighborhood of St. Paul was also known for its breweries. In 1871, Frederick Banholzer acquired the North Mississippi Brewery, which had been established in 1853. In 1886, Banholzer Park, an outdoor beer garden, opened, buoyed up with balloon rides to Lilydale, across the river. After Frederick's son William died, the brewery declined, going out of business in 1904. The aboveground buildings hung around for decades. The nearby brewmaster's house has survived intact, becoming a Hazelden halfway house that has treated ten thousand people over more than half a century.

The Banholzer brewery cave, located on the river bluffs at the foot of Sumac Street, was as easily accessible to the locals as Yoerg's was on the west side of the river. Before it was sealed in 1991, Banholzer was the king of party caves; police patrol boats would routinely scan the river bluffs as they sped past. No one called it Banholzer Cave, though; it was known locally as Frankenstein's Cave. I could never figure out why so many also called it Schmidt Cave, which was obviously false, given that the Schmidt Brewery was half a mile away.

Banholzer Cave consisted of a large gridwork of passages arranged somewhat like a ladder, about a half-mile in length and large enough to drive a truck through. More of the rooms had special names than in any other brewery cave. Newspaper columnist Don Boxmeyer recalled this gleeful "boy's world" from his youth, mentioning names like King's Cave, Three Sisters (three parallel passages), Frankenstein's Bedroom, the Bear Hole, and the Dump.

One well-known entrance to this cave, by way of the Sumac Street sewer outfall, was located on the river bluff. The determined partier of yesteryear, bent double with his kegs, could shuffle through the brick sewer, crunching broken beer bottles underfoot and chasing the rats ahead of him, until coming to a hole in the wall by means of which he entered the cave. Or he could brazenly come in through the cave entrance on the other side of Shepard Road. In the midst of the Lametti Construction yard, there was a garage-like shed that opened into a long, gently sloping passage leading into the heart of the cave. I heard that there was once a police raid where tear gas was fired into one entrance, and the partiers, trying to elude capture, ran straight into the waiting arms of the police at the other entrance.

I made many trips to Banholzer Cave in the years before it was sealed. Because the cave extended below Shepard Road, a busy trucking route, there was a perpetual snowfall of white sand grains into my hair. On one of the pillars of the cave, a life-size red Pegasus had been artfully spray-painted. On another wall someone had sketched out the blind entrance to the Mines of Moria, a reference to Tolkien's *Lord of the Rings* story. Another room had a very high ceiling with a skylight. The best-known spot in the cave was Pussy Heaven—an excavated passage along a natural vertical rock joint in the sandstone, which got its name from its suggestive oval shape. Obviously, the names had changed since Boxmeyer's day.

My creepiest memory of Banholzer Cave stems from a late-night visit. The roomy passages, usually vacant, had a very woebegone occupant, a deeply intoxicated paint-sniffer. As I walked through the cave, this guy acted strangely, shadowing me at a distance, and playing a game of bopeep. I soon found my way to the exit.

In 1991, Shepard Road was widened and repaved, and the authorities took the opportunity to seal Banholzer Cave, which had given them so much grief over the years. Chain-link fencing was wrapped into the entrances and concrete was poured into the mesh. The ceilings were collapsed in from above where possible, and the remaining voids were slurried full of sand, pumped in through hoses.

Almost as soon as Banholzer Cave was sealed, local diggers made extensive attempts to reopen it. I'm not sure what cave voids awaited them, except possibly the sand fill might have settled enough to leave low crawl spaces here and there along the tops of the rooms. All the while, the city was pushing its sewer separation program, and the few accessible peripheral sewer voids, from which most of the attempts were launched, steadily dwindled. In the beginning, for example, you could still enter little sandstone rooms off the old Sumac sewer, and I found piles of bottles where someone had spent a lot of time trying to dig open the main cave, but without success, as the chain-link–concrete combination proved impenetrable. In frustration, apparently, the digger directed some offensive graffiti toward the public works folks. Finally, there was nothing left but a backdoor attempt at wading through waist-deep raw sewage in the West Seventh Street branch interceptor, from which I was able to access a few nasty little voids of no consequence.

STAHLMANN'S CELLARS

In 1855, Christopher Stahlmann established the Cave Brewery, later the Schmidt Brewery, on Fort Road (West Seventh Street) in what was then the outskirts of the city. Thomas Newson, in his *Pen Pictures and*

Biographical Sketches of Old Settlers (1886), described Stahlmann: "He was born in Bavaria in 1829; came to the United States in 1846 and ... removed to ST. PAUL in 1855, and erected his brewery the same year. He was a member of the House of Representatives in 1871 and in 1883; was [Ramsey] County Commissioner in 1871, and held several other minor offices." Describing Stahlmann's commercial enterprises in more detail, Newson wrote: "In early days he went out to what was known as the old Fort road, now [West] Seventh street, and purchased several acres of land there and built his brewery thereon. These acres were then considered away out of the city, but are now within the city limits and very valuable." Stahlmann was indeed "one of the greatest pioneers of the West End."

With the growth of the beer market following the Civil War, Stahlmann's Cave Brewery, as it was known, became the largest brewery in Minnesota, with an annual production of ten thousand barrels by the late 1870s. In 1884, his production peaked at forty thousand barrels per year, but by that time Stahlmann was no longer in first place.

As the name Cave Brewery suggests, Stahlmann carved an extensive lagering cave, still known as Stahlmann's Cellars, below the brewery. A newspaper reporter, in 1877, described the cave during its heyday:

Armed with candles, and conducted by Mr. Stahlman, the visiting party started down, down into the bowels of the earth; down through the strata of solid lime stone rock which underlies all that section, and of which the buildings are built, we went until we struck the underlying strata of sand rock, fully sixty feet below the surface. Here were the cellars—cellars to the front, the right, the left, and the rear—in all over 5,000 feet, or nearly a mile in length, and still the work of excavating new chambers is going on. These cellars are about 16 feet wide and ten feet in height. In them now are some 120 huge butts of different varieties of beer, in all over 3,000 barrels. The butts are in chambers, six or eight in a line, each group backed by a huge chamber of ice to keep them at proper temperature, in all over 6,000 cakes of the three foot Mississippi ice now being in store. Such complete cellars, dry, fresh and clean, we venture cannot be found elsewhere in America.... Fortunately Mr. Stahlman has an inexhaustible supply of the purest of spring water. It is brought in pipes from the bluffs, and carried into every floor of his private residence, feeds the boilers, runs through his cellars, all over the brewery and malt house, and is finally discharged into a sewer with the general refuse, which is discharged into the Mississippi through the cave.

Atmospheric descriptions like these influenced later writers, and Stahlmann's Cellars acquired a national and almost mythical reputation as the very type of labyrinthine complexity, which it still held more than a century later. As noted by art historian Susan Appel, "The breweries with the best and most extensive cellars became the most famous."

The use of caves to trap cold winter air or to fill with ice for lagering was becoming obsolete by the 1870s when brewers began to build icehouses, which "took the aging of lager beer out of caves and placed it in an aboveground stack of 'cellars' cooled by a massive body of ice at the top of the building." The construction of icehouses bypassed the arduous task of underground excavation. With the widespread adoption of mechanical refrigeration in the 1880s, ice-making machines freed brewers from dependence on natural ice with its uncertainties of supply and price. The icehouse evolved into a mechanically refrigerated stock house where temperatures could be scientifically controlled. Eventually, mechanical refrigeration focused on generating cold air itself rather than ice, avoiding altogether the bulkiness and messiness of the latter. Consulting the 1885 *Sanborn Insurance Atlas* for St. Paul, I found several icehouses depicted at the Cave Brewery, indicating that Stahlmann had converted to the newer refrigeration method by that year. These icehouses were built during the reconstruction of the Cave Brewery in the early 1880s. At some point, the lagering cave was abandoned.

Another factor favoring the abandonment of lagering caves was the desire for cleaner facilities, following in the wake of Louis Pasteur's research into the so-called diseases of beer. The Fort Street sewer (as it is referred to in the original contracts) was carved under Stahlmann's Cellars in 1884 and intersects it at several points. In the present day, this sewer sometimes overflows into the cave. It's therefore unlikely that the cave was used much after 1884; indeed, the Stahlmann Cave Brewery was incorporated as the Chris Stahlmann Brewing Company that very year—without the cave moniker.

Today St. Paulites are more familiar with the Cave Brewery's successor, the great Schmidt Brewery, which towers over the Fort Road neighborhood like a magnificent red brick Rhenish castle. Jacob Schmidt was born in Bavaria in 1845 and learned his craft at Milwaukee's famous breweries and elsewhere, ending up at the North Star Brewery on St. Paul's Dayton's Bluff, which he effectively controlled by 1884. Meanwhile, Christopher Stahlmann had succumbed to "inflammation of the bowels" in 1883, leaving the Cave Brewery in the hands of his competent sons, all of whom tragically perished, however, one after another, from tuberculosis, causing the brewery to go bankrupt in 1897. In 1900 Schmidt, seeking to replace the North Star Brewery, which had recently burned down, purchased Stahlmann's brewery.

Schmidt rebuilt Stahlmann's brewery in 1901–2 along the Oneida Street axis with the help of Chicago architect Bernard Barthel, who employed the feudal castle style. By this time, progressive brewers regarded the use of caves for lagering as a sign of backwardness. In 1901, for example, Schmidt's chief local competitor ran a newspaper advertisement boasting, "The only brewery in St. Paul that has a modern refrigerating plant is Hamm's Brewery. Beer is stored in rooms kept at a temperature of 35 degrees. Light, pure air and absolute cleanliness help to make the beer pure and wholesome. No dark, ill-ventilated caves; temperature unchangeable and ventilation perfect. Insist on getting the honestly brewed HAMM'S BEER. Annual capacity, 500,000 barrels." Schmidt, whose North Star Brewery had depended on lagering caves at Dayton's Bluff, introduced mechanical refrigeration at the Stahlmann location soon after.

Jacob Schmidt died in 1910, but his able business partner, Adolf Bremer, together with the latter's brother, Otto, made the brewery one of the leading regional beer producers in the country. With the onset of Prohibition in 1919, the Schmidt Brewery began producing soft drinks and a successful near-beer named Select. When Prohibition was repealed in 1933, Schmidt resumed the production of beer and within three years claimed to be the seventh-largest brewery in the United States. After several changes in ownership, involving acquisition by Detroit-based Pfeiffer's in 1955 and LaCrosse-based Heilemann's in 1972, Schmidt ultimately became Landmark Brewery in 1991, operated by the Minnesota Brewing Company. The new owners considered giving tours of the underlying cave at the time, but nothing came of the plan.

I explored Stahlmann's Cellars with fellow cavers in November 1999. We traversed the extensive sanitary sewer labyrinth under the Fort Road neighborhood, which connects with the cave. Carved in the sandrock in the late nineteenth century, this labyrinth consists of thirty miles of narrow walking passages, and navigating the countless look-alike intersections could be tricky without a compass. The Fort Street sewer forms the backbone of this labyrinth.

We entered the great sandrock labyrinth by walking up a storm-water outfall at Ross Island on the Mississippi River and crawling through a small pipe into the sanitary side—something no longer possible owing to St. Paul's sewer separation program, which has sealed the connection. Once inside the labyrinth, we followed the Palace Avenue sewer, the main drain for brewery wastes, to get to Stahlmann's Cellars.

Walking up this narrow sandrock passage for the first time, I heard a rush of water in the darkness ahead and saw a shimmering white ghost advancing toward me. Within seconds, a torrent of beer waste had engulfed my waders and the frothing foam billowed up around my legs. How high would the beer get? There are those who would gladly drown their troubles in drink, but this wasn't what I had in mind. The vile odor of the brewery sewer, where beer sat around in subterranean pools for days before draining away, was beyond words.

Worse was ahead. We came to a passage lined with quivering jelly stalactites, up to a foot long, dangling from the vaults above. I subsequently collected samples of the jelly with latex gloves, placing them in glass jars. I conducted a series of ghoulish experiments on the jelly in my basement at home, subjecting it to various chemicals, such as hydrochloric acid and hydrogen peroxide, to see whether I could deduce anything about its nature. Afterward, I poured bleach down the basement floor drain, as my experiments had shown that bleach entirely disintegrates the jelly. My fear was that the jelly, so much of which had been washed down the laundry tub, would begin to grow in the drains and clog them, as under the brewery itself. Perhaps I had been influenced by watching the movie *Alien*, with its malevolent jellies.

I found out later that the jelly is in fact well known to sanitation engineers as sewer slime, or pendant slime. One such slime, examined under the microscope by researchers, was found to be the product of a bacterial-fungal combination that secreted a substance called zoogleal matrix. The fungus provided a physical surface on which the bacterial slime producers could proliferate. The function of the copious slime was to absorb and concentrate nutritive substances from the atmosphere. Ethyl alcohol was found to be especially conducive to slime formation. One researcher dubbed them alcoholic slimes, which seems to fit best. The brewery waste, which splashed into the Palace Avenue sewer from pipes, had plenty of opportunity to generate nutritious aerosols. Indeed, at one point there was a crude shaft in the sandstone containing what appeared to be a beer waterfall—probably leakage from above.

We found evidence that others, in the distant past, may also have witnessed this ghastly spectacle. In a nearby side tunnel under Erie Street, laborers had cemented a horseshoe into the keystone of the sewer arch. Hoping for the best?

Beyond the snot galleries—beyond the microbial veil—we found the great Stahlmann's Cellars. I let out a whoop as I slithered from a small clay pipe into the enormous black void. I wiped the vile jelly from my body. It was like a birth. My light illuminated a primeval forest of colossal yellow brick piers, swarming with giant red cockroaches. Rats scuttled among the breakdown slabs on the cave floor. Festoons of vapor hung lazily in the warm, fetid air. We began to sweat profusely and removed our coats. While there were isolated patches of slime in the cave itself, they were nothing like that found in the sewer we had just passed through.

In 1999 the brewery was running full steam, producing Pig's Eye Pilsner and other brands. And I mean *steam*—there were noisy deluges of hot water from the brew house into the cave through a hole in the ceiling several times an hour. The steaming cascade splashed into a deeply eroded sandstone pit, which contained a jumble of broken brickwork and other detritus. The chambers in the immediate vicinity, a low, gloomy maze of fermenting brickwork, felt like saunas, reminding me of a visit to the Yampah Vapor Caves in Glenwood Springs, Colorado.

Stahlmann's Cellars proper is located beyond the footprint of the brew house and is thus devoid of the supportive brick piers. Following the passage heading north from the brew house maze into the main cellars, the dividing line between the two was nicely marked by a stream of cold water several feet wide and deep that crossed the passage on its way from the brew house water well to the Fort Street sewer. Shortly after crossing this miniature River Styx, we arrived at the largest room in the cave, which we dubbed the Rotunda, after a similar room in the Mammoth Cave of Kentucky from which passages radiate outward in several directions, just as they did here. Twin boulders sat in the center of our Rotunda. We placed a lamp there as a visual reference point and explored outward in each direction. Despite the precaution, the cave was such a maze that we got lost, even having left rock cairns to mark our route, as the old polar explorers used to do. Until I learned the maze better, I had to rely on compass readings to navigate.

The passage heading northeast from the Rotunda led to a manhole, visible in the cave ceiling, at the top of a steel ladder. Sealed today, this manhole once provided access to the cave from the basement of the office building and was the usual entry point to the cave for the occasional newspaper reporter. One such reporter glumly commented in 1993, "Anyone who knew anything about those caves is long dead."

The passage heading southwest from the Rotunda contained the best stalactites in the cave, more than a foot long and quite drippy, forming rows along the intersecting joints of the limestone ceiling. Beyond the stalactites, a trio of vertical well pipes passed through the cave. These are the wells that supplied the much-frequented pump house on Fort Road, which dispensed free "spring water" to the public for many years.

Going east, a massive round arch of limestone rubble masonry and a stairway leading upward toward Oneida Street, though choked with boulders, marked a former entrance to the cave.

At the outskirts of Stahlmann's Cellars, a sandrock passage runs toward the original Stahlmann mansion at 855 West Seventh Street (now called the Marie Schmidt Bremer Home), an Italianate villa that was constructed circa 1870. Under the mansion itself we found a mysterious shaft, its walls coated with white flowstone, a natural mineral deposit left by flowing water. With a diameter of three feet, this thirty-foot shaft is large enough for a person to fit through, but its purpose is unclear. It brought to mind the kidnapping of Edward Bremer by gangsters in 1934, after which the family reportedly dug a tunnel from the mansion to the Rathskeller across the street.

We left Stahlmann's Cellars by a different way than we entered, following a lengthy sandrock crawlway that began under the Bremer mansion and led to the Fort Street sewer. We had a nasty surprise when some rats emerged from their burrows, squeaking in protest at the unexpected intrusion. After braving the whiskered gauntlet and wading down the sewer trunk lines, we emerged into the open air once again.

What was to be my last visit to Stahlmann's Cellars for several years was on Thanksgiving Day in 1999. One of my friends was so revolted by the sights and smells of the expedition (he complained loudly, for example, of the "sperm odor" in the cave) that after exiting the sewer outfall he tore off the trash bag he had been wearing and flung his red helmet onto the banks of the ravine, stomping home to eat Thanksgiving dinner as best he could in his thoroughly de-appetized state. I quarantined my rucksack after arriving home to forestall a potential infestation from insect hitchhikers. My rucksack had been sitting around in the sewers, and perhaps some roaches were exploring my stuff while I was exploring their world. You learn to leave everything outside the house, even your clothes.

In June 2002, Landmark Brewery shut down. Gopher State Ethanol, the nation's first urban ethanol plant, began production at the site in April 2000 and continued in operation until May 2004 when it, too, shut down. We returned to Stahlmann's Cellars in April 2006 to see what changes, if any, the brewery closure had brought about in the underlying cave. Owing to St. Paul's sewer separation program, which severs subterranean travel routes, the cave was much harder to get to this time. We had to enter the sewer labyrinth by way of a remote aperture and traverse a lengthy detour, a total distance of one mile, to the cave.

The microclimate of Stahlmann's Cellars had changed dramatically during the interval since our earlier visits. Most notably, the cave was much cooler and drier because the brewery was no longer draining hot wastewater through the cave. Back in 1999, I measured the air temperature in the Rotunda at 70 degrees Fahrenheit (obviously, this was not a temperature maximum for the cave, rather what I would consider an average) and nearly 100 percent humidity. The same instrument in the same spot now registered 52 degrees—the temperature you'd normally expect in caves at this latitude—and 90 percent humidity. The subterranean stream that formerly sported among the giant brick piers had also dried up, probably because the brew house well pump had been shut off. In the absence of brewery waste, the cave life had died off. No rats or cockroaches were seen this time. The living sewer jelly was gone too, having changed from a moist white slime to a dry black crud.

In February 2005, the Minnesota State Historic Preservation Office determined that the great castle-like Schmidt Brewery, which still sits vacant, was eligible for nomination to the National Register of Historic Places. Whatever the brewery's future use, hopefully the historic cave found in the depths below can also partake in the vision, commemorating the heritage of the great nineteenth-century German brewers of St. Paul and their endless, fascinating mazes.

HEINRICH BREWERY

Minneapolis also had a few brewery caves. By far the most accessible was the Heinrich Brewery Cave, near the West Bank campus of the University of Minnesota. Beginning as the Minneapolis Brewery in 1866, the Heinrich Brewery, as it came to be known, existed until 1903. The surrounding area was dubbed Brewery Flats because the Noerenberg Brewery, whose lagering caves are completely sealed, was also located nearby. These breweries, along with others, merged to form Grain Belt Beer in the 1890s, which went on to become a nationally recognized brand.

Heinrich Cave was dug in the sandstone, probably in the 1880s, pretty much at river level, with more than one thousand feet of passages. The three entrances (two are completely blocked up; the middle one is gated) led to three passages going straight into the bluff. The passages are connected by low crawlways. In the late 1930s, when the sanitary interceptor tunnel was being dug just inland from the cave, the cave was used as a dumping ground for excavated sand. The passages, originally twenty feet high, are now nearly full to the ceiling throughout much of the cave.

A view of the Heinrich Brewery, framed by the mouth of Bromley's Cave, in Minneapolis.

COURTESY OF THE MINNEAPOLIS PUBLIC LIBRARY, MINNEAPOLIS COLLECTION, BR0121.

Heinrich Cave was gated as a hibernaculum for the Eastern Pipist-
relle bat by the Minnesota Department of Natural Resources (DNR) in
1990 and is no longer open to the public. When we initially explored
the cave back in the 1980s, before the gate was installed, we found
improvised fortifications, toy swords, and so forth, indicating the
cave's use by university students for games of Dungeons & Dragons.
We also came face to face with several fat raccoons. In later years, after
someone had busted the lock off the hibernaculum, I installed my
own lock on the cave to protect it—something that earned me scath-
ing abuse on the Web from other explorers. The DNR later installed a
stronger lock.

Apart from its bats, Heinrich Cave is unusual for its mineral formations. The largest room in the cave, just inside the gate, is wide and
low, but there's a breakdown pile here that has been fused into the
form of a huge, orange stalagmite by iron-rich waters dripping from the
ceiling joints above. In the remotest part of the cave is the Red Room,
chock full of reddish rusticles (rust stalactites) made of ferrihydrite.
The floor here is corrugated with red flowstone, with nests of cave
pearls. A greenish pool of water in the rear of the Red Room is afloat
with calcite rafts. Perhaps more unusual are the gypsum needles found
in a small crawl tube at the rear of the cave, and gypsum petals can
be found on the ceiling nearby. In other places, it appears as though
gypsum has grown between layers in the limestone ceiling, wedging
them apart and causing them to collapse onto the floor below.

What the Minneapolis breweries lack in size and number, they
make up for in their unique crystal deposits.

THE MEDIEVAL TEMPLES
OF MUSHROOM VALLEY
ST. PAUL'S WEST SIDE

A whole economy and countless legends lie locked from view inside those rustic cliffs.

OLIVER TOWNE

MUSHROOM VALLEY in St. Paul, according to the boast, was the largest mushroom-growing center west of Pennsylvania or, alternatively, west of Chicago. Sometimes it was called the mushroom capital of the Midwest. The mushrooms were grown in the more than fifty sandstone caves that punctuated the bluffs. Although called caves, they were artificial, often beginning as silica mines and subsequently used for mushroom growing and other purposes.

Boosters in the post-mushroom era have made hopeful comparisons with Kansas City, Missouri, where a subterranean industrial park of several thousand acres was created from a room-and-pillar mine in the Bethany Falls limestone, beginning in the 1930s. About 90 percent of the space is used for storage, especially food storage, since Kansas City is a transportation hub near the geographic center of the United States. The abandoned limestone mines there also provided space for manufacturers of precision instruments, including parts for the Apollo moon program. Although this "obvious" use of underground space is periodically suggested for St. Paul's Mushroom Valley, as by the Condor Corporation in the 1980s, a countermovement inevitably develops, arguing that the neighborhoods above will be undermined and collapse into the ground.

Mushroom Valley was the informal name for a several-mile stretch of the west side of the Mississippi River gorge, from South Wabasha Street to Pickerel Lake. Mushroom Valley is divided into three distinct segments: Plato Boulevard, Water Street, and Joy Avenue. Each segment has its own distinct flavor. The Plato segment, incorporating what had been the cave-riddled Channel Street before replatting changed the area in 1970, is capped by Prospect Terrace with its historic houses and magnificent views of the city. Most of these caves are filled with flammable wooden debris. The Water Street segment, running along the river and under the High Bridge, had by far the largest caves, forming a labyrinth extending under Cherokee Park. The Joy Avenue segment, now vacated, can still be seen where an unmarked dirt road runs through the woods in Lilydale Park. While most of these caves are very short—root cellars and such—Joy Avenue is bookended by large caves: Mystic Caverns at its eastern end and Echo Cave at its western end. Named after its namesake acoustic effects, Echo Cave was dug for silica by the St. Paul Brick Company and gated as a bat hibernaculum by the Minnesota Department of Natural Resources in 1989. More than any other cave in the valley, Echo Cave seemed stuck in a time warp, providing silica right up to the end. Beyond that are the brick company's clay pits in the Decorah Shale, a bizarre industrial landscape but the city's premier ice-climbing venue because of the springwater seeping from the cliffs, which freezes in winter.

Mushroom Valley had been considered for bomb shelters after World War II began, even before the attack on Pearl Harbor. In the early 1960s the caves were surveyed by a local firm, TKDA, for suitability as fallout shelters, producing the maps that we have today. Generalizing from the TKDA survey, the typical cave is a straight, horizontal passage about 150 feet long, often connected by crosscuts to similar caves on either side, creating network mazes with multiple entrances. A cave operated by the Becker Sand & Mushroom Company was the largest of all, with thirty-five-foot ceilings and nearly a mile of passages; its wonderful hybrid name captured the chief dual usage seen throughout the valley.

The 1962 Civil Defense maps have limited usefulness to the would-be explorer, as the surveyors only included passages large enough to accommodate the atom-harassed populace. Crawlways, stoopways, and windows into other passages were deliberately omitted, sometimes leaving out half the passages in the cave. Even if too small for human beings to enter, such connections often have a major influence on air flow and the hibernation of bats.

Not all the former sand mines were used for mushroom growing. Examination of city directories, insurance atlases, and real estate plats allowed me to reconstruct a fuller picture of the diversity of people and businesses that inhabited Mushroom Valley. These sources reveal what each of the caves was used for, as it is fairly easy to correlate each street address with a particular cave entrance. I will focus on the three chief uses of the Mushroom Valley caves: mushroom gardening, the aging of blue cheese, and places of entertainment, especially night-clubs. (I described another major cave-related industry in Mushroom Valley, brewing, in "The Cave under the Castle.") Finally, I will briefly discuss the dark cloud that has hung over Mushroom Valley in recent decades owing to injuries and death in the abandoned caves.

mushroom Gardening

The Greeks and Romans were fond of eating mushrooms collected in woods and meadows, but it was not until about 1650, in Paris, that one particular species, the White Mushroom *(Agaricus bisporus)*, was actually domesticated, or cultivated. (Other species had been cultivated in the Orient many years earlier.) The White Mushroom thrived on horse manure but not as well on the manure of other animals. About 1800, Parisians found that mushrooms could be grown in the dark, in the subterranean stone quarries that honeycombed their city, which provided even temperature year-round. Mushroom cultivation did not reach the United States until 1865. In the 1880s, there was an abortive attempt by the Mammoth Cave Mushroom Company in Kentucky to raise mushrooms in that cave; the product was served at the Mammoth Cave Hotel and shipped to eastern cities.

In the early days it was often necessary to abandon a cave after growing mushrooms in it for just a few years due to the accumulation of diseases and insects. About 1890, however, a method for the direct germination of mushroom spores was developed at the Pasteur Institute in France. A pure spawn industry began selling disease-free inoculum, grown in milk bottles, to mushroom farmers.

The original mushroom farmers in St. Paul were Frenchmen who "had seen mushrooms growing in the caves under the sewers of Paris." Interviewed on at least two separate occasions by the *St. Paul Pioneer Press* newspaper columnist Gareth Hiebert (Oliver Towne), the mushroom farmers stated that their predecessors began the local industry in the 1880s. The last cave ceased production in the 1980s during the creation of Lilydale Regional Park.

"St. Paul's Caves Eclipse Backlot for Gardening, Except for Crop Foes," by Jay W. Ludden, in the *St. Paul Pioneer Press*, May 27, 1923, offers a unique glimpse of mushroom farming. Ludden was clearly awed by the sheer size of the caves: "These caverns have cathedral-like arches, and looking into them through the dusk that conceals details and accentuates the big lines, one is reminded of etchings of the interiors of medieval temples. This impression is strengthened when at the distant end of the cave the workmen's lamps give light as from an altar."

"As with all gardening," Ludden mused, "the more one goes into it, the more one is disillusioned as regards its simplicity. Pests and blights and molds confront one, and remedies are more or less difficult

This humorous image appeared in a *St. Paul Pioneer Press* article on St. Paul's mushroom caves in 1923, illustrating the battle between mushroom growers and the fearsome manure flies.

to apply." By 1923, the pure spawn technique had been adopted by local growers: "Spawn culture is a big industry of one St. Paul company, which has had at one time on the racks used for the purpose, 125,000 milk bottles containing spawn."

But Ludden reported that "terrific battles are carried on in the dark depths of the caverns, victory going sometimes to the gardeners, and again to the bugs, which, microscopically, are appalling and ferocious." The newspaper article contains an incredible image showing a man, dagger drawn, battling an enormous manure fly inside a cave carpeted with the "ghostly blossoms" of mushrooms. "The artist has depicted a terrific battle between a mushroom grower and one of the enemies that attack his crop," the caption explains.

One of the standard authorities on mushroom pests, published by the U.S. Department of Agriculture in 1941, describes the manure fly as having "a hump-backed appearance. They are quite active, moving about constantly in a series of jerky runs." While there were several control measures, such as light traps, dusts, and fumigation, the best strategy was to prevent infestation of beds in the first place. Horse manure compost was placed in the caves and allowed to pasteurize— also called sweating out—during which the temperature of the compost rose spontaneously to 145 degrees Fahrenheit, which killed or drove off most of the pests. After letting the temperature return to normal, the beds were inoculated with spawn and the mushrooms began to grow. But Ludden reported that "the source of the fertilizer has been noticeably diminishing with the decrease in the number of horses, owing to the rise of motorized transportation."

One of the crop foes not found was weeds—at least those of the photosynthetic variety. "For the weeds grow to a height of only four or five inches," Ludden continued mawkishly, "pale and frail, like the heroines in the old time volumes of Select Reading for Young Ladies, then droop and die, like one of those heroines distraught by the idea that her mother suspects her of having told her first untruth."

In addition to their battles against the bugs, Ludden also noted wars among the mushroom farmers themselves. In one nasty case, a mushroom cave was prevented from expanding farther into the sandstone by another mushroom cave that had burrowed completely around it. I recall exploring those two caves years ago, and I had been puzzled by their arrangement until I read Ludden's report.

Further technological changes after 1923 improved the lot of the mushroom farmer. The adoption of the tray system in the 1930s and the consequent disappearance of the old floor beds were a big step forward in controlling mushroom pests. No longer could the pests seek refuge in the underlying soil during pasteurization only to later reinfest the beds. Indeed, remains of these wooden trays form the chief diagnostic artifact of former mushroom caves in St. Paul.

A more recent *St. Paul Pioneer Press* article, "Mushroom Farming Is Family Tradition," March 28, 1976, paints a portrait of Mushroom Valley in its final days. "Mushroom growing," one of the farmers pointed out, "remains hard and backbreaking work because some things simply cannot be mechanized—including the picking of mushrooms." Although more than a dozen families once engaged in the work, few members of the younger generation seemed willing to adopt the manure-based lifestyle involved. William Lehmann, known locally as the Mushroom King, moved his operation to "the world-renowned cement-block caves of Lake Elmo" in 1965. Presumably the more rural setting at Lake Elmo, east of St. Paul, made for lower manure transportation expenses than in the heart of the city. Specially designed aboveground facilities, as at Lake Elmo, while initially more expensive than caves, allowed for finer tuning of environmental conditions, including the control of pests and diseases. The Mushroom Century had come to a close.

cheese ripening

The Villaume Box & Lumber Company, founded in 1882, was a well-known St. Paul business, "one of the nation's leaders in the manufacture of custom millwork, shipping cases and boxes," according to a 1940 promotional brochure. The brochure continued:

Villaume has on its own property, 14 hillside caves with surface level entrances. Each cave has a ceiling height of 12 feet and is 20 feet wide. The 14 caves contain a total of 50,000 square feet of floor space, usable for manufacturing, storage, or as shelters in event of air raids.

From 1933 to the 1950s, the University of Minnesota rented one of the V caves, as they were known, and produced a domestic Roquefort cheese—subsequently named Minnesota Blue—an event that would have international repercussions. St. Paul was acclaimed the "Blue Cheese Capital of the World" during World War II.

Professor Willes Barnes Combs, a native of Missouri, was appointed professor of dairy industry at the University of Minnesota in 1925. He soon discovered "a queer local fact. There are dozens of sandstone caves in St. Paul." In the late 1920s, while shopping for mushrooms at a cave in St. Paul, he noticed that a lantern in the cave was covered with rust. The mushroom grower informed him that the atmosphere of the caves was extremely moist. Combs conjectured that the caves might have a combination of temperature and humidity similar to the celebrated Roquefort caves of France, where Roquefort cheese is produced.

Humans have been using caves to ripen cheese for millennia. The story of the Cyclops cave, where an early type of the popular Greek feta cheese was ripened, appears in Homer's *Odyssey*. The French Roquefort caves themselves have a history dating back to classical antiquity. In the first century AD, the Roman scholar Pliny the Elder was said to have served this cheese to guests in his villa outside Rome. The blue, aristocratic veins running through the cheese were partly responsible for Roquefort being called *Le Roi des Fromages*—the King of Cheeses. Italy's Gorgonzola and England's Stilton are similar blue-veined cheeses.

"Prof. Combs now has found that Roquefort conditions are approximated by the sandstone caves along the Mississippi in the Twin Cities area," a newspaper reported. St. Paul's caves, according to Combs, were "the only caves in this country where temperature and humidity are similar to those in France." Artificial ripening chambers, or mechanical caves, had been tried in the past, but they proved so costly to build and operate that they had not attained success on a commercial scale. "We can't set up a room like this," Combs explained. A crucial problem was to hold the temperature low while maintaining high humidity—an almost paradoxical combination.

Having secured an appropriation from the state of Minnesota to cover the cost of five thousand pounds of milk and other necessities, Combs placed the first batch of cheese—"about 100 pounds"—in a small, rented cave. "In 1933," Combs wrote, "when the Dairy Division of the University of Minnesota became actively interested in the manufacture of this cheese insofar as was known no blue cheese was being manufactured commercially in this country."

While Combs's use of St. Paul's caves was new, the cheese recipe was not, being "an old formula that had been gathering dust in the

Department of Agriculture." But Combs was using a special strain of the blue mold that had been selected by researchers at Iowa State College. "The first batch went haywire, probably because the cave had no door," Combs said later.

In the spring of 1934, Professor Combs tried again, the mouth of the cave this time being sealed with "a tight wooden framework." He met with spectacular success. On July 20, 1934, Walter C. Coffey, dean and director of the University's Department of Agriculture—for whom Coffey Hall was later named—wrote a letter to the U.S. secretary of agriculture, Henry Wallace, on behalf of his staff:

We are in the midst of a research project having to do with the manufacture of cheese of the Roquefort type. Copying after certain manufacturers of this type of cheese in Europe, we are ripening these cheeses in caves. These caves are cut out of the salt sand-stone along the Mississippi River in the St. Paul vicinity. There are workers who make their livelihoods constructing these caves. I am told that they get the sand which is well adapted to moulding purposes as compensation. Therefore, the possibilities for cheese caves are almost unlimited.... If we succeed in making a uniform product of high quality, we think we shall be paving the way for a great cheese industry because of the availability of these caves.

There was a big public announcement of the new cheese the following year. "Million Yearly Cheese Trade Seen Here," crowed the *St. Paul Pioneer Press* on January 6, 1935, reporting how "the dairy chief," Combs, "disclosed that nearly 10,000 pounds of Roquefort-type cheese, the flavor of which amazed epicures, was cured this year in a small, experimental cave, within a few minutes' walking distance from St. Paul's City Hall." *Popular Science* magazine featured the University cave in its April 1935 issue under the heading "Caves for Cheese Making Discovered in America."

The cheese was ripened in the caves for three months, removed, wrapped in tinfoil, and placed in cold storage for six months, by which time it had developed "that heavenly stink which goes so well with cold beer." The conditions were rather exacting. "This cock-eyed cheese is very temperamental about its adolescence," wrote one reporter.

Combs scaled up his operations in the following year. "A larger cave of about the same cross section but over 200 feet deep was secured in 1935. This cave had been used for growing mushrooms, and when first observed had a rather musty odor. Approximately an inch of sand was scraped from all surfaces of the cave in order to present clean surfaces. The musty odor virtually disappeared and did not at any time contribute to the flavor of the cheese."

Combs claimed that there were enough caves near St. Paul to supply the entire world demand for Roquefort. "There's not a European cheese that can't be made right here in Minnesota," he boasted. Talk like this did not go unnoticed for long. M. Henri Cassou, a member of the French Foreign Trade Commission, swooped down on "the bastard caves," declaring, "There is only one Roquefort cheese and it is made in France." "Genuine Roquefort cheese," Cassou informed the American, "is made from sheep's milk. This milk has other properties, because of the peculiar conditions of vegetation around Roquefort, France." The Minnesota product was made from the more plentiful cow's milk, which sometimes imparted a yellowish tinge to a cheese

Professor Willes Barnes Combs *(left)* and R. A. Trovatten, the state commissioner of agriculture, inspecting Roquefort cheese in the University of Minnesota caves, 1935.

COURTESY OF THE MINNESOTA HISTORICAL SOCIETY.

that was supposed to be white. France had "an old agreement with the State department which somehow restrains American cheese-makers from labeling their cheese with the dear old name that sends cheese fans off into the gentle dithers."

Combs gave Cassou a tour of the University cave. "Your product is very good," Cassou conceded, after tasting the cheese, "but I would suggest that it be called 'blue' cheese. Why fly under false colors?" Combs was obliged to "fall in line with the panty-waists, and just call it 'blue cheese.'" It was eventually named Minnesota Blue. But Cassou had been the victim of a capital joke. Combs confessed years later that genuine French Roquefort had been planted among the Minnesota cheeses in the cave. Cassou hadn't even noticed.

National Cheese Week, "which aims at putting into consumption the nation's cheese surplus," was designated as November 10 to 16, for 1935. This promotional event was inaugurated in Minnesota on November 12, 1935, when the state commissioner of agriculture, R. A. Trovatten, inspected "the University of Minnesota Roquefort cheese caves," hosted by Combs. By the end of that week, it was reported that work had begun on a new cheese plant in Faribault, Minnesota. Thus originated the Treasure Cave brand, introduced in 1936 and going strong today. It was the first commercial venture stemming from Combs's research.

Shelves of cheese ripening in a cave used by the Kraft Cheese Company.

PHOTOGRAPH BY PAUL WRIGHT STUDIOS OF PHOTOGRAPHY. COURTESY OF THE MINNESOTA HISTORICAL SOCIETY.

Having begun with such fanfare, Combs's Roquefort project unexpectedly dropped out of sight for a while. The fall of France to invading German armies in June 1940, however, cut off French imports decisively. "City's Million-Dollar Cheese Industry Gets Off with Bang," trumpeted the *Pioneer Press* on December 15, 1940. In the autumn of 1940, the Kraft Cheese Company of Chicago rented "one big cave, 150 feet deep" from Villaume, and Kraft's "K-men" began marketing the ROKA brand of blue cheese. The Land O'Lakes Company, its rival just down the bluff, rented "two caves, 100 feet deep," at the former Castle Royal nightclub, which had gone bankrupt in 1940. In January 1941, the first commercial blue cheese from St. Paul's caves hit the market.

Combs had triumphed. On February 27, 1941, thirty-six Minnesota legislators visited "the University Farm experimental cave" under Combs's wing and were served blue "as well as some Trappist or Port de Salut-type brick cheese." The legislators went on to visit the Kraft and Land O'Lakes cheese caves, whose very existence owed everything to Combs's mastery of the dairy arts. As if that were not enough, Combs rolled out yet another cheese, called Gopher. The University cave was featured in the *New York Times* on June 18, 1942. One reporter declared that "St. Paul is well on its way to become the blue cheese capital of the world."

By 1945, it was reported that in Minnesota the production of blue cheese ranked second only to cheddar. Concern arose about what would happen to the fledgling blue cheese industry after the war, but fortunately these fears proved unfounded. In 1949 it was reported, "Imports [of Roquefort] have dropped to practically nothing." The Land O'Lakes Cheese Cave was listed at 6 West Channel Street in *Polk's City Directory* until 1959.

The last substantial work carried out in the University cave appears to have been that of Howard A. Morris, one of Combs's graduate students, who did research there in the late 1940s. I interviewed Dr. Morris, who recalled signing cave rental agreements with the Villaume Company and stated that the University cave ceased to be used sometime during the 1950s. A local caver recalls having seen a derelict sign pointing to the University cave in the late 1960s.

Villaume relocated in 1970, leaving the entire stretch of caves vacant, to the delight of local explorers. Although the University cave's bluff entrance has long been sealed, I found access through a back door—a crosscut from an adjacent, open cave, which ran parallel. The cave is full of debris such as wooden beams and scrap iron to within a few feet of its ceiling. I found no obvious artifacts from the cheese-making era.

In addition to cheese, another dairy product in Mushroom Valley was milk. The Milk Truck Cave, as we call it, still contains, like a sort of drive-in time capsule, the partially buried delivery trucks of the old St. Paul Milk Company. The trucks were parked underground and just left there, the white sand sifting down on them over the years, burying them as if in snowdrifts. During one visit to this unique underground parking garage, we dug down through the sand enveloping one of the trucks, looking for its glove compartment in search of identifying information. It was empty, but we recorded the truck's serial number. Using the Detroit Industrial Vehicle Company (DIVCO) Club Web site, we were able to date the truck to the 1950s. The more remote passages of the Milk Truck Cave, which we could only get to by squeezing through a tight hole, were rather creepy. Once I met a big fat raccoon back there. His water bowl was a natural drip pocket in the floor of the cave under an old ventilation hole in the roof, and he could go out to the river for food. Quite a nice setup!

THE NIGHTCLUB ERA

From the earliest days, some of the Mushroom Valley caves were used for subterranean entertainment. *Northwest Magazine*, November 1886, describes the elaborate caves that German immigrants had dug, called Felsenkellers. One of them had "a broad stairway, cut through the sand-stone upwards to the terrace, where the visitor can step forth among the trees into the open air and have from the commanding height, a magnificent view of river and city scenery. The 'Felsenkeller' with its bowling alleys, etc., is occupied by John B. Fandel Jr., whose father spent seven years in fashioning the grotesque interiors of his spacious caverns." The 1891 *Rascher Atlas* called Fandell's place a Cave Saloon. Oliver Towne, too, described "the famous Fandell caves, one of which houses a beer hall called the Mystic Tavern, whose emergency exit was a winding staircase up through 100 feet of rock to the top of the hill above." Having explored this spiral stairway myself, I did not find it as convenient as the above descriptions would suggest.

Mushroom Valley's nightclub era began as national prohibition

(1919–34) was winding down. There were two nightclubs here in the 1930s, Mystic Caverns and Castle Royal. A local mushroom grower recalled "the bumper-to-bumper cars that poured past here day and night to those nightclubs." Oliver Towne called Mushroom Valley "one of the oddest night club belts in the world."

Mystic Caverns—not to be confused with Fandell's Mystic Tavern—is forgotten today, but it was beloved in the 1930s. "The most novel café and night club in the country" was opened on April 8, 1933, about the same time that the classic version of *King Kong*, starring Fay Wray, hit the movie theaters. Garish newspaper advertisements for Mystic Caverns, with leering skulls, promoted "St. Paul's Underground Wonderland," advising readers to "See the Beautiful Silver-Cave and the Rainbow Shower of 2,000 Mirrors. Dine, Drink and Dance to the rhythmic tunes of Jack Foster's Ten Cavemen." The ads spelled out the location exactly: "Cross the Wabasha Street Bridge at the new St. Paul Courthouse.... Travel up the river road under the High Bridge to the huge Neon Skull and Crossbones."

On opening night, four hundred people had to be turned away, and Mystic Caverns was rapidly enlarged to hold eight hundred people. During construction, liquid glass was sprayed on the walls. There were three main chambers, one of which contained the ballroom, called the Silver Cave. According to one patron, the cave contained "a mon-

A newspaper advertisement for Mystic Caverns in St. Paul, which operated as a nightclub from 1933 to 1934.

FROM *ST. PAUL DAILY NEWS*, APRIL 14, 1933.

strous chandelier, with lights flashing all different colors, two stories above the polished-wood dance floor." The other two chambers held, respectively, the main dining room and "a regular old-time bar, 40 feet long, with brass foot rail and all, where light lunches and beverages will be served." "A system of loudspeakers wafts the music from the main dining room into the farthest recesses of the innumerable smaller caverns which serve as private dining rooms," it was reported.

"Entertainment features will be in keeping with the mystic atmosphere, providing palmists, mind readers, psychics and a magician for the amusement of guests." Some of the magical effects were produced by a stage manager for the famous magician Howard Thurston. As if that were not enough, "Ghosts will stalk the river bank, 'living' skeletons will move about its cavernous rooms, weird specters will peer from hidden recesses and women will float above the heads of the orchestra." By far the biggest draw was the nude fan dancer, Sally Rand.

One of the cave's owners, Jack Foster, was the leader of the St. Paul police band, which made it all the more ironic when a Ramsey County grand jury investigation led to the closure of Mystic Caverns in 1934 for running a "subterranean casino."

After its glory days, Mystic Caverns was used for potato storage, and in its misunderstood old age was dubbed Horseshoe Cave by the cavers of the 1980s, unaware of its romantic past. In the 1990s, I diligently examined the palimpsest of graffiti on the cave's walls, especially in the former ballroom, hoping for old signatures (or any artifact) from the nightclub era, but could find nothing convincing. It had been stripped bare, like the fan dancers who had wowed crowds more than a half century earlier.

The other big 1930s nightclub was Castle Royal, proclaimed the "World's Most Gorgeous Underground Night Club," on what is now South Wabasha Street. The cave consists of several parallel passages connected by crosscuts. Originally a mushroom cave, it was acquired by William Lehmann, the Mushroom King. On October 26, 1933, after spending $150,000 on the place, he opened a nightclub in the cave, Castle Royal, with a fancy, patterned brick facade that you can still admire today. Mushrooms, not surprisingly, loomed large in the dollar menu that he touted. The chandeliers, fountains, and tapestries that graced the establishment came from the recently demolished Charles Gates's mansion; Charles's father was "Bet a Million" Gates, the nation's largest manufacturer of barbed wire. The ceiling was stuccoed to prevent the incessant rain of sand grains on diners and that gritty feel while eating. Doorways were carved in the shape of mushrooms. In the Big Band era, performers like Cab Calloway, the Dorsey Brothers, Harry James, and the Coronado Orchestra played there. And of course there are the gangster stories.

Even before Prohibition, St. Paul allowed gangsters to remain in the city as long as they didn't commit any crimes while in residence—the so-called O'Connor system. Many were on the lam from Chicago. The crime historian Paul Maccabee, who spent thirteen years researching FBI and police files for his 1995 book, *John Dillinger Slept Here*, which deals with crime and corruption in St. Paul, stated that there was no proof that Dillinger or other gangsters frequented Castle Royal. In my own research, the only evidence I could find was a 1977 newspaper clipping reporting that one of the original musicians "remembers seeing Ma Barker and John Dillinger there, and one of the current kitchen workers claims she witnessed three thugs gunned down at the bar one night back in the 1930s." But the daughter of one of Lehmann's partners wrote, "I must express my feelings about all the sensationalism before the 1977–78 reopening [of the restaurant]. I never heard of the 'Castle Royal' being a hang-out for gangsters. It would have been most distressing to my father if he had known or suspected such."

Ghosts are said to infest Castle Royal and were even featured in a 1982 television production. But there's a more prosaic explanation, based on my past experience in the caves of Mushroom Valley. Years ago, I recall exploring a nearby cave when I heard girls chatting and giggling somewhere in the darkness ahead of me. When they heard me, they clammed up, fearing the consequences of meeting a stranger in such vulnerable circumstances. I wonder how many of the poltergeists in Castle Royal were actually explorers who came in through the back door at night, as I was able to do as recently as the 1980s, when the cave was still connected with others at the back end and not well sealed as it is today—especially considering that some of the ghosts are said to walk through walls, which sounds to me like someone emerging from an opening into the cave proper. All it would take is an incident or two like this to get the stories going.

The Castle Royal nightclub went bankrupt in 1940, and much of the cave was rented out to Land O'Lakes as a ripening vault for blue cheese until 1959. After the 1965 Mississippi River flood, Lehmann moved his mushroom-farming operation to Lake Elmo, specializing in pickled mushrooms. The cave remained vacant for most of the next dozen years, except for being rented briefly to Jerry's Produce.

Castle Royal was purchased by Mike Golden and Lebanese restaurateur Jim George, and they refurbished it as a restaurant, opening in 1977. They reportedly invested half a million dollars in the venture, injecting an Art Deco motif. The cave had a Bogart-style Casablanca atmosphere, with a sixty-foot bar and dance floor. Khaki-clad waitresses served up the gourmet fare. But within a year, they found that the fancy menu and valet parking weren't selling well in what was derisively called the hamburger area of town, and they reluctantly reoriented the menu toward fast food. Subsequently, a lightning bolt struck the cave, and a patron sued them for an alleged bat bite. A columnist, describing their troubles, labeled it "A Royal Nightmare."

Castle Royal hosted the welcoming party for the National Speleological Society's annual convention in 1980, which attracted cavers from around the country. Later that year the Jaycees staged their annual Halloween attraction in the cave, before the event had firmly ensconced itself at the Tunnel of Terror (described in "Velvet Underground"). The restaurant closed in 1982, but in 1984 the cave briefly hosted Royal Pizza. In the late 1980s the cave was advertised as The Library, a sort of nonalcoholic teen nightclub, and then became vacant again.

Castle Royal was purchased by Bremer Construction in 1992 for office space and heavy equipment storage. Under their ownership the cave now flourishes as the Wabasha Street Caves. The Bremers have invested a lot of money fixing the cave up. They rent out twelve thousand square feet of finished space for wedding receptions and other events. The industrious Bremers hosted the Great American History Theater, added gangster tours of St. Paul, a cave tour, and a coffee shop. Their success is a splendid example of how the caves of Mushroom Valley, rich in history, can be utilized and made profitable again.

cave TRAGEDIES

Mushroom Valley has earned a bad reputation in recent decades for the injuries and fatalities that have occurred there, but cave accidents are conspicuous by their very rarity. The area's annual toll of drownings in lakes each year exceeds the total number of deaths in its caves over the past century, yet we never hear anyone talk about forbidding people to swim. Some of the things that were done to the caves years ago have made them less safe than they were before, and some would like to blame the caves for their misfortunes instead of taking personal responsibility. Everyone has a role to play in preventing further tragedies. We live in a part of the country where caves aren't all that common, so they are viewed as something exceptional. Elsewhere in the country it's the opposite. Traveling through the limestone belt of the southeastern United States, where caves abound, I found a different attitude. There are so many caves there that it wouldn't occur to anyone to try to seal them all up. Almost everyone played in the caves as a kid, so they do not seem alien, and there are far more caving clubs, so people can learn how to cave safely. It's been said that the most dangerous part of a cave trip is driving to the cave, considering the annual slaughter on our nation's roads.

The incidents in St. Paul occurred after the caves had been left vacant and were no longer utilized. Broadly speaking, there are two different groups of caves where the incidents occurred, each having a different problem. Along Water Street, where most of the caves are empty, the problem is ceiling collapse, usually caused by campfires and/or loud music. Along Plato Boulevard, where most of the caves are filled with flammable wood, the problem is usually carbon monoxide poisoning.

In 1954, a "landslide" killed three-year-old Eddie Brown during a visit to the abandoned Mystic Caverns at the west end of Water Street. "Death ended a day of fun.... A 60-pound chunk of sandstone fell from above the cave arch ... and struck him on the head.... Mrs. Brown, who became hysterical, was put under sedatives at the hospital." We learn from a followup that Mystic Caverns was the scene of "wild parties by teenagers" in the 1950s. Then, as now, no one could figure out how to seal a cave properly. "It had been boarded up, even blocked off with cement blocks, and still had been broken into, the report said. Police had suggested the cave be dynamited to destroy it."

An increasing number of caves became vacant along Water Street in the late 1970s, especially after Ramsey County bought out the old Altendorfer and Bisciglia mushroom farms. Water Street formed a connection between the Harriet Island and Lilydale segments of a proposed regional park. The first incident occurred on May 26, 1984, when Cave No. 532 (a designation based on its Water Street address) collapsed, killing one person from skull fracture and paralyzing another with a broken spine. A campfire, lighted to provide warmth in the chilly cave, had dried and weakened the sandstone ceiling. In response, city officials smashed in the roof of the cave, a solution that was effective in this case because the cave was on a slope and there were no buildings above it. On October 20, 1993, two teenagers were critically injured in another cave collapse along Water Street.

Police cars began regular patrols along Water Street, but evading them became just one more thrill for the explorers. A sensationalist element crept into the media's coverage of the area. One newspaper article suggested that bodies were being dug up in local cemeteries and carted into the mines by Satanists for unspecified rituals. One caver even began noting "shrines" on his maps of the abandoned mines. It was like a bizarre parody of the medieval temples that Ludden had imagined back in 1923.

I got a sense for the enormous amount of collapse that can occur in these caves under certain conditions by visiting the Bait Shop Cave, located upriver from the High Bridge and a former Al Bisciglia mushroom cave. This cave went up for sale in 2007, and I toured the property with the realtor. The empty gray tubs, where countless minnows had lived, were still sitting there. This cave had the largest collapse dome I've ever seen in Mushroom Valley, leaving a miniature Himalayas under the vast vault. Initially, the sellers were asking more than a quarter million dollars for the property, but after the real estate bubble burst the price dropped substantially. Subprime had met subterranean.

In 1985, the old High Bridge was demolished, and the resulting concrete chunks were shoved into a few of the abandoned caves along Water Street. This was the origin of the bizarre rebar snakepits in the caves, with twisted steel rods projecting outward in all directions. I could tell what cave I was in—Big Snake or Little Snake—from what diameter rebar it contained, one inch or one-half inch, respectively. This was another unsuccessful exercise in filling caves, but at least here the fill material was noncombustible.

On Plato Boulevard it was a different story. In 1969, as part of the St. Paul Housing and Redevelopment Authority's Riverview Industrial Project, which began in the wake of the 1965 flood, numerous old structures on the floodplain were razed, and the debris was bulldozed into the vacant caves along Plato Boulevard, forming the cursed wood fill that plagues us to this day. These caves are so dry and dusty that it's easy to see how a rip-roaring fire could get going, as they began to do as early as 1971. The wood was repeatedly set on fire by trespassers in the caves, where it smoldered, causing carbon monoxide poisoning, sometimes long after flames were no longer visible and the air appeared clear. Although passersby sometimes reported smoke billowing from cave entrances, firefighters do not usually go into the caves to extinguish these fires owing to the risks involved.

The Peltier Caves, on Plato Boulevard, became notorious after the deaths of two seventeen-year-old girls, overcome by carbon monoxide, from past fires, in a low spot in the cave, on September 26, 1992. City officials initially sealed the caves with Bobcat loaders. A warning sign was erected outside the cave by the parents, reminding potential explorers about the fate of the two girls, but a dozen years later, on April 27, 2004, three more teenagers, each seventeen years old, walked right past that very sign and died in neighboring Fandell's Cave, also from carbon monoxide poisoning. I well remember visiting these caves in the 1980s. At the very back end of one of them, beyond the zone of wooden fill, I experienced a warm feeling and rapid breathing, as did the person accompanying me. These are classic symptoms of carbon dioxide poisoning, and we promptly exited. To be sure, the more mundane day-to-day occupational hazard in these caves is not asphyxiation but tetanus, from the ever-shifting, nail-studded cave fill. It's so easy to impale yourself!

After the 2004 deaths, I served on Mayor Randy Kelly's committee to discuss permanent solutions to the cave problem. The straightforward option of imploding the caverns, with explosives or machinery, as had been done along Water Street, was not available to us because the Plato caves are situated along a vertical bluff with houses on top. If you were to collapse the cave ceilings here, the void space would simply migrate upward inside the sandstone.

Sealing has not worked well in practice because over time cave entrances tend to slump open naturally or are dug open. Occasionally, however, sealing does work. The city undertook to seal the Becker Sand & Mushroom Company cave in 1991, and it remains sealed today. But the effort was Herculean: an enormous earthen ramp was built against the bluffs, and soil was trucked in. I recall the endless procession of trucks along Water Street at the time.

As for the option of filling the caves with something, the problem is that most fills settle over time, leaving a space on top, often with poor air circulation, creating a nightmarish obstacle course for potential rescuers. Obviously, no one was going to suggest stuffing even more flammable wood into the caves. A successful example of filling is Banholzer Cave across the river, where a solidifying slurry was used in 1991.

Another option, used with great success to fill abandoned mines in the West, is polyurethane foam (PUF). PUF is foam of the sort that, on a smaller scale, you spray into the cracks every autumn to keep out mice and the blasts of winter. In this particular setting, it was deemed unworkable, especially since PUF is flammable and generates toxic gases when it burns. Don't need any more of those!

One of the cheaper and more diverting suggestions was to spray skunk juice all over the wood in the caverns. The unpleasant odor would deter partying. You would have to periodically refresh the scent, of course. On the down side, the odor could migrate into adjacent businesses, such as the Wabasha Street Caves.

It was clear that any solution would be costly. CNA Consulting Engineers, a well-respected firm in all things subterranean, subsequently conducted a study for the city, released in 2005, which took all of these suggestions into consideration and recommended spending a million dollars to seal the caves, using landscaping to hide the entrances so potential trespassers would have no clues where to dig. St. Paul has not yet been able to find the funds to carry out the project and has had to fall back on the ad hoc Band-Aid scheme of sealing caves.

John Burghardt, a geologist with the National Park Service, reviewed CNA's 2005 report and reweighted some of the factors in their evaluation matrix. Earlier that year, I had given Burghardt a tour of the St. Paul mines, some of which fall within the boundaries of the Mississippi National River and Recreation Area (MNRRA). He concluded that the value of the abandoned mines to bats and other wildlife had not been properly assessed and promoted another alternative. At the U.S. Borax Company mines near Death Valley National Park, California, an ordinary concrete sewer culvert, with specially designed steel bars that allowed bats to fly through and also provided ventilation, was successfully installed and never breached. In answer to some critics who argued that few bats had been seen during CNA's survey of the caves, Burghardt pointed out, "Most cavernicolous bats require at least 5 feet to drop into flight, so they typically will not roost in spaces much smaller than humans can walk through"—like the wood-filled mushroom caves. And while it's true that a gate had been installed at Echo Cave in 1989, it was so poorly designed that its failure should not deter us from using a much improved version.

Personally, I think utilization, where it can be accomplished, is a viable alternative, the reclamation of Castle Royal being the best example. For some caves, reviving them as outdoor classrooms or parks is an option. In Rochester, Minnesota, at Quarry Hill Park, there's an abandoned mine in the St. Peter Sandstone, originally dug for vegetable storage, which was firmly gated and is now the center-piece of their nature center. Educational tours of the cave are given on a regular basis. Just east of the Twin Cities, in Chippewa Falls, Wisconsin, there's Irvine Park, featuring an abandoned brewery cave in the sandstone outcroppings—sound familiar? The cave is left open for park goers to explore, with a historical plaque at the entrance. On my visits there, I never see drinking, drugs, or creepy persons lurking about, nor is the amount of graffiti overpowering. I think a mix of some of the above alternatives, determined on a case-by-case basis, will solve the problem of controlling access to the caves.

VELVET UNDERGROUND
ABANDONED SAND MINES

The wall, in places, was covered with shapeless fungi.

VICTOR HUGO, LES MISÉRABLES

IN THE EARLY 1990S I was accosted by a director who wanted to make a movie that involved a subterranean chase scene. He wanted my assistance on a pro bono basis (of course), my reward being that I would be mentioned in the fast-rolling credits at the end. Being naïve at the time, I was flattered to be of service to Hollywood. Given his criteria, I thought the vast Ford sand mines under the Highland Park neighborhood in St. Paul would do. I called the Ford public relations people and arranged a tour of the mines, which duly took place.

We were ushered into the mines at the twin portals near the tall chimney of yellow brick at the old steam plant in the river gorge, below the factory. The oxygen levels proving satisfactory, we continued on our way. I later gave a general presentation on Minnesota caves to the director at his office in downtown Minneapolis. It became obvious that I shouldn't be packing my bags for Hollywood anytime soon. The director vanished into thin air after I had devoted considerable effort to the supposed movie. Since then, several other directors have approached me for the same reason, but I'm a little less enthusiastic nowadays. Few proposed movies come to anything.

The Ford Motor Company built its Twin Cities assembly plant for Model Ts in the early 1920s. In addition to using hydroelectricity from the nearby Ford Dam, coal was used to generate steam. The coal was offloaded from trains into the assembly plant and then transported to the steam plant in the river gorge by being lowered down an elevator.

From 1926 onward, there was a glass manufacturing facility here also, which used silica shipped in from the Minnesota River valley to make automobile windshields. Ironically, Ford had not realized at that time that its Highland Park plant sat right over the best silica deposit of all, the St. Peter Sandstone. Whoever finally recognized this fact is an unsung hero of the obvious, from a geologist's standpoint, because the sand had already been much in demand locally for glass making since the late 1800s.

In glass recipes even small amounts of contaminants can be ruinous. The St. Peter Sandstone is a polycyclic sandstone, winnowed of its impurities several times over by geologic processes, leaving much of it, as the textbooks say, 99.44 percent pure silica. (These same textbooks often call the St. Peter Sandstone "the Ivory Soap of sediments" because of its purity, a strange comparison.) In fact, the exact percentage of purity varies depending on where you take your sample and from which part of the geologic column. The lowermost layers in the St. Peter are shaley—much higher in impurities.

Beginning in the late 1930s, Ford, in their quest for silica, mined out 2.5 miles of passages in the St. Peter Sandstone below their Highland Park plant, creating the main caves, and another 1.5 miles of passages below Shepard Road, creating the Marina Caves. The operation ceased in 1952 when it became more economical to manufacture the glass elsewhere.

My first awareness of the Ford mines came in early childhood, when my brothers brought back breathless tales of vast subterranean spaces under our Highland Park home. I may have gone down into

Two views of the tunnel system underneath the Ford Plant in St. Paul. Ford mined silica for the manufacture of glass windshields in automobiles.

PHOTOGRAPH ON NEXT PAGE BY NORTON AND PEEL. PHOTOGRAPHS COURTESY OF THE MINNESOTA HISTORICAL SOCIETY.

the basement to look for them in my childish enthusiasm. I believe my parents warned my brothers about visiting such dangerous places. I didn't hear of the mines again until I discovered them for myself years later.

The Ford mines stand completely abandoned and empty today. Up until some careless urban explorers broadcasted the location of the entrance on the Web, thus wrecking it for everyone including themselves, it was possible to explore them at leisure. The usual entry point was an old door in the bluffs behind the steam plant. There was a lengthy hike to get to it, along a trail that ran through the woods in Hidden Falls Park, where we could pretend to be fishermen. At the right moment, we would bend the door back and squeeze through the opening, no one the wiser. On one occasion we did have a close call. After spending hours exploring the mines, we exited to find a Ford security vehicle parked smack across from us. But the driver was asleep, so we were able to make good our escape.

Once inside, the sandstone passage headed into the bluff before coming to a three-way junction. The passage turning north went to the hydroplant at the Ford Dam. There, although the glass door said "Operator Only," bold individuals could open it and explore the building if they chose. Following the passage straight ahead from the junction brought us to a steel ladder leading one hundred feet up to the Ford plant, where they made Ford Ranger pickup trucks. The ladder

was wet, slippery, and rusted, providing little assurance of safety. We were more interested in the mines themselves, which were located south from the junction.

This sandstone passage led to twin concrete tunnels of large diameter. The tunnels ran back from the river to the enormous, but defunct, tandem elevator shaft, by means of which coal had been lowered from the plant far above or supplies from river barges brought up into the plant. In later years, a brazen exploratory herd collapsed the elevator in a shower of green sparks for no good reason, thus emphasizing again to the authorities, who had already found their Web sites, that something was amiss. Ford sealed the door permanently after that.

Beyond the big elevator shaft, the Ford sand mines proper began. A single sandstone passage continued along the line of the twin tunnels, then branched into dozens of cathedral-sized passages. The 1962 Civil Defense map indicates that the mine could have been used to shelter exactly 2,913 persons in the event of atomic cataclysm.

Following the right-hand passage, we could pursue the southern limb of the mine, which ran a quarter mile before dead-ending at a former bluff entrance, now sealed. There was a prominent layer of flood silts here suggesting that the mine had flooded in the past, most likely owing to one of the historic Mississippi River floods. Along the way, we came across a memento of years past, a tiny note, rolled up tightly and stuffed into a hole in the sandstone. Unrolling the secret scroll of the ages, we were directed to "Make sure to close the doors tonight." We did.

Going straight ahead, we came to the Combs, where shorter side passages branched off the main trunk like the teeth of a comb. These were the highest, widest, and most closely spaced passages in the entire mine. Beyond the combs, at the farthest point in the mine, there was a mysterious door. Behind it, we found what looked like a red coffee can. It was a Teledyne Geotech Seismometer S-13.

I found out later that this seismometer, now defunct, had at one time been connected via a dedicated land line to a seismograph in Pillsbury Hall at the University of Minnesota. The *Twin Cities Ford News*, August 22, 1962, described how it was installed by the late Professor Harold Mooney, who was looking for a place devoid of local vibrations. The seismometer was part of a cold war network of stations for monitoring nuclear blasts around the world. One of Mooney's students recalls seeing the system active as late as the 1980s, by which time it had a strictly educational function. Sometime thereafter the program was discontinued, and the lines rusted away.

The goal of my later trips into the mines was to collect geologic information. Using a compass, for example, I determined the major joint directions in the sandstone. Finding a natural joint running through the rock, I simply had to ascertain its compass direction and I could pick that same joint up again in a distant part of the mine.

I also noticed that the wettest passages, floored with tomato-soup gloop, were at the north end of the mines, closest to where the Ford Dam was located. Apparently there's a substantial hydraulic head in the sandstone because of all the water penned back behind the dam, and the water leaks out of the mine walls there, forming springs. From the north wall, the water flows as a stream to a sump within the mines. The passage is usually inundated, so a boardwalk had been constructed, which was in serious decay. It made me wonder whether the dam could ever fail from water taking this shortcut through the mine passages and gradually enlarging them, although I found no evidence that this was occurring.

As seen in archival photos, the passages were dug by laborers with air chisels who shoveled the sand into cars that ran along narrow-gauge tracks through the Ford mine. Later on, compressed-air drills were used. In a few places we could still find isolated segments of the track or ghostly impressions in the muddy floor of the tunnel where the wooden sleepers had once been, a sort of phantom railway. Many of the passages ended in benches, indicating that sand removal had taken place in at least two stages as the floor was lowered.

We also investigated a deeper set of passages and chambers even more rarely seen, situated completely below the mine itself and not directly connected to it. These sandrock sewers had to be entered by way of the old Highland Parkway outfall, located a city block upriver from the plant itself. The connection no longer exists because it was sealed off from the river during St. Paul's separation program. These passages were just barely large enough to walk through and very foul. The human waste was so thick that miniature toilet paper volcanoes had formed in the passages, belching methane and hydrogen sulfide gas as you stepped on them. Beyond the volcanoes, the passage forked, each branch leading to deep drop shafts, walled with granite blocks. Evidently, drainage water from the mine passages above was diverted to the river by this means. We could see a chamber hewn in the solid rock far below us—possibly at river level—but didn't have the gear to get back out of the pit, should we descend. We might have been able to exit via an outfall on the river, but if there were no such connection, we would be trapped. We decided not to mess with it.

Several miles downriver from the Ford sand mine, under Shepard Road, there's another, somewhat shorter mine, also frequently attributed to Ford's glass-making operations. The 1962 Civil Defense map of the mines shows what it calls the Holiday Harbor Sand Caves, with a dozen entrances in the bluffs behind the St. Paul Marina. These passages were rated to shelter 1,953 occupants.

From 1981 to 1989, Gary Svoboda, a local businessman, rented the abandoned mine for boat storage as part of the Watergate Marina. According to him, the caves remained vacant for nearly a generation after silica mining ended in the 1940s, except for countless clandestine sorties from local teenagers—as testified by the abundant graffiti. Kids got into the cave, partied the nights away, and carved elaborate pieces, like the Stairway to Heaven, in remote passages. Going up this slippery "stairway" to the giddy alcove at the top and downing a six-pack must have been a real thrill for them. Apart from entering the old mine through broken doorways, the kids could also crawl through a hole in the wall of the Davern Street storm sewer, which also allowed sewage to flood the cave, so it was sealed years later. The most notorious event from this period occurred in 1974, when forty persons, ranging in age from fourteen to twenty-three, were arrested after a weekend party inside the cave turned into a brawl. People were struck over the head with flashlights, stabbed, and threatened with guns. Drugs were confiscated by the police.

Svoboda found that he could store as many as 450 boats, up to sixty feet in length, in the old sand mines, adding "a King Kong–sized steel door" for protection. The installation of mercury-vapor lights and blacktopping, and guniting the walls to reduce erosion, cost $100,000. It was advertised as the "Upper Midwest's Largest Underground Storage Facility." But boat storage didn't pan out in this case because mice and mold gnawed at the boats during the winter while chunks of ceiling occasionally came crashing down onto the boats from above. The boats also took on a peculiar, lingering, earthy odor that was difficult to eradicate. The same odor that permeates my caving clothes!

In 1982 the St. Paul Jaycees (Junior Chamber of Commerce) offered their first Halloween "Tunnel of Terror" at this former sand mine, using the eastern third of the mine network. Prior to renting this space they had staged the event peripatetically, moving from one venue to another each year. In 1980, for example, it was held in the Castle Royal cave. They never expected to be in the mine very long—let alone twenty-two years. Initially there were no elaborate set-piece scenes as there were in later years, when a sense of permanence allowed them to flourish. The volunteer ghouls simply ran about in the dark, clad in discarded graduation gowns, scaring the visitors in an effective but unsophisticated manner. Visitors were not required to hold onto a rope, as they do now, or to be led about by a guide. From the beginning, the event was aimed at teenagers and adults, the experience being judged too scary for children. There was usually a Kid's Day, however, during which the lights were left on and the fog machines off.

The Tunnel of Terror uses one-third of the mine passages; the remaining mile is largely vacant. Beyond the tour area, there's a "boneyard" where extra scenery is stored and where the off-duty volunteers could play vertical horseshoes for relaxation—trying to hook pegs far up on the walls. The city also uses the mine; Como Conservatory stores plant bulbs there in winter, making a sort of gigantic root cellar. Nothing but piles of moldy wooden palettes are found out in the great black voids beyond that. In the vast hinterland of the mine, the cathedral-like passages were so large that our headlamps failed to illuminate them. Horseshoe Bend and the Labyrinth area were especially noteworthy passages.

In later years the Tunnel of Terror attracted 12,000 visitors during the Halloween event. Live bats from the caves, which flew about at dusk and, as if on cue, dived into the waiting lines, gave added verisimilitude to the plethora of fake bats ornamenting the passages. I recall seeing lines a quarter of a mile long waiting to get into this very popular event.

But after the deaths of three teenagers in Fandell's Cave in St. Paul on April 27, 2004, from carbon monoxide poisoning, fire inspectors demanded another fire exit in the mine. The Jaycees solicited a bid for boring a new tunnel through the sandstone, but it came to a whopping quarter of a million dollars, far beyond the means of a nonprofit organization. Thus ended, for the time being at least, a proud twenty-two-year tradition.

For some of the more dedicated volunteers, much of their life centered around this Halloween event. Halloween preparations began in

March of each year. There were weekly open work nights, although usually only those who had personal investments in large sets began showing up this early in the year. By September, the pace quickened, and the cave was busy every weekend. The sting of bleach filled the air as the sets were spiffed up for the coming event.

The tour followed a route through the mine involving two large loops, and I will describe it in sequence as it was in its last, most highly evolved year. The average lifespan of a set was about seven years, I was told, owing to wood rot in the humid mine air. Behind the scenes you would find huge billows of white fungus covering every wooden surface. The fan-shaped fungal tendrils splayed outward in all directions in their hungry quest for more wood. The giant fungus could also be incorporated into the background scenery by a skillful designer, creating a veritable Velvet Underground.

Before the tour began, visitors were read the rules ("Hold on to the rope," "No touching the scenery," etc.) and given the option of turning back if they were developing cold feet. One part of the terror is that in the darkness you quickly get turned around and lose your sense of direction—but where would you run to escape? There are numerous secret passages behind the walls for the volunteers to use, so they can dash from one scene to the next, economizing on personnel. The introduction of radios made a big difference in coordinating the "attacks" of the ghouls as well as for emergency communications, a volunteer told me.

Early in the tour you passed the whimsical scene of a skeleton driving a boat—perhaps a reference to the 1980s boat-storage era in the mines. The creepiest part was just beyond, the Land of Shadows, where you walked between two rows of black, robed figures. Most of them were inanimate scarecrows, but the occasional ambush by a living figure brought plenty of screams. The faux forest, festooned with cottony cobwebs, was put together from actual waste brush cut by the Public Works Department. Most of this material had been sprayed with fire retardant.

The first big set piece, Frankenstein's Castle, was three stories high. It was built of plywood onto which Styrofoam stones had been glued to give the castle a rusticated appearance. The tower of the castle, illuminated with a red chandelier, served as a vantage point for the volunteers to observe activities in passages running off in three directions. Entering the castle, you passed through Frankenstein's workshop, furnished with imitation electrical apparatuses such as cast-off computer monitors. They got many of these props when another big local Halloween attraction, Spooky World in Shakopee, shut down.

The Unholy Tomb and the Sanitarium, operated by Mike Kamrad since 1992, was an elaborate set piece. Mike devoted a dozen years of his life to developing this Halloween tableau, continually improving the scenery, as indicated on a commemorative plaque he affixed to the entrance to his domain—a pyramid topped with a garish cyclopean eye, like the Masonic pyramid on a dollar bill. Once inside the set, you saw a grasshopper-green, two-armed, four-legged object of devil worship in a graveyard. A rotating fireplace light behind the set created the appearance of fire on the sandstone walls. Volunteers pretended to worship this devil while a recording chanted the seven names of the devil. I thought the Hoofed One surely had more names than that.

Kamrad controlled the set from his computerized power tower, where he could observe the action. Spooky music—loud enough to suppress conversation, as he informed me—was forever blasting from the tower, including sound tracks from *Psycho, 2001: A Space Odyssey*, and *Terminator 2*. He told me that he could always tell where the scariest spots were by the furrows in the sandy floor of the mine, caused by visitors dragging their feet along. Some visitors actually go down on their knees while clutching the rope, trying to stop their forward progress, to the annoyance of the guides. He filled in the furrows occasionally, when they got too deep.

The Sanitarium was the second half of Kamrad's realm. Passing through a door flap, visitors were saluted by a shrill siren blast and a burst of blinding light. Ushered into a courtyard, they were swept with searchlights, harassed by ghouls, and dive-bombed by Gordon, an airborne inmate with his brain exposed—actually a dummy on a rope. Visitors approached an elaborately crafted, two-story facade complete with gables, which Kamrad meticulously modeled on a real sanitarium at Danvers, Massachusetts, where lobotomies were the operation of choice. He was inspired, he said, by the horror movie *Session 9*, which was set at Danvers and involved a character named Gordon.

After leaving Kamrad's fantasy landscape, you entered the Crematorium, a lengthy strobe tunnel that seemed to decrease in size ahead of you, literally narrowing your options. After that you followed the Path to Hidden Falls, referring to the well-known waterfall near the Ford plant in St. Paul. A prominent sign bore the enigmatic words,

"Have Gear Loaded and Friends Ready to Go," leaving you to ponder the original context.

The second great castle in the mine was Dracula's Castle. The doorplate indicated the occupant—Vlad III Tepes—and the year, 1456. Behind the scenes there was an industrial-strength fogging machine. There was fog throughout the mine, but this was the most heavily saturated area, having its own underground distribution system of pipes. After this, you were led through Dracula's Red Room, with heavy wooden beams and red-light chandeliers. Volunteers, bodies painted with a brick pattern to match the walls, suddenly leaped out at the startled visitors.

On their final Halloween before closing down, in 2004, my friend John and I volunteered to help at the Tunnel of Terror to gain insight into the whole operation. I wore a Soviet-era gas mask that I had purchased at Ax Man Surplus, in conjunction with a shredded sewer jacket that required no retouching to look authentic. I strolled about the Sanitarium and scared visitors for a while, but my real job that night was to operate the power tower's blinding searchlight and Gordon, the flying lobotomy patient. From here also, using a vocal mixing system that Kamrad had rigged up, I did a chilling wolf howl that echoed throughout the caverns. John had purchased an infrared digital video camera and used it to film the fun. With skillful editing, he produced a psychedelic documentary of the Jaycees' final performance.

PART IV

THE MILLING DISTRICT

SUBTERRANEAN VENICE
MINNEAPOLIS'S MILL TUNNELS

And Styx with nine wide channels roars around.

MILTON, *PARADISE LOST*

DURING THE HALF CENTURY BETWEEN 1880 AND 1930, Minneapolis was the flour milling capital of the world, taking the hard spring wheat of Minnesota and the Dakotas and milling it into flour by means of the waterpower generated at St. Anthony Falls. The casual visitor to Mill Ruins Park in Minneapolis today should realize that much of what he or she sees in that park was once hidden under the old Shiely gravel yards and was part of a complex subterranean landscape that has now vanished. If you wanted to see those same mill tunnels even a dozen years ago, you would have had to put on your coveralls, grab your flashlight, and embark upon the subterranean waters in a makeshift raft. During the long stretch of years after the last mills shut down, the way to enter the place was known to very few people, and the remoter nooks and crannies to fewer still. It took quite a bit of exploration to find which chink in a particular tunnel wall led to this or that historic tunnel. But that was half the fun.

I first came to the west side mill district in the 1980s. The favored entrance to the extensive system of abandoned tailrace tunnels back then was in the ruins of the former King Midas Mill, which burned down in 1967. There, concealed by weeds, was a heavy steel trapdoor, about the size of a storm cellar door. Giving one last glance around to be sure no one had spotted us, we lifted up the door and entered a shaft containing a rusted spiral steel stairway that led down forty feet into a concrete room flooded with water. This stairway was installed by the Corps of Engineers in 1962 during the construction of the Upper Lock and Dam; it was removed during the creation of the park in 2000.

The trapdoor sometimes had a padlock on it; we would just bust it

off with a crowbar. At one point during an intense period of exploration, we had the chutzpah to put our own padlock on the trapdoor.
I kept the key on a chain around my neck and bragged about having
"the key to the Minneapolis underworld." The next time I went back,
however, I found that some other explorer had busted off my padlock.
And so it goes.

There were little voids in the exposed ruins of the King Midas Mill
where the homeless used to take shelter. I recall that one of them had
sealed his personal niche off from the elements with a tarp, trying to
remain inconspicuous, except that there was an apron of beer cans,
liquor bottles, etc., littering the slopes below, giving the whole thing
away. Considering the proximity of the tunnel system, I wondered why
people simply didn't go live down there, but I soon figured that out.
While the tunnels are a great place to escape summer's heat or winter's cold temporarily, the dampness seems to strike into your very
bones after a few hours, producing a vaguely unpleasant feeling that
soon grows intolerable. Plus that, you get very grimy.

At the bottom of the spiral stairway there was a slot, or low opening, near the waterline, easy to overlook. Duckboards led from the slot
into the enormous system of mill tunnels, echoing with the sounds
of distant water. To the right, there was a passage leading to the old
Cataract-Holly tunnel, with distinctive yellow brickwork. This was the
oldest mill tunnel in the St. Peter Sandstone under Minneapolis, dug
in 1859, before the Civil War.

Following the duckboards, which bowed downward like a pirate's
plank at every step, we found ourselves in the mother of tailrace tunnels, the First Street tunnel. Walking along on the mud banks, we
arrived at a grim subterranean beach from which flooded mill tunnels radiated outward like the fingers of a hand. No flashlight could
adequately illuminate this great subterranean space. The tailrace tunnels had been dug in the soft St. Peter Sandstone, leaving the bottom
of the overlying Platteville Limestone to serve as a natural ceiling.
The sandstone walls had been lined with Platteville rubble masonry
to prevent erosion by the water flowing through the system.

The mill tunnels in this part of the system were flooded to a depth
of eight feet with stagnant green water. The water appeared green in
the light of a flashlight; it was probably just a loathsome gray. Moored
on the beach was a sturdy wooden raft, about the size of a garage door
and supported by fifty-five-gallon steel drums for floats. Standing on

this raft, it was easy to propel ourselves up and down the canals with a pole, like a subterranean gondolier, and hence the tailrace system was soon dubbed Subterranean Venice. In places where our pole wasn't long enough to touch the bottom of the tunnel, we'd have to push along the walls to move forward. In some of the tunnels there were narrow stone ledges along which we could walk for some distance, but rarely did they go all the way to the ends of the tunnels—and that's where the voids got interesting.

Poling ourselves up the largest of these tunnels, the First Street tunnel, for example, we'd see dark openings high up in the walls— windows, as it were, into even more passages. It was great fun to stop and climb up into them—securely mooring the raft so that it didn't float away while we were thus engaged. I'll tell you some of these adventures after explaining how the mill tunnels operated. The termi- nology and tunnel names I use are those of the official archaeological survey carried out in the 1980s.

In 1857, the Minneapolis Mill Company began digging the First Street canal parallel to the Mississippi River. Underneath it, the First Street tunnel was dug. The canal was covered over with wooden planks where it ran along First Street (this plank road has been re-created in Mill Ruins Park). Water, diverted from the river, entered the upstream end of the canal through a gatehouse (which filtered out debris such as logs), was carried to the individual mills by branch canals, and then drained through holes into the tailrace tunnels below. The water fell through iron draft tubes up to four feet in diameter, spinning tur- bines on the way down and hitting deflection cones at the bottom

A section view of the bed of the east channel at St. Anthony Falls, showing the diversion of water from the falls to the tailrace tunnels below.

FROM J. L. GREENLEAF, "REPORT ON THE WATER- POWER OF THE MISSISSIPPI RIVER AND SOME OF ITS TRIBUTARIES," *TENTH CENSUS OF THE UNITED STATES, 1880*, VOL. 17 (1887).

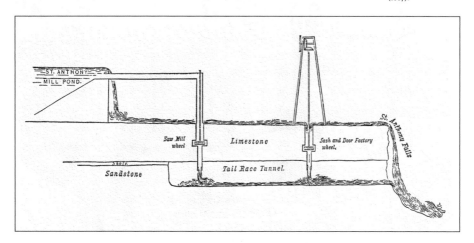

ST. ANTHONY MILL POND

Saw Mill wheel · Limestone · Sash and Door Factory wheel.

St. Anthony Falls

Shale · Sandstone · Tail Race Tunnel.

(to prevent erosion of the floor). The water then flowed through the various tailrace tunnels, called spurs, which merged to form the First Street tunnel. The latter emptied into an open-air channel that carried the water back to the river. I would have loved to have seen this magnificent underground space back in its glory days, when the mills were running full blast. Back then there were strings of lights running through the tunnels and good boardwalks for the workers to use. Most of that wood was scavenged afterward, leaving the bare tunnels we see today.

Farther south along First Street, a different system prevailed. There, each mill, although supplied by the First Street canal, had its own tailrace tunnel that flowed independently out to the river instead of joining a trunk tunnel. These individualized tailraces were harder to access because you had to find a manhole into them, which was usually located deep in the subbasement of some ruined building. And they were pretty scary places, unventilated, with tons of rotting wood generating carbon dioxide gas, not to mention the figures lurking in the shadows.

A view in 1890 of construction at the First Avenue canal along the west side of St. Anthony Falls. This canal provided much of the waterpower for Minneapolis's flour milling district.

PHOTOGRAPH BY HENRY R. FARR. COURTESY OF THE MINNESOTA HISTORICAL SOCIETY.

In 1960, the First Street canal, no longer used, was filled up with earth, and the tunnels beneath it were simply abandoned—bequeathed, as it were, to a whole generation of urban explorers. Poling up the largest of them, the First Street tunnel, the Arctic Mill spur branched off immediately to the right. On the left side, several hundred feet farther up the tunnel, the Crown spur branched off. We came to a jagged opening high in the wall, which led to a brick-lined corridor ending in a circular room with a shaft to the surface. Continuing along the First Street tunnel, another opening, this time on the right side, led to a cavelike void in the sandstone. Grody green Glenwood Shale littered the maze of passages, supported by brick piers, which appeared oozingly ancient. At the far end of the maze there was a bulkhead pierced by a small aperture, allowing us to squeeze out into the old city tunnel like human toothpaste.

The city tunnel was the tailrace for the City Water Works, a former hydropowered pumping station. Back in the early days of Minneapolis, before sewage had tainted the Father of Waters, drinking water was drawn from the river in the downtown area itself. In 1904, after completion of the Columbia Heights plant farther upriver, this downtown waterworks was abandoned. Its wide passage, supported by square brick piers, runs for hundreds of feet, floored with tomato-soup-colored sediments. At the upstream end, where water formerly entered the tunnel, there are three draft tube alcoves lined with glazed brick. Before Mill Ruins Park was created, the downstream end was sealed with a bulkhead. We had to enter and exit the tunnel through a small trapdoor if we didn't come in through the bulkhead aperture. Nowadays, standing in the park below the Stone Arch Bridge, you can peer into the city tunnel through the new steel gate, shoulder to shoulder with all the other tourists.

Returning to the First Street tunnel and getting back on the raft, we could pole to the very upstream end, where the Columbia and Occidental draft tubes were located, and beach the raft. The water was shallow, and we could get out and stroll around. During heavy rainfall, water surged out of the Columbia draft tube, easily the largest single input of water into the tailraces. Poling all the way back down the First Street tunnel, we eventually arrived back at the grand junction of the system, where we could leave the raft and walk up another branch, the Standard tunnel—named for the Standard Mill, of course. This passage was very muddy, with a stream meandering along the floor. At the upper end of it we could cross into yet another tunnel, the Old Standard. The ceiling was low in the Old Standard, requiring an annoying ape-knuckle walk to get to the far end, where a hole had been punched through the brick wall and a steady breeze of warm, rotten-egg gas blew out.

That little hole in the Old Standard tunnel led to another world. We did a low belly crawl for about thirty feet. Our ears were fearfully cocked for the rats squeaking among the loose stones in the flickering shadows around us. The crawlway was so tight that we could not get away from an inquisitive rat if it sauntered up to us—as they disgustingly did sometimes. I have heard grown men scream like girls on such occasions, though no one was ever bitten. Instead of muscling our backpacks through as we crawled, slowing us down, we tied ropes to them; once we had passed the whiskered gauntlet, we could quickly drag them through. At the other end, the crawlway opened up into the Minneapolis sanitary sewer system, which I discuss in "Lost World."

I explored this Subterranean Venice many times with different people over more than a decade. Each time I visited, I noticed that the beloved and most necessary raft was ever more dilapidated. Eventually, I saw that someone had either busted it up for no good reason or a hell of a storm had passed over, such as the one I experienced in 1999.

I descended into the Subterranean Venice on a beautiful summer day in 1999 with a party of explorers. On this trip, we brought inflatable kayaks (since the big wooden raft was no longer seaworthy), foot bellows, and all the other impedimenta for expeditions into wet caves. We could not open the trapdoor to the spiral, so we entered the system by the city tunnel trapdoor. We hiked over to the Arctic Mill spur, inflating our kayaks on its dark shores. Setting sail like a gaggle of goslings, we floated merrily into the First Street tunnel.

The tunnel system, usually as quiet as a tomb, suddenly began to echo with the ominous sound of cascading water, suggesting that a rainstorm was in progress above. Kayaking through the murky tunnels toward the noise, I noticed, to my astonishment, that I was sinking and said so to my fellow sailors, who didn't seem to show much concern in their eagerness to visit the waterfalls that had suddenly appeared. At first I thought perhaps I had gouged the kayak on a sharp rock, but then I realized that the air plug had come out. By the time I capped it again, it was too late; the kayak had lost so much buoyancy that I was let down into the drink along with all my gear and had to swim ashore, sodden kayak in tow behind me. The bellows was nowhere nearby, and I was disinclined to apply my lips to the slimy air valve to reinflate the kayak, so I was temporarily marooned on this forlorn beach. I decided to go check out a few waterfalls of my own until the others rowed past.

Hiking to the Old Standard tunnel, I beheld a veritable Niagara of raw sewage spilling into the Standard tunnel. Clambering up through the opening, I was able to walk far enough along to see that the sewage in the usually dry tunnel was coming from the little hole leading to the rat crawl. For the first time I found out where so much of the stinking water that fills these canals came from—sewage overflows during wet weather.

The water level was rising rapidly in the tunnels, which surprised me because of how large they were. The water began lapping against the stone catwalks that ran along the walls of the tunnels, which were usually well above the waterline. I wondered how much higher it would go. I didn't think that the water would rise to the ceiling, but you never know. Meanwhile, my fellow explorers had reached the far upstream end of the First Street tunnel, admiring the stormwater inputs from the long-dead turbines. I could hear their muffled voices echoing incoherently amid the roar of water and see the flashlight beams directed this way and that as if they were engaged in a light saber duel.

Our kayaks were only meant for one passenger each, so I would have to find my own way back through the deep waters of the Arctic Mill spur tunnel to the exit. Should I swim fully clothed in the cold, sewage-tainted water? I wasn't a really strong swimmer and had too far to go. I noticed the beached wreck of the former wooden raft and tried to resurrect it, hoping that it would last long enough, despite its thoroughly decayed condition, to get me back up the spur tunnel. No sooner had I clambered aboard and shoved off into deep water than the raft split in half and flipped over very noisily, dropping me back into the water, and I had to swim ashore a second time. Thoroughly soaked with the sewage-tainted tunnel water, I had even fewer options this time. I edged along the narrow stone ledge as far as I could go, to where it tapered down to nothing, then gingerly lowered myself into the dark soup, half swimming as I pulled myself along the wall, since I could not touch the bottom with my feet.

The others eventually returned and began deflating their kayaks and repacking their gear. After relating my travails to the others—which seemed only to amuse them—and hearing about the waterspouts that they had witnessed, we were amazed to find brilliant sunshine outside, just as when we had entered. A late afternoon thunderstorm had sprung up out of nowhere after we entered, rained an inch an hour at least, then moved on. It stressed the importance of checking the weather forecast before a deep-earth tunnel expedition.

The work on Mill Ruins Park was far advanced when we entered the mill tunnels for the last time, in 2001. The purpose of this final trip was to document in video how the tunnels looked to urban explorers during the forty-year subterranean heyday between the construction of the Upper Lock and Dam in 1960 and the creation of Mill Ruins Park. Going there at night was not our usual practice, and I recall losing my footing on the mud-slickened slopes of the construction site and rocketing down to the entrance. Among other improvements, I noticed that the rat crawl had been patched over so raw sewage could no longer overflow into the tailraces.

There was a side benefit to the new park. Everyone used to have to pay dearly for parking and lug their gear several blocks for tunnel expeditions. Exiting the outfall late at night, drenched with sewage, we appeared very suspicious to passers-by as we trudged back to our cars, muddy rafts in tow. With the creation of Mill Ruins Park, there was a parking lot with no time restrictions right next door.

Subterranean Venice was not the only place in the vicinity to explore. The east side—the old town of St. Anthony, incorporated into Minneapolis in 1872—had its own milling district, albeit on a smaller scale. Although many of these tunnels were associated with saw milling rather than flour milling, there are similarities. The most famous of those on the east side is Eastman Tunnel.

William Eastman purchased Nicollet Island, just above St. Anthony Falls, in 1865. He devised a plan that would bring waterpower to the island, to supplement the existing system of overhead power cables, and began digging a six-by-six-foot tunnel under the riverbed, from Hennepin Island, below the falls, to Nicollet Island, above the falls. River water diverted through the tunnel would produce power.

The work progressed wonderfully for a while, achieving a length of two thousand feet. But as the tunnel neared Nicollet Island, where the limestone caprock was thinner, the river began seeping through. The leak grew rapidly until the tunnel was overwhelmed and the laborers had to scramble for their lives. The soft sandstone was eroded easily by the torrent, and on October 5, 1869, a loud cry went up: "The falls are going out!" It appeared as though the leak were about to engulf the whole river, leaving the waterfall dry and the two cities stranded without hydropower. Timber cribs were frantically constructed, freighted with rocks, and maneuvered over the churning whirlpool in an attempt to plug the hole in the riverbed. After a month of agonizing struggle by the citizenry and numerous setbacks, the situation stabilized somewhat, but there were recurring leaks for years. The only permanent solution was for the Corps of Engineers to construct a dike under St. Anthony Falls in the 1870s.

I saw Major Farquhar's map of St. Anthony Falls depicting where the sandstone had been washed out during this episode; it looks like a map of Mammoth Cave but tucked under the bed of the Mississippi River instead of being in Kentucky. The part of the tunnel under the falls received a root canal of sorts and was carefully backfilled.

From the tunnel system under Nicollet Island ("Down the Rabbit Hole"), there are various cavelike voids with curious Neapolitan swirls of natural pigments, which tapered out pretty quickly into fill material. At the downstream end, under Hennepin Island, the Eastman Tunnel is still very much in its original form for some distance. In 1992, I received permission from the St. Anthony Falls Hydraulic Laboratory to visit the Eastman Tunnel, using the trapdoor access point in their basement. I wanted to see how far up under the riverbed I could walk before encountering the dike.

I wore disposable white coveralls, as used for painting, so that I could remove them after finishing my explorations. Descending through the trapdoor under the lab, I found that the Eastman Tunnel ran under the riverbed as far as my light beam went; I hoped to be able to get all the way up under the dam itself. Crawdads and clams surrounded me everywhere. At one point I peeked up through a grating into the Main Street Power Station, observing the dynamos with wonder. The going soon got rough. At first I got nothing more than a little splash of red mud on my boots. But the farther I advanced, the deeper the mud became, until it was up to my knees. Each step required great effort and strange gymnastic contortions. When the mud got waist deep, I was ready to turn back, but I could see the end of the tunnel, so I persevered. As I struggled, I mentally devised a pair of mudshoes, something like snowshoes, that I could modify for walking on top of the glutinous mud instead of sinking in with every step. Finally, I arrived at the concrete bulkhead, a total distance of one hundred feet from the walkway. I noted a little bit of leakage, but it was "nothing to worry about," I was later informed by officialdom. NSP had pumped tons of concrete into the tunnel years earlier to forestall any further problems.

Back at my starting point, I removed the by-now utterly shredded and stained coveralls. The red tunnel mud had soaked through everywhere. As I walked up to the director's office to report, I left a mess behind in the hydraulics lab. A trail of drippy footsteps led from the trapdoor right to the director's door. Later, architecture critic Larry Millett arranged a photo shoot in the Eastman Tunnel for an article he was writing about me (*St. Paul Pioneer Press*, October 19, 1992). The tunnel is visible in the background of the photo.

The east side also hosts the Phoenix Mill tunnel, which ran to a no-longer-extant rye mill adjacent to the Pillsbury A Mill. The tunnel's bedrock walls were ornamented with squiggly red lines recording old water tables and could be followed for several hundred feet. We soon came to a catwalk bridge passing overhead. Swinging ourselves up, we found a drop shaft at one end, suffused with an eerie bluish light and carpeted with cave pearls (a spherical mineral deposit). Following the catwalk in the opposite direction, paralleling the defunct St. Anthony water main, which in rusty decay resembled a sea serpent's backbone, we passed over a half dozen sawmill tailraces. At any one of these tailraces we could hop off the catwalk and stroll through the tunnels. As on the west side of the river, however, the mill tunnels were flooded to a depth of about eight feet with stagnant green water; if we weren't careful, we could easily slip off into the drink. In the old days, some of the tunnels led, via rickety catwalks and ladders, to the basements of Main Street buildings.

The strangest thing that ever happened to me in the Phoenix Mill tunnel occurred one winter years ago when I entered with DNR personnel to conduct a bat count. As soon as we entered the tunnel, we found clothes scattered about everywhere, as if several people had recently disrobed. As we advanced, finding more garments, I began to think we'd corner the shivering nudists farther up the tunnel and began thinking of a good one-liner. Then I came across a bag full of feminine hygiene products. All this was the cause of much hilarity among us, captured on film by our videographer. Our bat count was a complete success, indicating a record number of pipistrelles in the hibernaculum, but the nudists that day were zero in number.

BOAT RIDE TO OBLIVION
CHUTE'S CAVE

This most interesting place is no longer frequented by human beings of the ordinary sort.

ANONYMOUS, 1889

IN 1990, using on an old sewer map, I went hunting for a legendary Minneapolis cave that everyone else in the caving community declared was a hoax. Some had even committed themselves in national print. No one showed the least interest in my project. I was on my own with this one.

Descending the long stairway into a park near St. Anthony Falls, I met a paint sniffer on the banks of the Mississippi River—spray-paint-can lid in hand, primed for inhalation—obviously high on his pre-ferred product, with the telltale smears of paint on his face, absorbed in his own private Vietnam. Looking about, I saw the entrances to half a dozen old mill tunnels. Choosing the most likely one, its frost-shat-tered limestone arch festooned with tropical-looking vines, I lowered myself into the waist-deep green water and waded into the darkness. Under the arch, a flock of pigeons suddenly flapped up, startling me, in a scene reminiscent of Hitchcock's *The Birds*. Bullheads swam between my legs, cavorting in the flashlight beam, unused to being disturbed in their murky realm by Shakespeare's "forked beast." Water thundered ominously in the dark distance. Soon I was beyond the last rays of the sun. Strange shapes of rotting wood and moldering stone loomed about me. The air was rank and fetid.

After scaling a high wall in an obscure alcove of the ancient mill tunnel, I found myself in a gravel-floored room full of concrete parti-tions that supported Main Street, directly above. I started a tight, cork-screw crawl through a jumble of jagged limestone boulders, arrayed like shark's teeth. Did this little void actually go somewhere? Without kneepads for protection, I maneuvered slowly. The suffocating crawl

145

space always seemed just about to dead-end. Glimpsing a flowstone medusa and beautiful crystal-lined pools, I continued. Finally, the crawlway opened up into a vast sonorous chamber, and I tumbled down the slippery shale slope leading into it. Chute's Cave at last!

The triangular chamber, about fifty feet on a side and fifteen feet high, contained a primeval forest of decayed timber, drooping now in the humid gloom but at one time meant to hold up the overlying street. I strolled among beautiful crystal formations and shimmering pools. Giant slabs of limestone, the size of pontoon boats, littered the floor. Some of them were coffin-shaped—the result of the characteristic rhomboidal jointing pattern of the Platteville Limestone layer, from which they had detached themselves. Another slab jutted out into the huge room like a rocky pulpit or the prow of a ship.

A very long tunnel with a Gothic-shaped cross section led off from the big room of Chute's Cave. I heard water in the distance. On the sandstone wall at the entrance to the tunnel I saw a carved cyclops head, smiling enigmatically. This tunnel, I would learn later, was the famous Chute's Tunnel, through which tourist boats had floated more than a century ago, but traversing it afoot was a real slog. It contained the typical bilayered mud deposits characteristic of Minneapolis mill tunnels generally: red on top, black and anoxic below.

As I continued through the red mud, I inhaled lungfuls of rotten-egg gas, hydrogen sulfide. I came abreast of a small side passage from where the sound of running water was coming. The extra water in the mix made the mud very loosey-goosey, and I sank down to my waist. As I attempted to advance, the glutinous mud sucked off my shoes with a slurping noise. I needed my shoes, if only to get out of the cave again, so I paused and groped about in the ooze, leaving my arms stained to the shoulder. I put the shoes in my rucksack until I could get back out of the tunnel. I continued my stocking-foot expedition in the ketchup. I was indeed beginning to acquire a reputation among other cavers as a sort of deep-sewer mudpuppy.

The loose mud gradually merged into a lake of painfully cold water that extended as far down the tunnel as I could see. The ketchup had become more like tomato soup in consistency. I continued around an elbow in the passage and, after another city block of tunnel, found that the ceiling met the waterline. Tree roots dangled down, so I guessed this was probably the sealed entrance, where Chute's Tunnel once opened to the outside world to let the tourists in. It was the first of many visits and the last time I would have to go alone. The cave was very real—certainly not a hoax. Others took an interest now that I had shown the way. Walking back to my apartment, stained with red filth but otherwise quite content, people crossed the street to avoid me, as though I were the Creature from the Black Lagoon.

Chute's Cave and Tunnel have a long history, beginning with a strange hoax just after the Civil War. On December 10, 1866, an article titled "Curious Discoveries in Minnesota" appeared in the *New York Herald*. According to this account, Mr. Reuben Nesmith found the cave while digging a potato bin. He struck an iron trapdoor, "beneath which a spiral stone staircase led down into the earth." Along with his brother-in-law, Luther Chamberlain, he descended the stairway of 123 steps, and they "found themselves in a narrow horizontal passage, dug in the white sand," which accurately describes Chute's Tunnel, dug in the white St. Peter Sandstone. They entered "a spacious artificial cave, also excavated in this white sand." Successive chambers contained relics of a prehistoric civilization, including iron and copper implements, a colossal human figure, hieroglyphics, a stone sarcophagus, and a sacrificial altar. When the sarcophagus was opened, a human skeleton was found, whose bones crumbled to powder.

The very next day the *Herald*, pointing out an inconsistency in the Nesmith story, suspected it of being a hoax that "a correspondent at St. Anthony" had foisted on them. There are close parallels between the Nesmith Cave hoax and details found in *Ancient Monuments of the Mississippi Valley*, a classic work of archaeology published in 1848 by Squier and Davis, two people cited by the *Herald*. In excavating Native American burial mounds, these antiquarians found stone coffins, skeletons that crumbled to powder, and sacrificial altars with calcined bones. Nesmith concludes, as Squier and Davis had done earlier, that "the relics found are not at all aboriginal in character, and may have been the work of a people existing long before even these prairies were the hunting grounds of the Indians."

The *St. Paul Pioneer*, while expressing doubts, reprinted the original *Herald* story verbatim on December 16. On that same day the *St. Paul Daily Press* published a continuation of the cave story under the title "The St. Anthony Wonder." The derisive tone of this anonymous piece suggests that the cave story had been pressed into service as another weapon in the on-going feud between the rival cities, St. Paul and Minneapolis.

Inside the cave, the *Daily Press* article reported, unnamed explorers found a slab of malachite (an ore of copper). When this was raised, another spiral staircase was discovered. This, too, had 123 steps and was constructed of polished marble with banisters of shining brass. "The descent of these steps," the narrator continued, inverting the proper sequence of geologic layers, "took the explorer down through the Mesozoic and Cenozoic formations, and almost below the post-tertiary periods. The hall to which these steps led was of the utmost conceivable grandeur." The ceiling was composed of stalactites that appeared like diamonds, leading the more enthusiastic "to believe that they had at last found a greater than Golconda." The hall was paved with blocks of gold-bearing quartz. Incongruously, the walls were made of peat. Life-sized human figures of stalagmite were "sitting upright upon conveniently arranged settees, and, to all appearance, enjoying themselves." Switching easily from exploration to eschatology, the narrator ends on a sarcastic note. The cave "is supposed to be the place where good St. Antonians go when they die."

Reuben Nesmith himself now entered the fray. On December 20, 1866, the *St. Paul Daily Press* printed a letter in which he affirmed the truth of the *New York Herald* report. "The matter has been kept as secret as possible ... until the explorations shall have been fully completed." On December 21, however, a letter to the *St. Paul Pioneer* denounced Nesmith and Chamberlain as "myths" and asserted that no such cave existed except in the *Herald* correspondent's "*cavernous skull.*" On December 22, the *Daily Press* referred to Nesmith as "the exhumer of this Toltec Herculaneum" and scoffed at the "Pickwickian antiquarians" who chased after "the alleged discoveries."

In another letter to the *Daily Press*, on January 1, 1867, Nesmith attempted to furnish plausible evidence for the cave, claiming that it "connects with the cave so long known to the people of St. Anthony, the entrance to which, is under the mineral springs." He invites the public to visit his cave, either by "the Grand Staircase ... or to enter, if they prefer it, the cave at the falls, and to follow up the long passage."

On January 9, 1867, the *Minneapolis Chronicle* ran the most lurid embellishment of the Nesmith Cave hoax yet. Couched in the form of a letter written from Luther Chamberlin (note the spelling change) to a Michigan antiquary, all the stops were pulled out.

In this version, Nesmith, Chamberlin, and the City Council armed themselves with Roman candles and descended into the cave where they traversed the by-now familiar succession of chambers containing marvels. In one of them "a huge stalagmite has been formed, we called it the tower of St. Anthony. It is a lofty mass two hundred feet in circumference, surrounded from top to bottom with rings of fountain basins." The next chamber was even larger, enough to contain "the whole of our Catholic Church." A rocket was fired, exploding as it struck the immense dome, creating a shower of falling stars with "the roar of a cannonade."

Mr. Nesmith led the City Council into ever stranger realms. He illuminated "a delicious little cave arched with snowy stalactites" in which there was a table "adorned with goblin knickknacks. It was the boudoir of some gnome or coquettish fairy." The next chamber was groined with gothic arches and paved with "globular stalagmites." "In a corner fountain," Chamberlin wrote, "we found the skeleton head and body of a serpent of uncreditable size." They passed into "another vaulted cathedral" that was flooded with "a strong iron water." Once again Chamberlin displayed a gift for vivid imagery: "This dark lake lit up by the blaze of a dozen Roman candles, and reflecting the flashing walls of the cavern, would have made a picture for Barnum." A nearby skeleton, eight feet high, caused him to wax philosophical: "Whether he was a lost traveler, an absconding debtor, a suicidal lover, or a wretched murderer seeking concealment from vindictive pursuers, no one can tell."

After eating a snack, "we again renewed our anxious search for something new." They were well rewarded, "finding innumerable natural curiosities, such as fish, snakes, bats, buffaloes' horns, and bones of all descriptions." The cavern extended under the leaking bed of the river, where they heard "the current of the river washing the rock overhead."

"We had now penetrated about five thousand feet in the interior of the earth, and Mr. Nesmith said that the chambers were still innumerable beyond. Our twine having run out, we made a hasty retreat," Chamberlin concluded. He added that Dr. Chute "is now at work digging a tunnel, commencing below the Falls, with a view of tapping the cave"—another clue linking Nesmith Cave and Chute's Cave.

On January 10, 1867, the *Minneapolis Chronicle* printed a retraction. The editors declared "the so-called St. Anthony Cave" to be a "stupendous hoax" that appeared "during our temporary absence." The *Chronicle* had hitherto "refrained from joining the St. Paul papers in keeping up the joke."

While the Nesmith Cave hoax was exploded locally, it had a longer life further afield. In the *Minneapolis Tribune* for July 17, 1867, it is reported that "a party of ladies and gentlemen from Milwaukee arrived in St. Anthony ... to visit the 'Nesmith Cave.'" The writer continued in a sarcastic vein: "The ladies made a becoming toilet to descend into the bowels of the earth, where they were to feast their visions on the works of art and science placed there by that supernatural class of beings who inhabited this globe and region so many, O, so many years ago." Despite "due search and enquiry," the cave could not be located. "What the gentlemen could have said to their ladies on their return to the hotel, cannot be imagined."

Who was behind the Nesmith Cave hoax? Two suspects have been put forward, David Edwards and Edward L. Welles. A third claim is that both men played a role.

David Edwards (1816–1890) was described as "always bubbling over with mirth" and "a ready writer ... endowed with a gift of entertaining originality" who "helped much to pass away the time, necessarily dull, that must elapse between the closing of navigation in the fall, and its opening the next spring, a period of six months." The Nesmith Cave hoax would have been entirely in character for him and but one more example of his "stirring articles." It was reported that "the author of these was eagerly sought by many that they might 'get even with him,' but the secret of his identity was sacredly kept." Edwards was later dubbed "St. Anthony's First Wag."

In 1930, Carl E. Van Cleve asserted that family friend Edward L. Welles (also spelled Wells), not David Edwards, was the author of the hoax. But Van Cleve, born June 25, 1861, was only five years old at the time of the hoax, hardly old enough to recall such events in detail.

Also in 1930, newspaper columnist Merle Potter presented a third solution, crediting both Wells and Edwards. Potter claimed that Wells, as Nesmith, initiated the hoax, and that Edwards, as Chamberlin, "embellished the Wells report." Although Potter did not cite any evidence for this assertion, there does indeed appear to be at least two different styles of hoax writing, creating a fault line in the cave imagery. The original Nesmith articles are rich in archaeological imagery and use the spelling "Chamberlain," while the article signed "Chamberlin" appears to be that of someone who had visited, or at least read about, a tourist cave. Specifically, it appears to contain elements borrowed from Wyandotte Cave, often called "the Mammoth Cave of

Indiana" and a well-known nineteenth-century tourist attraction. The Tower of St. Anthony bears a curious resemblance to the Pillar of the Constitution, a giant stalagmite in Wyandotte Cave.

Chamberlin demonstrates his knowledge of contemporary tourist caves by describing a transformation scene, a lighting effect that was very popular and often the high point of a cave tour: Nesmith used Roman candles to "shed a faint illumination like the twilight stealing through the Eastern horizon." Horace C. Hovey, the "Father of American Speleology," in his *Celebrated American Caverns*, described the "extraordinary transformation scenes" he witnessed during his 1854 visit to Wyandotte Cave, where Roman candles and fireworks simulated a city by night, an erupting volcano, and a "petrified sunset."

At present, the most likely explanation seems to be that David Edwards, using the pen name Luther Chamberlin, authored the hoax article in the *Minneapolis Chronicle* for January 9, 1867, but that other unidentified persons wrote some or all of what had gone before, including the original article to the *New York Herald*.

In the years following the hoax, the cave took on a new life. In the *Minneapolis Tribune* for August 10, 1875, a "New Attraction" is advertised. "Mr. Mannasseh Pettengill has leased the famous Chalybeate Springs" and will "carry out a plan of improvements, which will

M. Nowack published a stereopticon view of a tourist on a boat at the entrance to Chute's Tunnel, ca. 1876.

PRIVATE COLLECTION OF VICTOR THORSTENSON.

make it more popular than it was before the war." As depicted on an engraving of "St. Anthony's Falls Mineral Springs," the resort included a photographic gallery, observation tower, hotel, and bath. Warner's *History of Hennepin County* mentions "a fish pond and a few curiosities of the animal kingdom. The view of the falls with these extraordinary inducements, rewarded the tourist for the fatigue of descending the long stairway to the bed of the river, and the patronage of the swing, boat and restaurant compensated the enterprising owner." Advertisements for Chalybeate Springs appeared in the *Lake Minnetonka Tourist* throughout the summer of 1876. In one of them, almost as an afterthought, we are informed that "a few yards below the springs is the entrance to a tunnel, excavated for water power purposes, and extending some two or three hundred feet into the white sand-rock."

In the *Saint Paul and Minneapolis Pioneer Press and Tribune* for August 26, 1876, there is another advertisement for Chalybeate Springs. The attractions included "ice cream parlors and cigar stand" and "a little building occupied by M. Nowack, as a photograph gallery, where may be found stereoscopic views of that locality." "The band plays at the springs every Saturday evening," it continues, "and with the grounds brilliantly illuminated, and the grand old Mississippi rolling and tumbling at your feet, the scene is a beautiful and impressive one." But the tunnel receives a new emphasis this time: "Chute's Cave—A Boat Ride of 2,000 Feet, Under Main Street." This was the first use of the name "Chute's Cave." The advertisement continues:

If you have a desire to EXPLORE THE BOWELS OF THE EARTH, Mr. Pettengill can accommodate you in that particular also. The mouth of the "Chute Cave" is just below the springs, and the bottom of this cave is covered with about eighteen inches of water. For the moderate sum of ten cents you can take a seat in a boat, with a flaming torch at the bow, and with a trusty pilot sail up under Main street a distance of 2,000 feet, between walls of pure white sand-stone, and under a limestone arch which forms the roof. It is an inexpensive and decidedly interesting trip to take.

Mention of "a limestone arch which forms the roof" indicates that the large open chamber in Chute's Cave was accessible at this time, so the tour did not merely involve traversing the sandstone tunnel.

In the *Saint Paul and Minneapolis Pioneer-Press and Tribune* for December 1, 1889, in an item titled "Underground Minneapolis," we read:

Some people, however, think that the only example of these subterranean retreats is the one known as Chute's cave, the mouth of which is in the East side mill district. This most interesting place is no longer frequented by human beings of the ordinary sort. But a few years ago not a day passed that did not bring it visitors. A stream of water ran the whole length of the cave, and for the small consideration of a dime a grim, Charon-like individual would undertake to convey, in a rude scow of a boat, all visitors, who were so inclined, for a distance of a quarter of a mile or thereabouts into this gloomy passage. The mouth of the cave was at the foot of a high overhanging bank.

By hosting tours, Chute's Cave became the third-oldest show cave in the state, after Fountain and Carver's Caves in St. Paul. Rural southeastern Minnesota, the state's premiere show cave region today, has a history of commercialization that began only in the twentieth century, with the advent of the automobile.

The summer of 1880 appears to have been the last season for Pettengill's resort. In the *Northwestern Miller* for February 18, 1881, we read that a "large force of men is at work on the tail race, which runs along below the Chalybeate springs for several hundred feet, making sad havoc of the fountain and other paraphernalia connected with that resort." City sewers were connected into the tailraces, adding unsavory sights and smells. Pettengill's obituary states that he closed his resort "at a great sacrifice" and opened a farm in Todd County in the fall of 1881. "The beauty of this place [Chalybeate Springs]," it reported, "was ruined by the improvements made for water power and railroad purposes."

Perhaps a more dramatic event also played a role in the demise of Chute's Cave, one that may have suggested to Pettengill or his visitors that the cave was unsafe. On December 23, 1880, Main Street in St. Anthony collapsed. "Will the History of the Eventful Year, 1869, Be Again Repeated," screamed the *Minneapolis Journal* on December 24, 1880. This was an allusion to the Eastman Tunnel disaster of 1869, which nearly destroyed St. Anthony Falls. "A catastrophe occurred on the east side last evening which really threatens imminent danger to the interests of the whole city," it reported. "About six o'clock a noise of cracking timber was heard near H. J. G. Crosswell's flouring mill just below the new Pillsbury A mill, and immediately after the earth just below the mill settled down about six or eight feet, a portion of Main street going down. The break ... extended down the street, between two and three hundred feet, the sink hole being in an oval form." The article fingered the culprit: "The Old Tail Race, Known as Chute's Cave, a Bad Investment," opining that "The Treacherous Sand Stone Under the Lime Rock Does the Business." Warner's *History of Hennepin County* was more succinct: "Into the hole, tumbled a part of Main Street. A tree was swallowed up to the limbs."

Several eight-by-ten glossies of the interior of Chute's Cave and Tunnel, dated October 21, 1936, are in the files of the Metropolitan Council Environmental Services Department. They were apparently taken during documentation of the construction of a sanitary sewer, the Minneapolis East interceptor, which passes near the cave. They show the square-set timbering that is still found in the cave but, owing to settlement, no longer performs its original function of supporting the ceiling.

June D. Holmquist wrote about "The Nesmith Cave Mystery" in *American Heritage* magazine in 1951. Interest had been sparked by suggestions that Minneapolis caves could be used as civil defense shelters. The August 29, 1950, *Minneapolis Star*, for example, includes Chute's Cave and Tunnel in a list of "atom bomb shelters." More than a decade later the October 5, 1961, *Minneapolis Tribune* includes them as potential "fallout shelters." But Chute's Cave and Tunnel, with their multiple inputs of water, are unsuitable as shelters from radioactive fallout. One authority noted, "Water supplies in caves are derived from the surface and are therefore subject to contamination by radioactive fallout." A more fundamental flaw is the location of Chute's Cave. A characteristic of "good mines and caves" is that "they are generally removed from critical target areas."

That's the last we hear of Chute's Cave for several decades. Today, it can be observed that the cave is situated in the St. Peter Sandstone with a ceiling formed by the overlying Platteville Limestone. It is not the largest cave under Minneapolis, but it is about two hundred feet long and one hundred feet wide and is collapsed in the center. The floor-to-ceiling collapse mound fills the greater part of the cave. Adelbert Russell Moore, an engineer for the St. Anthony Falls Water Power Company (which became part of Northern States Power Company in 1923), explored Chute's Cave in 1909 and described the mound as consisting of "fallen lime rock in a very irregular shape, but on the whole somewhat resembling a huge fountain built up in tiers, over which water trickled, the water being impregnated with iron had colored the stone to almost a jet black giving it an extremely beautiful appearance." The water-laid mineral deposits described by Moore are better known among cavers as flowstone. When I explored Chute's Cave in 1990, the accessible portion consisted of the void space around the perimeter of this enormous mound and the big room. Moore called the big room "very wonderful."

The origin of Chute's Cave has long been in doubt. Was it, like other natural caves in the St. Peter Sandstone under the Twin Cities, created by groundwater washing away sand grains? Or is it artificial, merely a widened segment of Chute's Tunnel? Or is it partly both? The claim that Chute's Cave is a natural cave was made by Moore in 1931 and became the basis for the account presented in Lucille Kane's classic book, *The Falls of St. Anthony*. His assertion is plausible and very neatly explains some aspects of the Nesmith Cave hoax. But state geologist Newton Horace Winchell, who completed a classic study of the postglacial retreat of St. Anthony Falls and was thus quite familiar with the area, declared that caves are absent from the Mississippi River gorge above Fort Snelling. Dr. Jeff Dorale, of the University of Iowa, in 2000 and 2001 collected samples of flowstone from the Tower of St. Anthony in Chute's Cave for radiometric dating. This method calculates age based on how much uranium—present in the formation as a trace element—has decayed to thorium. Dorale found that the flowstone postdates 1880, suggesting that the cave is fairly young and potentially artificial.

The earliest known depiction of Chute's Cave is a small detail on a large Corps of Engineers map. Described as "showing improvements made, by the US, under direction of Maj. F. U. Farquhar, Corps of Engineers ... from 1874 to 77," the map was prepared in the wake of the Eastman Tunnel disaster of 1869. Chute tunnel is depicted and labeled as such. The words "Break of Dec. 23, 1880" is written over a widening of the tunnel. The next map, dated 1894, depicts the collapse mound as a dashed circle in the center of the cave. Moore surveyed the cave on March 8–10, 1909, and produced the first accurate map. His intention was perhaps to delineate the limits of the cave preparatory to the construction, in 1910, of Pillsbury's concrete and tile elevator—a heavy structure that is still standing and is now part of East Bank Mills, upscale condominiums. Moore had thus drafted the "treasure map" I used to find Chute's Cave many years later, in 1990.

DOWN THE RABBIT HOLE
NICOLLET ISLAND CAVES

*The rabbit-hole went straight on like a tunnel for some way, and
then dipped suddenly down, so suddenly that Alice had not a
moment to think about stopping herself before she found herself
falling down what seemed to be a very deep well.*

LEWIS CARROLL, *ALICE IN WONDERLAND*

AS NOTED IN THE JOURNALS of the early explorers, there were originally a half dozen sliver-shaped islands at St. Anthony Falls, the largest waterfall along the entire course of the Mississippi River. There
were islands above and below the falls, and some that straddled it.
Some of the islands were reputed to harbor caves. The most famous
case, clearly a hoax, was the fictitious gold cave of Spirit Island.

Spirit Island, below the waterfall, owes its name to the legend of
Dark Day, who deliberately plunged over the falls in a canoe with her
child to spite a two-timing husband. Her spirit haunted the island and
was sometimes glimpsed in the mist of the falls. For many years, the
island's trees were a favored resort of eagles, which would snatch fish
that had been stunned by their plunge over the falls—a sort of natural
roadkill along the waterways. In the 1860s, newspapers reported a
gold cave on Spirit Island. I've always thought that someone could
easily have gotten the idea for this hoax from observing the shadowy,
zigzag reentrants, characteristic of the Platteville Limestone, which
often appear from a distance to be cave entrances. Sadly, Spirit Island
was quarried for its limestone caprock in the late 1890s, which ruined
the whole place. One old photo of the island from this time reminds
me of images of the foundering *Titanic*. The remainder of the island, a
mere sandstone stump, was completely grubbed out during the Upper
Harbor Project after World War II, which extended the head of navigation on the river to above the falls. Another island, Hennepin Island,

still in existence, was famous as the location of the 1869 Eastman Tunnel tragedy, described in another chapter.

Nicollet Island, located above the waterfall, is the best place to find real caves among the islands today. It's like a little bit of downtown St. Paul in the heart of Minneapolis, in a subterranean sense, because nowhere else under Minneapolis can you find a labyrinth of brick-lined utility tunnels in the sandrock layer of the sort that abound under St. Paul. Interestingly, it was once proposed to have the state capitol relocated to Nicollet Island—which would have made the comparison with St. Paul all the more appropriate.

Nicollet Island was originally the site of an Indian maple sugar camp, and there's still a street named Maple Place reflecting this. The island's woods were "so dense with timber and undergrowth, that it was impossible to penetrate it," according to one early visitor, who also reported thousands of passenger pigeons. Half a mile long and shaped like a battleship, the island's fifty acres were purchased from the government in 1848 by Franklin Steele, the founder of St. Anthony. John Orth, Hennepin County's pioneer brewer and one of the founders of Grain Belt Beer, dug the first caves in the sandstone under Nicollet Island beginning in 1850 for use as beer storage cellars. By the 1880s Orth had built an icehouse to replace the cave; the cave was used for mushroom growing as late as the 1920s. Later, under the guise of Satan's Cave, it became a well-known rendezvous for urban explorers.

Nicollet Island was historically tripartite, with a northern residential area, a central commercial belt, and a southern industrial tip. Unfortunately, East Hennepin Avenue, the major commercial artery, had decayed into a miniature skid row by the early 1900s, and many of the buildings were razed during an urban renewal project in 1973. Looking at the gentrified Grove Street flats and ornate Queen Anne–style houses today, it's difficult to imagine this island had once been a slum. Urban planners compared Nicollet Island to Ward's Island, adjacent to Manhattan.

From the beginning, Nicollet Island attracted legends just as dubious as those swirling around Spirit Island. In 1866, when the island was first subdivided by speculators, a mysterious subterranean vault was supposedly discovered by railroad workmen, according to the *Minneapolis Chronicle*, which kept the farce going for several days.

The walls of the vault were covered with hieroglyphics, it was said, and on one side there was a door that no one could open. An "educated Frenchman," examining the hieroglyphics, determined that they concerned an extinct race of flying men of a high order of intellect. He concluded that this small room was the vestibule of a large theater or forum, containing valuable treasures, where these people studied over their secrets and drew up their designs in the arts and sciences.

After a trial of three hours each on numbers, music, and words, a word was whispered, and the door moved a little. It now being evening, it was thought best to leave until some propitious hour when the word would be spoken again, and then, no doubt, the door would open.

At 8 o'clock, A.M.... persons engaged in examining the mysteries ... repaired to the spot on Nicollet Island, and commenced labor.... All were still—each took his position, as on the previous day—the word was whispered. The door opened.... Immediately in front of us was a statue resembling an angel with its two fingers of the right hand on its mouth—this we understood to mean silence.... Beautiful lettering and drafting were made upon the walls, representing nine departments, as follows, as we go around the theater ... Language, Mathematics, Geometry, Music, Astronomy, Botany, Zoology, Intelligences, and Spirit Land. In front of each of these departments was a statue of beautiful figure about five feet high, angel in form situated as if viewing the field before it. The floor of the hall was something like crystal. The canopy was so bright that our eyes could not view it.... On looking at our watches we found that we had been absent from our friends nine hours. Being now in need of refreshments, we retired to our home, and after resting have prepared these few notes for those who love to read, and bask in thought and revery.

My own introduction to subterranean Nicollet Island involved more travail than treasure, as a member of a roving exploratory herd on a cold, snowy night in the winter of 1989. One guy removed the lid, which was partly in someone's backyard, and a big cloud of steam billowed out. We scrambled down the shaft into the toasty warmth of the tunnel system, twenty feet below the surface, which carried the island's water main.

What makes the Nicollet Island tunnel system so uncomfortable is that the passages are only five feet high and half as wide, forcing us to go about Quasimodo-like for hundreds of feet while straddling a water main and carrying a big rucksack full of heavy tools. By the end of the trip, just standing upright felt positively delightful. The fetid tunnel air was unwholesome to breathe, stagnant, and tainted with raw sewage. While most of the passages were floored with dry dirt, the water mains occasionally ran through pools of raw sewage. Although the water in water mains is under positive pressure and, if there was a hole in the pipe, would leak outward rather than inward, I still found the situation unsavory to contemplate. Maybe that's why I usually drink bottled water.

In 1894, the city engineer drafted a large map of Nicollet Island, one hundred feet to the inch, which became the favored exploration guide for urban explorers. I had the deluxe version, fifty feet to the inch, which covered a whole tabletop. It shows the city water tunnel, or ring main, around the perimeter of the island, with short laterals, or side passages, running out like spokes to individual house lots. Conveniently, each lateral was numbered on the map, so I could count them off to find a particular one that I wanted to explore. Many of these laterals were empty sandrock tunnels—stagnant dead-ends, no longer containing water pipes connecting to the former houses above. In 1988, the construction of the new Hennepin Avenue suspension bridge, linking the East Bank, Nicollet Island, and downtown Minneapolis, severed any passages beyond them from the main network.

What early caught my attention about this map is that some of the passages depicted had been sealed off by concrete bulkheads. I was able to squeeze around several of the bulkheads and found nothing unusual on the other side. The most interesting case, however, involved the "bloody snake passage" (as I called it in my field notes). Behind this bulkhead, the sandrock passage meandered about, its walls coated with scarlet-red flowstone deposits that resembled dripping blood. Nearby, a crude shaft, filled with chaotic, unstable debris, led up toward the foundations of DeLaSalle High School.

One of the passages, marked as number 30 on the big map, ran

Liquor retailer A. M. Smith maintained wine cellars (as depicted here in a period newspaper advertisement) on Nicollet Island in the late nineteenth century.

from east to west across the midriff of the island. Using this passage, it should have been possible to cross through Nicollet Island from one side to the other. But the passage dead-ended at a sinkhole, where the land surface above had caved in, presenting a formidable obstacle, and too much work would have been required to dig open the connection for uncertain gains.

The west side of Nicollet Island is riddled with irregular sandrock crawlways not depicted even on the big 1894 map, and some of them could potentially be natural caves. A. M. Smith's wine cellars were supposedly around here, but exploring the spot underground, I found nothing remotely resembling a tidy wine cellar, and certainly no left-over vintages to regale the weary explorer. I concluded that the wine cellar had been located *above* the limestone caprock of the island, rather than in the underlying sandrock, where the tunnels branch and flourish.

Some of the Nicollet Island voids were of respectable antiquity. Toward the south end of the island were the Neapolitan caves, so called from the colorful swirls of reddish iron pigments in the white and green walls. These were all that remained of the upstream reaches of the old Eastman Tunnel, which collapsed in 1869. The voids were very irregular and choked with shale fragments, forcing us to worm our way through nasty little rat holes to get from one room to another. Years later, I dug an exit from these voids to the outside world, breaking out into an old sewer that led to a manhole near the historic Grain Belt neon sign that faces downtown Minneapolis. An unintended consequence was that in winter the aperture allowed cold, dry air to blow into the tunnel system, perhaps even altering the bat hibernation patterns of that part of the island.

It's not often that you meet others underground. A disturbing incident occurred when I was hunchbacking through the ring tunnel with my fiancée, Cindy, one day. We heard voices coming up behind us, muttering something horrific. Since there are many curves and elbows in the passages, you can't see flashlights at any great distance, and voices are muffled. We continued along, not knowing exactly what our pursuers' intentions were. We could tell they were gaining ground because the menacing voices got closer. Finally, we exited through a manhole lid and walked back on the surface to the manhole where I suspected they had entered the system. Indeed, I found the lid off, and I banged it shut on them.

Nicollet Island's ring tunnel intersected Satan's Cave, its best-known cave. To get into the cave we'd squeeze out through a window in the brick wall of the ring tunnel and lower ourselves a body's length down to the sandy floor of the cave. In one spot, the ring tunnel passed through the cave itself, and being unsupported below, it resembled a brick bridge inside the cave. The cave consists of three parallel passages dug out of the sandrock, only two of which are presently interconnected, the third isolated by a roof collapse years go. Each passage was a dozen feet high and about as wide, running a hundred feet or so. My friend Mark went over the cave with a metal detector pretty thoroughly and dug up numerous old artifacts, such as bits of old horse tack. These he later reburied in the cave in a sort of time capsule.

Satan's Cave, of course, contains the famous "chapel" where a half-dozen devil's heads have been carved into the walls, in bas-relief, near floor level. The devils have open mouths in which candles can be placed to illuminate the room. The flaring nostrils were so delicately carved that light shows through. In the center of the room was an "altar" and "candelabra" with candles. Was it really used for satanic worship? I doubt it. We always brought votive candles with us, lit them, and then lay in the dry, beach-like sand for a catnap, as it was a nice place to relax from the painful contortions required to get there. The back wall of Satan's Cave was bricked over, but the passage almost certainly once led out to the river.

I speculated on the age of the devil heads. An article by journalist Stephen Hartgen in the *Minneapolis Star* for August 7, 1973, reported on the exploration of Nicollet Island caves. Although Hartgen, who accompanied the trip, described even trivial wall carvings, there's no mention of the dramatic devils, so they were probably carved after that.

I once did a traffic study in Satan's Cave to get a feel for the number of "worshippers" who used the chapel. Using a board, I smoothed out the sand floor that must be traversed to get to the altar. Anyone who came would leave footprints, which I could then log during my next trip, usually a few months later. I found that during some winter months no one visited the altar, while in the summer the floor was usually thoroughly tracked over by the time I returned. The devil was a big summertime favorite.

In the winter of 1940–41, Michigan State University researcher George Rysgaard, who passed away in 2006, crawled into the Nicollet

Island caves and counted the hibernating bats. I was struck by the data in his report, published in the *American Midland Naturalist* the following year. He found many Big Browns, but you won't find this species under the island nowadays; instead, you find Little Browns and Eastern Pipistrelles. Bats require places cold enough to get their body temperature sufficiently low to hibernate, but beyond that, the Big Browns prefer cooler situations, the Little Browns prefer warmer locations, and the Eastern Pipistrelles prefer moister locations. The subterranean ecology of the island may have shifted over the years in favor of those bats preferring warmer and moister conditions. We conducted informal bat counts of our own some winters, reporting the results to a DNR representative.

Apart from investigating the numbered laterals, another project was to get into Cave X, the largest cave under Nicollet Island, clearly depicted on the 1894 map but not physically connected to the ring tunnel. I did a little surface reconnoitering on the north end of the island and found the collapsed entrance to this buried cave from the outside. Because the bomb shelter surveys of World War II and the fallout shelter surveys of the 1960s did not mention this otherwise substantial cave, while mentioning other, smaller voids, it was reasonable to assume that the cave was sealed sometime prior to World War II. Since it would have required a big, obvious dig for us to reopen this cave from the outside, exposing us to the vulgar gaze of park patrons on neighboring Boom Island, we tried to dig into it from underground. Many trips were devoted to this task over the years.

Leading off from Satan's Cave there was a lengthy, claustrophobic crawlway floored with dry sand and lined with water pipes. After crawling for hundreds of feet we came to a well hole, which we crossed by crawling over rotten boards. According to the map, we were now close to the long-sought cave. Measuring to the spot where the cave should pass nearest to the crawlway, we were surprised to find an "X" already marked on the sandstone wall (which is why we called it Cave X). The journalist Hartgen, mentioned above, reported that the whole point of the 1973 expedition was to locate this unnamed, inaccessible cave, so I surmised that it was they who made the X mark. By coincidence, the cave as seen on the map also vaguely had the shape of the letter *X*.

Mark, who had independently sought the cave years earlier, devised special drill bits in his elaborate workshop at home and drilled a pilot hole through the walls at the X mark, using a battery-powered cordless drill, adding stems as the horizontal hole lengthened. The drilling was tediously slow, lasting for hours at a stretch, the scene illuminated with votive candles. Some of the helpers got bored and went to sleep in the narrow passages, hoping to eventually awaken to shouts of success. After a typical drilling trip, usually around Christmastime each year, the drill bits were carefully stowed away in the sandy passages until the next visit. We planned to break open a successful pilot hole to crawling size by renting a jackhammer, powered with a gasoline-powered generator on the surface, running the power line through a hole out to the riverbanks. I began work on the hole for the power line from the inside, digging through the loose, unstable soil. We didn't know at the time that one of our helpers would report our activities to a rival group.

After drilling fifteen feet into the wall, we struck a void, but it still seemed a little iffy. Mark proposed putting a small camera on the tip of a boom and having a closer look at the situation. Meanwhile, I tried finding a backdoor into the cave by walking through a deep-level sanitary sewer, dug in the 1930s, which appeared to run under the cave. But after lifting up the steel trapdoor, squeezing down through a small aperture into the gassy passage, saying a few last words to my friends, and treading over a soft brown carpet of feces and toilet paper, the elusive Cave X was nowhere to be found.

A few winters later, my drilling friend called to inform me that he had been walking around on the north end of Nicollet Island, looking for melted patches of snow indicative of caves below the surface, and had come across a strange opening that led down into a cave. The following weekend we met to investigate the find. He lifted a wooden trapdoor in the brush along the river banks, and I saw what looked like a large rabbit hole. We descended through the very steep, narrow soil tube, elaborately supported with wooden posts and chicken wire. Some of us went head first and others feet first. It had the flavor of Alice in Wonderland, chasing the rabbit down the hole.

At the bottom, about twenty feet below the surface, the hole connected to my own dig in the old familiar sandrock passages we knew so well, except in the interim, someone had used power tools to ream out our pilot hole to the size of a crawl tube, making the connection with Cave X. Someone else had carried out the exact plan we had earlier formulated, and it couldn't have been coincidence. It had required many hours of free time, money for high-quality, battery-powered tools, and a termite-like persistence to bore through fifteen feet of sandstone. It was one of the most elaborate urban dig projects I have seen in the Metro area, an impressive piece of work. The all-time local record for such digs, however, surely belongs to Hobbit's Hole, a sandrock tube 125 feet long, which someone dug through a sandstone ridge below Cherokee Park in St. Paul—for no apparent purpose. Termites on steroids!

After crawling through the new connection, we carefully examined Cave X, or as its discoverer chose to call it, "Santa's Cave," a name derived by transposing the letters of "Satan's Cave," which he carved into the cave's wall in staring capitals six feet high. The abundance of dates on the smoke-blackened walls fell into the dozen years from 1935 to 1947; most of them were from the early 1940s. Presumably the fire that produced the blackening took place prior to 1935. We discerned a number of pre-smoke carvings, crude and lewd, graven into the walls by even earlier visitors—a veritable signature gallery of Minneapolis history. In contrast to Satan's thick soil and artifacts, Santa's thin soil held no Christmas gifts for Mark's metal detector.

PART V

UTILITIES

A LONELY DAY UNDER THE MORTUARY
THE FORT ROAD LABYRINTH

Consider again when thou art in cool blood, what thou art like to meet with in the way that thou goest.

JOHN BUNYAN, *PILGRIM'S PROGRESS*

HUNCHED OVER in the low, narrow, Gothic-shaped sewers under a Fort Road mortuary, I was saluted by a splattering noise and sulfurous odor, and I tried not to look too closely at what might be causing it. Presently, I expected to see latex stalactites dangling from the vaults. The sewer passages were festooned with damp, glistening cobwebs that floated into my face, causing a tickling sensation. Worse than anything were the deep, black, glutinous sediments that sucked at my waders and boiled furiously with every step, releasing methane and rotten-egg gas. What mess had I gotten myself into this time?

Welcome to the Fort Road Labyrinth, as I came to call it—the longest, most-interconnected network of sewer tunnels under the city of St. Paul. They run under every street in the Fort Road neighborhood at an average depth of about thirty feet, with pipes coming down from individual houses and buildings. These tunnels, which carry raw sewage, were carved with hand tools in the St. Peter Sandstone bedrock more than a hundred years ago, and the floors were paved with brickwork. Some of the passages were so low it made me wonder whether child labor had been involved in their construction. I once painstakingly measured, on the sewer maps, the aggregate length of this labyrinth and found it to be thirty miles—the length of the famous Carlsbad Caverns in New Mexico—and most of it is coiled up, like a ball of twine, under just a few square miles. It's almost totally unknown to the public at large.

I hesitate to write about this place at all, for fear that my readers will not understand. Most people can relate to exploring a cave, or maybe a storm drain. But the attitude adjustments required to explore a vast sewer labyrinth are not easily come by. The unspeakable filth you must pass through is truly unspeakable. I begin to feel like Edgar Allan Poe, prefacing another gruesome tale with protestations of rationality. At a minimum you need a somewhat Swiftian sense of humor. And since it's difficult to describe a labyrinth of any kind in linear fashion, I will proceed by a sort of free association. The images crowd upon me.

Before I go any further, a short digression on sewer jargon is required. There are two kinds of sewers, sanitary and storm. The term "sanitary" is a euphemism because it refers to raw sewage, which most of us would consider unsanitary. It is sanitary in the sense that rather than running into nearby water bodies and polluting them it goes instead to a sewage treatment plant. Sanitary sewers are sometimes called interceptors because they intercept raw sewage that would otherwise flow into bodies of water. On the other hand there's the storm sewer, often called a storm drain, which carries rainwater to water bodies by means of an exit, called an outfall. Even when it's not raining, most storm drains carry groundwater that has seeped into them. In the bad old days, most sewers did double duty, leaving water bodies severely polluted. Here in the Twin Cities, the separate system was introduced in the 1930s; the municipal treatment plant at Pig's Eye, near St. Paul, became operational in 1938. It treated the sewage of both Minneapolis and St. Paul. Occasionally, the two kinds of sewer still overflow into one another, so to further reduce river pollution an on-going effort has been made in recent decades to separate them even more thoroughly.

Thirty miles of sandrock sewer passages under the Fort Road neighborhood of St. Paul were carved out by hand tools in the late nineteenth century.

SKETCH OF A LABORER FROM *ST. PAUL PIONEER PRESS*, MAY 30, 1892.

Historically, one of the oddest things is how the St. Paul sewer system differs from that of neighboring Minneapolis, despite the same starting conditions—the same underlying geology. The two systems are complete opposites. When Joseph Sewall originally envisioned St. Paul's sewerage, every building had a corresponding walking passage in the St. Peter Sandstone, below the Platteville Limestone. Andrew Rinker, by contrast, designed Minneapolis sewerage such that only the trunk passage itself was in sandrock; individual building connections were kept above the limestone, just below street level. Each system has its own advantages.

The story of the Fort Road Labyrinth mirrors the growth of St. Paul itself. Sewer Contract No. 4 was awarded for the Eagle Street sewer in the downtown area back in 1873. This sewer followed the line of a former surface stream, Rice Brook, discharging to the Mississippi River at its lower end. From Eagle Street, the system was extended to the southwest, along the axis of Fort Road. The labyrinth was built in segments by various contractors as the need arose. Finally, in the 1920s, the upstream end of the system curled deep under the Highland Park neighborhood like the tail of a monstrous sewer alligator. The labyrinth is no longer growing—except perhaps inadvertently, through erosional processes. Nowadays, of course, the sewage flows to the treatment plant instead of the river.

Most of my exploration of the labyrinth was undertaken in the years around 2000, and I kept a "sewer diary" to record impressions and keep things straight in my own mind. Initially, I was hunting for caves, like Stahlmann's brewery cave, but this netherworld of fermenting brickwork held a certain morbid fascination of its own.

Because the Fort Road Labyrinth is a sanitary sewer, I delayed exploring it for quite some time. Very few people, for obvious reasons, chose to accompany me. I once jokingly referred to the labyrinth as the Diamond Mine, hoping to motivate squeamish friends, presenting them with the venal prospect of finding wedding rings that had been flushed down the drain. Unfortunately, nobody was that stupid, and I never did find any rings. I had gotten this vision of treasure from reading Henry Mayhew's classic work on obscure London trades, published in 1851, which described the "toshers" who daily searched the London sewers for valuables as a means of livelihood. The most I've ever found in a sewer was a five-dollar bill floating around, and I used it to buy myself supper.

I was forced to explore solo, which is very, very dangerous because there's no one to rescue you in case of an accident; a sprained foot, for example, could prove fatal. I began leaving windshield notices on the dashboard of my car, notes that described which tunnel I planned to enter and who to call now that I obviously had not returned and you'd had to break into my car, God bless you, to read this. Basically, they were just to let someone know where to search for a bloated, rat-eaten corpse. Strange thoughts go through your mind as you pen these little suicide notes.

Despite the eerie isolation, I wouldn't have cared to meet anyone down there. In fact, the ghostly reflection of flashlight beams from water surfaces onto the walls, producing the momentary illusion that someone was approaching or receding from me in the tunnels, was unnerving. Borrowing a term from astronomy, I referred to this reflectance by the German word, *Gegenschein*, meaning counterglow. Pretty soon, you begin to hear voices in the dripping water, too.

I usually entered the labyrinth by walking up storm water outfalls from the Mississippi River, but St. Paul's separation program progressively sealed more and more of these easy connections. I found another entrance, squeezing through a small hole in the river bluff. I never used manholes in the streets, even if it meant I had to go the long way around, because this drew unwelcome attention ("Say, what are you doing there?"). Another problem with manholes was decapitation. Push the lid up at the wrong moment and a vehicle might hook it, taking your head off as well.

During my most active period of exploration, I was making trips every weekend, spending whole days in the labyrinth. I carried food during my lengthy expeditions, but it was difficult to find a place clean enough to feel like eating it. I emerged at nightfall in a very ripe condition, sometimes having lost a shoe along the way. The subterranean wardrobe invariably included a plastic trash bag for outerwear. Trash bags were potentially useful for many things, in addition to being ponchos and carryalls. In a pinch, they could be converted into makeshift waders, flotation devices, and even "lungs" to breathe from as a last resort.

I frequently had to discard all my clothes afterward, they were so caked with filth. If I thought something was salvageable, it was still usually so dirty that I didn't even want to use the basement laundry tub. I simply left it out in the backyard, exposed to the elements, recalling the bleach fields of previous centuries. The weather cycle of rainstorms and sunny days correspond to the cycles of a giant washing machine. What my neighbors must have thought of this I cannot imagine. If you forgot to remove the wet clothes from the car's trunk and discovered them some weeks later, they were usually afflicted with black mildew spots. The staggering ammonia vapors were usually enough to convince you to part with them.

It was a long time before I overcame my dread of sewer gas. I seriously considered getting scuba gear from a dive shop. I envisioned my rented air tanks bumping and scraping against the walls for mile after mile. Eventually, I decided that as long as I felt *moving* air, I was safe—no matter how bad the odor. Or so I thought.

Speaking of odor, it's been said that old fishermen, blindfolded, can distinguish one trout stream from another by the smell. I could do the same thing in the labyrinth. Overall, the labyrinth smelled vaguely like garlic summer sausage. But there were pockets of better and worse. Lengthy dead-end passages, flooded with stagnant blue-green septic pools, for example, were pretty overpowering. Laundromats, with their sudsy discharges, provided a welcome olfactory oasis in the sewers below.

Owing to bathwater and bodily fluids, the tunnels were pretty warm, even in winter, although during one winter trip my planned exit point, a river outfall, was barred off by a veritable dragon's jaw of ice stalactites and stalagmites. There was an anxious moment as I punched and kicked my way through this obstacle to escape the labyrinth, leaving with raw, bloody hands.

You might assume that the use of sewer maps would make exploration of the labyrinth a relatively cut-and-dried affair, but it didn't usually work that way. A newcomer to the Fort Road Labyrinth would soon become disoriented, dispirited, and lost, even with a map. All the passages look the same at first. After a few trips I began to perceive subtle distinctions among the different passages. This passage has uniformly black walls, while that one has a piebald weathering pattern, the underlying white sandrock showing through the crud. This passage has straight walls, while that one has wavy walls. And so forth.

A compass proved very useful in the labyrinth because there were only a few major passage orientations, which matched the streets above. When I unexpectedly came across a passage new to me, or became disoriented, I checked which way the sewage was flowing. Going downstream would bring me back to the main trunk line, running under Fort Road itself, which formed a sort of backbone to the otherwise amorphous arrangement. The role of Ariadne's thread in the labyrinth was here played by a blue-green thread of sewage.

I also learned how to use audible cues. Continuously thumping manhole lids under heavy traffic—the very hoofbeats of the Minotaur—formed the auditory signature of Fort Road, the side streets being comparatively quiet. Theoretically, I should have been able to find my way out of the labyrinth even in total darkness, but it was an experiment I did not care to make.

I soon discovered that portaging sped things up. When the map showed two sandrock tunnels approaching very closely under certain conditions, there was often a connection between them. Over time, I developed skill in predicting and using portages to the point where I began to fancy that I could almost walk through solid rock. Ultimately, it had to do with the geology. You wouldn't expect to find this generous connectivity in harder rock types like schist (as under Manhattan) or limestone (as under St. Louis) because they are more expensive to excavate.

The portages were grim little voids. Located along the crests of subterranean watersheds, the portages were the higher and drier places between two streams of sewage flowing in opposite directions. Rats love to dig their burrows in such terrain. The portages are usually smaller than the main passage, some just inconspicuous crawlways, which forced me into unwanted intimacy with those benighted creatures. Not everyone was willing to brave the whiskered gauntlet for the sake of new sewer lands beyond.

The nature of the local sewage seemed to be reflected in the health of the rats. One day, while strolling under one of St. Paul's charity soup kitchens, I observed fresh pasta floating in the sewage. Following the stream, I came to a pipe vomiting pasta into the tunnel. Swarms of sleek, fat rats clustered about, feasting gluttonously with their razor-sharp teeth. They parted ahead of me in the narrow passage as I approached and closed the gap behind, squeaking in protest all the while. While walking under a downtown hospital, on the other hand, I noticed that the rats appeared disheveled and mangy. Their zigzag tails must have broken and healed multiple times. They weren't bright-eyed and bushy-tailed like the happy pasta-fed rats under the soup kitchen. I came to enjoy encounters like this as a form of comic relief, considering my perilous situation far from human aid.

Another funny place was the pinup gallery. Some laborer, perhaps on a lengthy repair job and lonesome for the female species, had adorned the rock walls with centerfolds, of which only moldy shreds remained. I suppose the sewer is an appropriate place for filthy pictures.

There's very little graffiti in the tunnels, except for the initials of public works personnel, but I did encounter a very elaborate wall carving once, a tree—carved *in relief*—with intertwined branches, and several feet high. It seemed symbolic of the labyrinth as a whole, with its endless, branching passages.

The truly distinctive graffito of the labyrinth, however, was the so-called bat-rat tally, obviously the work of a bored sewer laborer who had been many places down there over the years. It's easy to distinguish "official" graffiti from ordinary graffiti, by the way, because sewer workers use green spray paint. The tally was a series of slashes purporting to represent the number of bats seen as compared with rats. As depicted, the ratio was usually one bat to ten rats. However, I think even that ratio is excessive. I seldom encountered bats in the labyrinth, and when I did they were usually on the wing. I rarely saw a hanging bat, owing, I suppose, to their vulnerability to rat predation.

Another sort of writing on the wall was more dubious. The passages were originally dug by laborers using picks, and over the years their chisel marks filled up with crud, giving the appearance of cuneiform writing, or the lettering of some long-dead sandhog trying to channel me. It seemed to be the visual counterpart of the auditory hallucinations generated by the dripping water.

One of my goals in the labyrinth, apart from getting to the occasional cave, was to see Seven Corners, the informal name for where Fort Road enters the downtown area proper. I expected to find seven passages going off in all directions, as the name implies. When I finally arrived at Seven Corners, I was disappointed to see only two or three passages, depending on how they were counted. The rest had been sealed off with masonry over the years. There was a sort of curious curved niche in the wall at this point, forming a seat, and I sat down to rest and ponder the situation. It had been a very long trip, and I still had farther to go. On my second trip to Seven Corners I tried a totally different route, portaging in zigzag fashion along the outer edges of the labyrinth. I discovered Crowfoot Junction, where three passages come together like a crow's foot.

Even though Seven Corners had been attained, I had as yet seen only a fraction of the whole labyrinth. Exploring upstream from Stahlmann's Cellars—away from downtown St. Paul—I very soon came to the dry, dusty, upstream end of the Fort Road tunnel. Where was the rest of the labyrinth—more miles of passages—as depicted on the map? It was below me. I called this sunken passage the foundered segment. For whatever reason, the foundered segment had more cavelike voids than other parts of the labyrinth. Some of these silent voids, these little tumble-rock chapels of the underworld, were natural in origin and lined with glacial cobbles.

At the far end of the foundered segment there was a sanitary waterfall that I couldn't possibly ascend. This waterfall also marked a fundamental change in the nature of the labyrinth from the classic nineteenth-century sandrock labyrinth that I had been exploring. Upstream from the foundered segment, where the classic labyrinth ended, the West Seventh Street branch interceptor, hitherto a parallel, concrete tunnel, took over the role that the old sandrock passages had played nearer downtown. It branched furiously, sending out tentacles to all the houses. To explore this twentieth-century concrete neo-labyrinth, I had to enter above the waterfall, through a separate river outfall.

My first serious trip into this outfall, with my friend John, lasted six hours. It was a hot summer's day, and it must have seemed strange to the fisherman sitting next to the outfall that we were putting on winter jackets. We slung our rucksacks over our shoulders and got into the waist-deep water. A Crestliner boat was bobbing in the river just offshore, and we entered the sewer in full view of its bemused occupants. No big deal, we thought at the time.

When we exited the outfall, the sun was setting. The patient fisherman, still in pursuit of urban fish, erupted with laughter. He told us that right after we had entered, the fancy boat had swung up to the outfall, and the busybody skipper had used his cell phone to call the police, who soon arrived and spent a long time yelling up into the tunnel and trying to coax us out. We, of course, had no knowledge of this, being miles back in the system. We, too, had a good laugh over the situation.

Farthest from downtown, this outfall was the last in the labyrinth series to be constructed, in the 1920s. Even in the comparatively short time since then, it had developed substantial mineral deposits, most notably brain coral, which is a rounded mass of rippled flowstone—the whole tunnel was sometimes referred to as the Brain Drain.

A weird thing about the Brain Drain was the so-called Alpine illusion. As I walked through the tunnel, I passed under shafts with manhole lids at wildly varying heights above me, as if one manhole were situated on a peak, another in a valley. I conjectured that the higher lids represented the true street level, far above, while I inferred, from the lower lids, that there was a set of passages immediately above the one I was in, which later proved to be the case.

Alone among the outfalls of the labyrinth, this horseshoe tunnel was lined with macaroni. "Horseshoe" refers to the shape of the cross section, and "macaroni" is sewer slang for vitreous-clay segmental blocks. In cross section, these blocks have a curly appearance like those funny pasta shapes you see at the grocery store. In almost every case where I've seen these segmental blocks used, the lining has collapsed, leaving macaroni scattered up and down the tunnel. This collapse played an important role in the explorations to come. The entrance to the neo-labyrinth was behind the fallen macaroni lining.

I readied myself for another long solo trip. I set my sights on reaching the Ramlow drop shaft, the farthest upstream point that can be possibly reached in the labyrinth. Ramlow Place is a short street south of Highland Village, nearly six miles distant from Seven Corners as the bat flies. From the outfall, I scrambled through the fallen macaroni and into the neo-labyrinth. I had to go more than a mile underground to reach Ramlow. During this hike I encountered a new subterranean ailment.

The neo-labyrinth was lined with monotonous concrete. In conjunction with a dim flashlight, this caused me to become dizzy after extensive walking. Whenever I felt dizzy in the sewers, it was time to exit because I could have encountered bad air. I was far from an exit, so I did what I have done before while traveling great distances underground: I sat down in a cool drop shaft to give myself a quick mental pep talk. I noticed that the dizziness dissipated rather quickly. I surmised the real reason and pulled out a fresh flashlight. My prescription for tunnel vertigo: take two batteries and call me in the morning.

Cleveland Avenue had a unique style of house connection that I had not seen elsewhere in the labyrinth. Whereas other connections are merely segmented clay pipes, these looked like fireplaces. Often, there were unbearably vile splatterings on the walls opposite, a Rorschach of wet toilet paper, as if the material had come blasting out of the fireplaces with great gusto. Branching off from the Cleveland Avenue sewer, I was able to dispel the old legend about subterranean passages running from the Hollyhocks mansion, a notorious Prohibition-era gangster hideout, to the river gorge. The sandrock sewer under Mississippi River Boulevard would have intersected any such passage.

There were several miniature outliers of the labyrinth, complete in every detail except that they were not connected to the main system. The largest of these baby labyrinths was under the old Shell Oil tank farm along Shepard Road, a contaminated parcel that was nicely redeveloped in 2005. Back in the late nineteenth century, before the tank farm, there had been a community there, each house with its own sewer connection. One of these tunnels was unique, spiraling upward toward the surface and containing a veritable ossuary of raccoon bones. Nearby there was a chamber in the sandstone in which someone had sculpted a perfect devil's head, a dozen feet in diameter and complete with horns, in a large sand pile on the floor.

Under the Highland Park neighborhood, there was another labyrinthine fragment, separated by a greater distance than any other from the parental void. Over successive visits during the years, I saw passage after passage cemented off by Public Works until nothing was left but a strange hairpin-type tunnel. On my last trip there, I observed raccoon eyes scintillating in my flashlight beam. The raccoon retreated ahead of me as I advanced, until I arrived at the very end of the passage—and no raccoon. It had vanished like a magician. Then I observed a pipe in the ceiling, about twelve inches in diameter, and shined my light up the hole. There was the furry bum, far above me. That's about as far as anyone can go in the labyrinth, and a fitting place to end this tale.

BEHIND THE SILVER DOOR
UTILITY LABYRINTHS

An unusual geologic formation is responsible for St. Paul's down-town area being honeycombed with more tunnels than perhaps any other city in the world.

ANONYMOUS, 1937

AS YOU WALK the streets of downtown St. Paul, there's little to suggest anything special underfoot. It's not until you are standing below the Mississippi River bluffs that you glimpse little holes in the cliffs near the Wabasha Street Bridge and see the magical "doors to nowhere" that you might not suspect otherwise.

Downtown St. Paul (the Loop) is underlain by a great utility laby-rinth, situated from twenty to seventy-five feet below street level. Esti-mates of its total length vary greatly, and I've seen figures ranging all the way up to seventy miles. This system was carved out from 1869 to 1907, in several big chunks and all by hand tools such as pickaxes and shovels at the rate of four to six feet per day per man. The passages are typically three and a half by six and a half feet in size and marked with street signs. It's difficult to specify exactly how many levels of passages there are because they frequently interweave, but I'd say there are about half a dozen in most areas. City engineer George M. Shepard's typical cross section of Wabasha Street, published in a 1937 newspaper article, gives you the flavor of these catacombs, "St. Paul's downtown area being honeycombed with more tunnels than perhaps any other city in the world." Bruce Bloomgren, of the Minnesota Geo-logical Survey, informed me that a *complete* map of the tunnel system was prepared years ago but had mysteriously "gone missing" at some point.

St. Paul's utility labyrinth is bounded on the top by limestone, on the bottom by the river level, on the north by the deep gash of Interstate 94, on the east by Lowertown (a valley where the sandstone is absent altogether), on the south by the river bluffs, and on the west by Seven Corners. When I explored these tunnels in the early 1990s, the game was to find a way of portaging between the utility labyrinth and adjoining tunnel systems. For example, did the utility tunnels connect with the well-known Capitol complex of pedestrian tunnels north of the interstate highway, with the Trout Brook system in Lowertown, or with the Fort Road Labyrinth to the west? Finally, we wanted to get as deep as possible—the elusive door to China we often joked about. Utilities placed in these tunnels included water, power (gas and electric), steam heat, telephone, fiber optics (in our day), and the storm and sanitary sewers.

The Water Department carved its tunnels from 1869 to 1890, bringing water from Lake Phalen and beyond. The warm tunnels prevented the mains from freezing during cold Minnesota winters. The big water

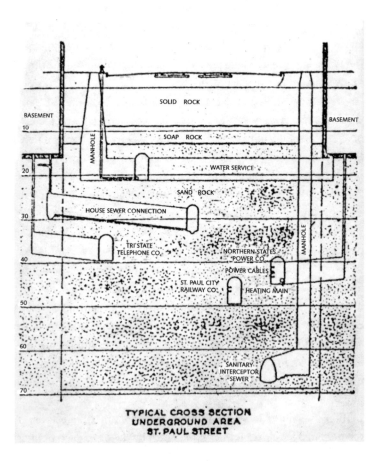

City engineer George M. Shepard drafted this typical cross section beneath a downtown St. Paul street for a newspaper article in 1937, giving a good idea of the sandstone utility catacombs that exist there.

TYPICAL CROSS SECTION
UNDERGROUND AREA
ST. PAUL STREET

main runs directly under Wabasha Street on its way to the bridge, then heads over the river to the West Side, which was annexed to St. Paul in 1874. A door in the basement of City Hall opens into these tunnels, from which the meter readers used to fan out to monitor the city's water use.

The St. Paul Gas Light Company was established in 1856. Coal was retorted to generate an artificial gas that differed from our modern natural gas in its composition and lower calorific value. In 1885, their Hill Street station was built against the bluffs, and by the next year the first gas ran through mains in sandrock tunnels under the Loop, bringing the gaslight era to St. Paul. (Nowadays, natural gas is used mainly for heating and cooking, not illumination.) Occasionally the gas would leak into the tunnels, resulting in flying manhole lids if it was accidentally ignited. In 1973, two trespassing youths struck a match in the tunnels and were blown off a ladder, both breaking their backs when they landed, and their parents sued the city for creating an attractive nuisance. (When did utilities become an attractive nuisance in our society?)

Alexander Graham Bell demonstrated his telephone at the Philadelphia Centennial Exposition in 1876. Within a decade, the Northwestern Telephone Company began carving its own set of tunnels under St. Paul. An amusing incident from the early days of their construction tells how the sandhogs, tunneling in from the river bluff, set up an impromptu subterranean bar to celebrate after reaching Eighth and Wabasha. These tunnels were larger than the rest, prodding the *St. Paul Pioneer Press* columnist Oliver Towne to quip that "the telephone caverns [are] the aristocrats of tunnels."

In New York City, which has often been a utility bellwether, there was a big incentive to place utilities underground after the famous blizzard of 1888, which caused lines and poles to droop and snap with the weight of the ice. The lines were buried, and the poles were chopped down. By 1893, St. Paul had passed an ordinance forbidding poles in the downtown area.

The American inventor Birdsill Holly is considered the father of district steam heating, which involves supplying steam heat to the buildings of an entire district in a downtown area from a central boiler facility. The first big district steam heating system in the nation was built by the New York Steam Company, which began supplying its Manhattan customers in 1882. By 1905, the American District Steam

Company began service to the St. Paul Loop through steam tunnels that it had carved in the sandrock. Competition among the power companies led to duplicate tunnels on opposite sides of the street, but in 1916, Northern States Power Company was incorporated, and several formerly separate parallel tunnel systems were joined under one banner. These tunnels weave through the sandrock like teredo-worm borings in the wood of old sailing vessels, deftly avoiding one another and leaving rollercoaster passages where one passes over or under the other. They are linked horizontally by crosscuts and vertically by interconnects and are often separated by numbered silver-colored doors that serve as bulkheads to isolate gas leaks. (I counted at least fifty silver doors.) In some cases, owing to interference with telephone transmissions, the companies couldn't use each other's tunnels and had to dig their own, which added even more mileage to the system.

In 1890, the St. Paul Street Railway Company, with its plant situated near the Hill Street station, began to electrify its lines, running the cables, supported on heavy iron frames, through yet another set of sandrock tunnels. These tunnels were abandoned in 1953, when buses replaced streetcars. One sandrock tunnel carried cables all the way to another tunnel, the historic Selby streetcar tunnel, 1,500 feet long, which opened in 1907. The Selby tunnel allowed St. Paul's cable cars to get to the top of the plateau behind the downtown. After the demise of streetcars, the abandoned Selby tunnel was used by the homeless. I recall exploring its darkened recesses back in the 1980s, before it was firmly sealed. The tunnel inhabitants could see our silhouettes perfectly as we entered, while we could only vaguely sense their flitting forms, putting us at a disadvantage. But even today, through a nearby ventilation pipe you can smell the sandrock tunnel that serviced the Selby tunnel, marking the deepest shaft in the utility system.

The Twin Cities, however, have never had a large population of mole people like New York City, in the sense of people who live in subway and train tunnels. But a large underground homeless population had developed in part of St. Paul's utility labyrinth many years ago. An 1878 newspaper clipping, "The Cave Dwellers," reports: "Beneath Rogers' block, in St Paul, there are a number of labyrinthian excavations made in the sand rock for sewerage and storage purposes, shaft holes connecting them with the buildings fronting on Third street [now Kellogg Boulevard]. The entrance to these vaults is from the river bank, and heavy doors and locks preserve them for the private purposes for which they were intended." It goes on to report how the vaults were taken over by "a gang of at least forty thieves" who built campfires belowground, sending smoke into downtown buildings and leading to an exciting subterranean battle with a platoon of police sent to flush them out. This maze was still accessible until recently. I recall edging precariously along ledges, like a mountain goat, on the eighty-foot cliff face near the Wabasha Street Bridge. The cliff was relandscaped during the reconstruction of the bridge in the late 1990s, removing the temptation for people to risk their necks. The holes led to a maze of crawl spaces around old building foundations in the Kellogg area, and it was for some reason utterly infested with centipedes, which I tried not to get down my collar. In some places we found caches of old glass bottles, which could be identified using collector's guidebooks such as Munsey's. The crawlways looped back out to the bluff face at several points, allowing me to experience, like some oversized squab, the nauseating interior of a pigeonhole lined with poop and feathers. At another place there was a deep elevator shaft leading down to the river-level Cobb Caves, an old cavern depicted in the 1874 *Andreas Atlas* and most likely the actual scene of the battle with the thieves.

There were other historic caves connected with St. Paul's utility labyrinth. In the ceiling of the Exchange Street tunnel, for example, there was a dark void, easy to miss. Climbing into it I found myself in the City Brewery Cave, a horseshoe-shaped void filled with bathroom fixtures. Originally, of course, the cave had its own separate entrance in the bluffs. City Brewery was founded at Eagle and Exchange streets in 1855 and was later acquired by Frederick Emmert, who used artesian well water in the brewing process. This brewery, which closed in 1901, catered to the Eagle Street saloon district, the most notorious of the establishments being known as the Bucket of Blood for its vicious brawls.

Nina Clifford was the most famous madam in St. Paul history. She ran a bordello at 147 Washington Street that existed for half a century (1887–1937), kitty-corner from the Minnesota Club (built in 1915). It's been claimed that the sons of many well-to-do families, upon coming of age, were sent to this bordello to learn the basic maneuvers. One of the most persistent rumors is that there was a tunnel running from the club to the bordello so that discreet visits could be paid to this temple of Venus, which could otherwise be reached by the garish red stairway down the bluffs. If there's any truth to the story, it was likely that the "tunnel of love" was in fact only one of the utility tunnels in the vicinity. If that's true, pleasure-seeking men in any building in the Loop could have enjoyed the same clandestine access. Upon investigating the rumor belowground, I did not find any open connection between the tunnel and the club, although it's possible it was sealed up long ago. In 1997, when the present Science Museum of Minnesota was under construction, the bordello site was dug up and yielded fourteen thousand artifacts. In 2005, I was featured on "Weird Underworld," an episode of *Weird U.S.*, on the History Channel, and I was interviewed about the bordello by the hosts, Mark and Mark. Unfortunately, they muffed my grand entrance, which involved dramatically emerging from below a St. Paul street by throwing off a manhole lid. They couldn't get their lines straight for the cameraman, and it would have been hilarious had my arms not grown weary with the repeated flinging.

Looking at urban exploration Web sites today, you'd think that St. Paul's utility labyrinth was some big new discovery. While digging through the Minnesota Speleological Survey files, I came across a sheaf of detailed trip reports, dating from the early 1960s, prepared by the Minnesota Rovers, an outing club. Their nocturnal excursions involved trips of as many as two dozen college students to the St. Paul utility tunnels. (That's what I call an exploratory herd.) The yellowing pages are filled with humorous details of their escapades, such as instructions to "park and make sure no one's watching you." It seems the students actually enjoyed being chased by the utility workers; brazenly invading the NSP plant itself, they used to purchase food from the vending machines. Given the late hours, it's no surprise that one report mentions getting a cup of coffee (only five cents), presumably to remain wakeful during the expedition. It was all in good fun.

Back in the days when I went exploring, one way to enter the utility system involved a subterranean space in the sandrock that my friend Mike described as Dr. Seuss's tunnels, owing to their bizarre, almost whimsical, configuration. Small wormholes would unexpectedly open up into large rooms. One passage led to a narrow stairway, carved in bedrock, at the top of which there was a steel door, painted red, which was locked half the time. When open, it gave direct access to the water main tunnels, the uppermost level of the utility labyrinth. There was usually a bit of nervous anticipation when creeping out into the forbidden sandrock corridors.

The tunnels were illuminated with strings of lights, spaced about one light every hundred feet or so, which could be turned on or off with switches every block. During each visit, different strings were lighted, and we were relieved to find that the pattern had nothing to do with our own comings and goings. The heat, and the fact that we could see lights for many city blocks, led to optical phantoms: it would appear that a distant light was suddenly darkened, as if a utility worker had passed in front of it, heading our way. But we actually saw very few workers, especially since we usually confined our visits to the wee hours and holidays. At that time of night, it was safe to explore even the subterranean break rooms of the Water Department, which were equipped with microwaves, televisions, and other amenities. We never removed anything or left any messes.

The air in the utility labyrinth was indeed hot, even though the system was naturally ventilated by strong convection updrafts, the air entering at holes under the Wabasha Street Bridge and whistling up through manhole lids in the downtown streets. Owing to the pervasive asbestos contamination from deteriorating pipe wrap, which menaced utility workers until it was removed in recent years, asbestos fibers covered the floor like snow in certain tunnels, and the more health-conscious among us wore respirators. But alas, try wearing a hot mask in a hot tunnel for very long—we soon let them flop.

Occasionally we'd come across rat mummies, desiccated in the desert heat of the sandy tunnels. I noticed that many of them appeared to have partaken of baits, their rotten spines, still tenting up a parchment-like skin, twisted in the characteristic S shape indicative of death by neuropoison.

I frequently wore khaki clothing, a desert color, for camouflage, hoping to blend in with the similarly colored sandrock walls, for whatever it was worth. I made several trips with my photographer friend Jason, and it was unnerving to remain stationary for as long as half an hour while he bracketed his artistic shots. I felt that it was an excellent way of getting caught.

One of our goals was to explore the long-rumored passage running under the Mississippi River. Wading through waist-deep raw sewage in one tunnel, we actually came to a stairway leading steadily downward, as if it were going to pass entirely under the river, but it stopped short at a large sewer vault. In fact, there is a passage going under the river, a siphon bringing raw sewage over from the West Side, via Navy Island—but nothing that a human being could pass through.

As for storm drains, there was one really big one, forming the lowest level in downtown St. Paul, the St. Peter–Rondo tunnel, which drained the interstate highways in the vicinity. This tunnel ran right under the Ramsey County jail, and doubtless the inmates occasionally watched our doings. During especially cold winters this tunnel accumulated large ice dams, where groundwater seeped out of joints in the wall and froze because of the cold air being sucked in through the river outfall by the powerful convection currents. One winter's day, having gone far up the storm tunnel with my fellow explorer John, I noticed that the water level had risen several inches during the course of our trip. I became alarmed until I realized that it was just a daily fluctuation, involving snow that had melted during the warmer winter midday. Going back downstream, we were scampering back over the ice dams when one of them suddenly broke loose. I rode it, bronco fashion, down to the outfall, colliding with other dams along the way.

Once, just by coincidence, we happened to be under the streets during the St. Paul Winter Carnival Torchlight Parade. Looking up from the bottom of a manhole shaft, I could tell that the parade was passing overhead. I jokingly asked my friend, in a loud voice, what would happen if someone knew we were down here. Immediately, someone on the street above shined a flashlight down through the open grating! That shut me up. I suppose I could have told them I was searching for the Winter Carnival medallion. Later that same evening, when exiting from the outfall on the Mississippi, we were startled by a burst of light and a loud explosion in front of us, just as we came out. It was the beginning of the fireworks show on Harriet Island. In order to prevent this sort of subterranean tourism when the Republican National Convention came to St. Paul in 2008, officials welded shut many of the manhole covers in the downtown area.

The exploration of college tunnels by students has become a subsport of its own in recent years and has even been given a special name—vadding. The word derives from "VAD," an illicit computer game. The Massachusetts Institute of Technology, in Cambridge, Massachusetts, is supposed to have the most extensive such tunnel system in the country. At Columbia University, in New York City, the tunnels intersect an old insane asylum; they were used during the Manhattan Project of World War II, and they played a role during the massive Vietnam War protests of 1968, when they were used by students to supply their beleaguered friends in the buildings above with basic necessities. To add further spice, the Columbia tunnels are said to have been used to transport radioactive materials, and even today there is a derelict cyclotron, or atom smasher, just sitting around down there, which someone spray-painted bright green. John Nash, the Nobel prize-winning mathematician of *A Beautiful Mind*, used to explore the steam tunnels under the Carnegie Institute of Technology in Pittsburgh while a student there in the 1940s.

It's no surprise that the second-largest utility labyrinth in the Twin Cities, several miles worth, is found under the University of Minnesota's Minneapolis campus, situated on both sides of the Mississippi River; there's also a smaller system under the university's St. Paul campus. The Minnesota Rovers scheduled official trips to these tunnels in the 1960s. When I was an undergraduate there years ago, I spent a lot of time exploring the tunnels late at night, like many other students. Many vadding Web sites have that angle well covered. I will mention just a few of the more unique features here.

In contrast to St. Paul's utility labyrinth, the university tunnels have a much more uniform appearance because they were designed from the start by a single entity as steam heating tunnels rather than by competing companies for different, and sometimes mutually exclusive, purposes over a span of years. You will find no Dr. Seuss stalking this labyrinth.

Harry Orr, heating engineer for the University of Minnesota, stands in one of the utility tunnels that served the campus.

COURTESY OF THE MINNEAPOLIS PUBLIC LIBRARY, MINNEAPOLIS COLLECTION, M0447.

Most students are probably familiar with the shallow distribution tunnels running just below ground level. In winter, after a light dusting of snow, they leave a geometric pattern of melted patches across campus, as mysterious as crop circles unless you know the underlying reason. The sheet-metal mushrooms, or ventilating towers, about as tall as a person, are another manifestation. We called the old heart of campus, where the towers were more abundant than elsewhere, the mushroom garden. Unless you were really bored and wanted to blister your skin on a hot pipe or commune with the cockroaches, this part of the system was of less interest than the deep tunnels carved in the St. Peter Sandstone and located a hundred feet below campus.

This deep level, connected by shafts with the shallow level, was arranged in a series of loops, like a cloverleaf. Workers from the steam plant got around on bicycles or, where the passage was wide enough, on electric carts. Sometimes students would have subterranean races on the carts, resulting in nasty crashes requiring a visit to the emergency room. The most unique spot was a large underground test room, fifty by one hundred feet in size, with a limestone ceiling. This chamber was excavated in the 1970s with a grant from the National Science Foundation for the purpose of studying the deformation of large rock caverns. Much of the research was conducted by Ray Sterling, director of the university's Underground Space Center.

In my opinion, the university tunnels are a case study in how the excessive and flagrant publicity provided by Web sites in recent years has had a negative impact on the ability to experience interesting subterranean spaces. As soon as the vadding Web sites went up, spilling their guts, the campus police took notice and initiated a security crackdown, with motion detectors and security cameras. It's no longer possible to explore these tunnels without serious consequences. In exchange for a little pseudonymous notoriety, these students permanently ruined it for their fellow explorers.

PART VI

PLUTO'S KINGDOM

LOST WORLD
SCHIEKS CAVE

Take counsel, cherish not the sun and stars. Come, follow me
down into the realm of gloom.

GOETHE, *FAUST*

IN 1939, the *Minneapolis Journal* photographer David Dornberg
went on a camera safari, as he called it, through a large cave under
downtown Minneapolis. He described it as "a 'lost world,' weird and
spooky—the darkest spot for adventure into which my four years as a
Journal cameraman ever led me." Some may discount this as sensa-
tionalistic tripe, but read the testimony of Roger Kehret, a seasoned
Minnesota caver with years of experience, in his 1974 booklet *Minnesota Caves of History and Legend:* "When cavers think of remote hard
to reach caves it brings to mind scenes of high mountains of the Pacific
Northwest or the steaming jungles of the Amazon. The most remote
and hard to get to cave that I have ever reached is found on Fourth
Street near Marquette Avenue in down town Minneapolis, Minnesota."
This chapter describes my own ordeal to reach this lost world.

Schieks Cave, as it has become known among urban explorers, has
also been called Loop Cave, Manhole Cave, and Farmers & Mechanics
Bank Cave. It got the name from Schieks Palace Royale, a gentlemen's
club that now occupies the old Farmers & Mechanics Bank building,
under which the cave is located. Journalist Kay Miller once described
the nightclub as "topless above, bottomless below" because of the
underlying cave, but there's no humanly enterable physical connection between them.

Schieks Cave is the largest natural cave under downtown Minneapolis, extending for a city block through the St. Peter Sandstone.
Carl J. Illstrup, a city sewer engineer who discovered the cave in 1904,
described it as a "cave shaped like an inverted bowl," a description

that seems puzzling to anyone who has actually been there. (It's shaped more like a pancake that has gone awry on the griddle.) In 1931, an enthusiastic journalist, Robert J. Fitzsimmons, waxed poetical about "the beauties of the sewer system" and described Illstrup as "the ruler of this fantastic world." The discovery of the cave in 1904, by a crew who braved "the lethal breath of deadly gases," is presented as the high point of Illstrup's life.

The earliest known documentation of Schieks Cave is the 1904 Lund survey, which is good for showing the former creeks and lakes of the cave. Reportedly, the cave was kept a secret for years because city officials feared the public would think downtown Minneapolis was built on a thin shell that would plunge into a hole in the earth. Another concern was that burglars might have worked undetected and bored directly into the bank's treasure vaults. By 1921 it was reported that "the entire business portion of the city is built over a series of subterranean lakes and caverns as mysterious and baffling as the Mammoth

Camera Safari Explores 'Lost World' Under Loop

ROUTE OF CAMERA EXPLORATION UNDER MINNEAPOLIS LOOP

Minneapolis Journal reporter Dave Dornberg drafted this map of Schieks Cave based on his "Camera Safari" through the cave in 1939.

caves of Kentucky or catacombs of Rome." The 1929 Lawton survey depicts the cave extensively modified by the construction of piers, walls, and artificial drainage systems. It also shows the seventy-five-foot entrance shaft on Fourth Street and the fifteen-foot shaft from the cave to the underlying North Minneapolis Tunnel (NMT), a sanitary sewer.

In 1952 the Twin Cities Grotto, the local chapter of the National Speleological Society, visited Schieks Cave, and it was written up for the Sunday supplements. The late architectural historian David Gebhard, author of many guidebooks, was a member of this club. In 1983, a successor organization, the Minnesota Speleological Survey, visited the cave, and their lurid account of the gloomy cave, whose walls were black with cockroaches, and the roaring sewer that ran under it fired my enthusiasm to get there someday—one way or another. Perhaps by climbing up from the sewers rather than down from the streets?

In *Minnesota Caves of History and Legend*, Kehret revealed how the Rovers, dressed as sewer workers, surrounded the entrance manhole with barricades and used a truck-mounted winch to remove the heavy, hexagonal lid (which in recent years has been welded shut). Getting there must have been more than half the fun, because Kehret said little about the cave itself except that it was "almost filled with sand, concrete, pipes and other debris."

In 1993, my friend John and I examined the storm drains under the Minneapolis downtown (the Loop) with the hope of getting into Schieks Cave. Located far below street level, this system drains to the Mississippi River by a large outfall in the milling district. With reference to the most famous sewer of antiquity, it's the very Cloaca Maxima of Minneapolis. Because we found no connection from the storm drains to the cave or to the sanitary sewer known to run under the cave, we shelved the project. Shortly thereafter I left for the University of Connecticut, where I did graduate work on barite mines.

In 1996, Peter Sand, a college student, along with several friends, began a series of attempts to get to Schieks Cave. He created a Web site, "Minneapolis Draining Archive," perhaps the first of its kind in this area, where he posted trip reports of these and other adventures. After exploring the storm drains without result, he tried wading upstream in the North Minneapolis Tunnel. This sanitary sewer, eight feet in diameter, carries the great river of human waste from the Loop and runs directly under the cave.

NMT is the very gut of Minneapolis. Wading upstream is fatiguing owing to the swift, chest-deep current (three feet per second) and the well-lubricated invert (floor). Occasionally one of them would lose his footing, even to the extent of full immersion in the warm, gray fluid, and get swept back to the starting point. Sand persevered to the extent of going two city blocks, but there were still four blocks remaining to get to the cave. He even considered driving climbing pitons into the sewer walls. While NMT has been called a lot of things over the years, my favorite was Silk Road, an allusion to all the little bits of toilet tissue swirling through there. It takes effort to maintain a sense of humor in such grim surroundings.

In 1999, *National Geographic Adventure* magazine commissioned a writer to report on urban exploration, which came to focus on the efforts to get to Schieks Cave. By this time I had met Sand, and we agreed to join forces. I advocated an upstream strategy: to find a safe entrance to NMT upstream from the cave and go with the flow rather than buck the current. The summer of 1999 was devoted to this task. My role in the exploration was critical. I picked all the locations appearing in the photo shoot, and I was the only person who knew how to access them. But I was in my thirties at the time, and in keeping with the magazine's hip, youthful target audience, I was downgraded to a "wizened elder" who "smokes cheap cigars." The youthful Sand was compared with world-renowned physicist J. Robert Oppenheimer, apparently for things like crafting a makeshift sewer canoe out of "an old file cabinet."

The first upstream entry point we investigated was the venerable Bassett Creek tunnel. Running below this storm tunnel for a short distance was a sanitary sewer, the whole thing forming something of a double-decker arrangement. The plan was to drop into the lower tunnel and head downstream to the cave. But after removing the lids in the floor of the upper tunnel and allowing the mephitic vapors to exhale, we got cold feet. The sewage was moving too fast down there.

More to be feared was the inferred existence of a waterfall at some point along the sewer line. While at Bassett Creek the sanitary sewer was somewhat near street level, at Schieks Cave the NMT is ninety feet down. Somewhere along the way there had to be a big drop, and the small-scale sewer maps that I had didn't indicate details of this nature.

Tracing the sanitary sewer downstream by peeping through the holes on manhole lids, we found a good lid farther along on a little-used side street. The sewage was not moving so fast here, but it appeared deeper. Surrounding the manhole with orange cones, we descended a rope ladder and walked downstream. My thigh waders soon overtopped and filled with sewage, so that I appeared to have elephantiasis. Condoms, distended with raw sewage, dangled from the vaults above our heads. The hypothetical waterfall, located near Déjà Vu Nightclub, proved very real. Affixing a safety line to a pipe jutting from the walls, we approached the slippery brink of the cataract and peered into the abyss. I recalled the ending of Edgar Allan Poe's *Narrative of Arthur Gordon Pym*, where a chasm opened to swallow the hapless explorers.

This sanitary waterfall marked the beginning of the deep NMT proper. From here, NMT ran under Schieks Cave and then on toward the treatment plant. We saw ladder rungs in the wall of the drop shaft in the midst of the waterfall. We briefly toyed with the notion of sealing ourselves in trash bags, diverting the waterfall, and descending the ladder, but it all seemed just a bit too weird. Such situations are also dangerous because the turbulence of the splattering sewage causes deadly gasses to bubble off. We gave up on that approach.

In August 1999, we investigated another tributary of NMT running under the Warehouse District. We found good lids situated among deserted construction sites, but here again we faced the daunting prospect of a waterfall. Soon after, Sand returned to the manhole with his buddies, descended into the tributary on a rope ladder, and walked several blocks downstream, where he encountered a steep flume rather than a waterfall. Once on the slippery slope they could no longer control their descent, rocketing down the flume in a shower of raw sewage.

At the bottom of the flume, Sand and company bobbed up into the waist-deep NMT, ninety feet below street level. One person had lost his flashlight, another his glasses, yet another both shoes. One of them had swallowed sewage, contracted giardiasis, and later had to undergo a course of antibiotics. Bloodied by the harrowing descent, they made their way to Schieks Cave, where they spent twenty minutes.

Sand had invited me to go on this trip, but I pointed out that there was rain in the weather forecast. His answer? They had life jackets. I don't think Sand had the faintest clue about the extreme danger of entering tunnels of any kind while it's raining. Despite every precaution, for example, even professional tunnel workers have been swept to their death, as tragically happened in St. Paul in 2007. It's not something to be taken lightly.

A few weeks later, with perfect beach weather above, John and I were ready to ride the flume down to Schieks Cave. I constructed a new rope ladder with Perlon climbing rope and wooden dowels, making it thirty feet long because that's the average thickness of the Platteville Limestone in the Twin Cities Basin, and hence the depth of many shafts thereabouts. I designed a new type of rigid ladder that could be floated into position and rapidly assembled. The floating ladder could be hitched to my belt with a rope and towed behind in the stream, leaving my hands free.

The multitudinous supplies in our bulging backpacks were encapsulated in three layers of plastic contractor bags; we must have looked like walking tool chests. As we headed toward the manhole, someone approached us and asked what we were doing, but we made no response. The equipment drop having taken place flawlessly in a drive-by operation, the rope ladder was unfurled and secured in minutes, the disposable floating ladder was lowered away, and soon both of us were securely at the bottom of the shaft.

But alas! We hadn't anticipated the force of the sewage flow in the narrow confines of the pipe. Perhaps it was the wrong time of day. The damned thing was running half full. I clutched at the slimy walls to avoid getting swept away. The air was tropical. I was sweating and felt bad. John had never developed a taste for sanitary work, and I had downplayed this aspect of the voyage to avoid facing the fearful prospect of descending to the cave alone. When you go to Hell, you want to take somebody with you.

There wasn't much time for debate. The Devil himself seemed to be tugging on the other end of my new ladder, trying to drag me down into the abyss of raw sewage under the city. It was a struggle just to get back out of the manhole, because the rope ladder had sprung up out of reach like a rubber band.

We crept from the manhole and lay on the ground like drowned rats, glistening with human waste. The operation had been an embarrassing disaster. Worse, owing to changes at the construction sites with the good lids, the entrance soon thereafter became unusable. Schieks Cave, once within my grasp, had receded to infinity.

An incredible piece of good fortune came our way the following year, however. While walking through the deep storm drains one day in April 2000—the very ones we had carefully examined years earlier—John heard cascading water in the darkness ahead of us. We discovered that thirty feet of the floor of a storm drain had collapsed into a void in the sandstone, and storm water was pouring through the break. Ducking through, we entered a large void and found a collapsed sanitary sewer. The significance of this struck me instantly. We finally had upstream access to NMT. The road to Schieks Cave was wide open.

This fortuitous window into the abyss, ephemeral as it may seem, was superior to the flume route in that we could walk to Schieks Cave straight from the river, with the ability to visit the cave as often as we liked, at least until the break was repaired. By contrast, the flume ordeal was so horrific that Sand swore off sewering afterward, a wise decision.

In May 2000, having regrouped and secured proper gear, John and I made our first trek to Schieks Cave. We followed a well-traveled route into the Minneapolis underworld. We climbed down an old manhole into the huge brick outfall chamber along the waterfront. Although the pea-green water was only knee-deep, we hugged the walls like mice, avoiding the deep drop-off in the center. The water was charged with flotsam, mostly wood, Styrofoam, and dead carp, which surged back and forth as if under the influence of tides. Periodically, the surge generated a tidal bore a few inches high that chugged noisily up the tunnel for several blocks.

I recalled my first visit to this chamber years earlier, before I knew about the manhole entrance. Quite alone, I swam up the outfall from the river in a wetsuit, having first filled the wetsuit with "clean" river water so that I wouldn't get the nasty, pea-green soup next to my skin. It was a hot summer day, and once inside, to prevent overheating in my wetsuit, I took a cue from the famous French cave explorer Norbert Casteret, who sometimes explored in the buff. You'd never dream of doing that in our present electronic age, considering how many explorers you might bump into. Nowadays it's all the rage to have someone take your picture at such times and post it on the Web for all to see. But I digress.

Hiking up the storm drain, we established base camp at the Wash-Port regulator, located under Washington and Portland. This was a key place in the Minneapolis underworld because the storm and sanitary systems were separated by little more than a low wall, and you could cross freely between them. A dry, concrete room, well above the waterline, was available for staging equipment. In recent years, this connection has been completely reconstructed, severing any access.

Leaving base camp, we passed another well-known subterranean landmark, the Iron Gate, a heavy steel flap door that had to be propped open to crawl underneath. The Iron Gate marked the beginning of the really deep stuff. When I heard it bang shut behind me I usually got a heavy feeling, a sense that I was now committed to whatever endeavor was before me. From there we hiked several blocks up the Washington Avenue tunnel and turned up a side tunnel, arriving at the sewer break. There was no chance of getting lost because the street names are marked on little bronze plates for the convenience of sewer workers.

The sewer break was very close to Schieks Cave, yielding access to NMT only one-half block downstream from the cave. I volunteered to wade up to the cave and affix a yellow polypro safety line for the convenience of the trips to follow. Lowering myself into the raging current of raw sewage, however, I could hardly maintain a footing on the slippery invert. I inched along, advancing sideways while paying out the safety line behind me. I clutched at every little irregularity in the stone walls like a rock climber. The walls of NMT were coated with a vile jelly that I hadn't seen before. The violet slime of the deep sewers!

Arriving at the shaft to Schieks Cave, I found a crude wooden ladder consisting of a single upright and crosspiece, like a crucifix. I had to laugh. It was the one that Sand had brought down the flume. Even though the ladder had been sitting there only nine months, it appeared ancient, showing how corrosive the sewer environment was. Tongue in cheek, we dubbed it the crucifix ladder, commemorating his ordeal.

Both of us had been waiting to see Schieks Cave for so many years that we experienced a sort of rapture of the deeps upon our arrival at the cave. Perhaps tiny bubbles of sewer gas had lodged in our brains. We gazed up the seventy-five-foot shaft to the street, the entry point for official tours in the past. It was like looking up from the bottom of a deep well hole, light streaming through ventilation ports in the hexagonal lid far above us. Lid fragments lay scattered about our feet, lids that had tumbled down the shaft and smashed like cookies when someone got careless.

Although this sandstone cave was extensive, its flat limestone ceiling was rather low, obliging us to go about like apes, balancing on our gloved knuckles as we made our way among the sand dunes with grunts of satisfaction. Large natural sandstone pillars, called stone islands on the old real estate plats, formed a maze within the cave. Pyramid-style concrete piers supported the ceiling in many locations. It was another example of the vaguely Egyptian appearance of deep sewer architecture.

A major arm of Schieks Cave ran under the eleven-story Title Insurance building, which is heavier than the adjoining four-story old Farmers & Mechanics Bank building. Consequently, there were more of the pyramidal piers here than in all the rest of the cave combined. This part was flooded with a lake of stagnant, bubbling sewage—the Black Sea—which years later mysteriously dried up, leaving a polygonal-cracked mudflat covered with a whitish efflorescence like a dusting of snow.

Inside Schieks Cave there was a concrete chamber that resembled a baseball dugout. The chamber contained a ceiling spring, dubbed Little Minnehaha Falls by sewer workers long ago and labeled as such on Dornberg's 1939 map. Groundwater poured from a bedding plane in the limestone ceiling, forming a curtain of water, and deposited vertically striped black and white, or zebra, flowstone on the walls of the room. The black mineral is probably manganese. The crown jewel of mineral deposits in Schieks Cave, a formation that we dubbed the Black Medusa because of its shape, is made entirely of this mineral.

Using a high-quality mercury thermometer, I took the temperature of Little Minnehaha Falls and found her very feverish. The groundwater temperature was 66 degrees Fahrenheit, much higher than the expected 48 degrees at this latitude, and warmer even than surface water for that time of year. Reporting the results in a professional newsletter, I speculated that this thermal anomaly could be the result of heat generated by human activities in a densely urbanized area. Boiler rooms, for example, warm up the surrounding ground.

The subterranean waterfall was a good place to ponder the old controversy about the origin of Schieks Cave. Everyone agreed that the cave was formed by the mechanical erosion of the soft St. Peter Sandstone by running water, a process known as piping. One view is that the cave was formed 10,000 to 15,000 years ago and is a relic of the ice age. The contrasting theory, based on the testimony of sewer engineer Illstrup, is that the cave "may have been formed by water escaping from an abandoned artesian well and washing the sand into the sewer." The sewer referred to is doubtless the North Minneapolis Tunnel, on which construction began in 1889. My own contribution was the discovery that the "Old Artesian Well," at least as marked on Dornberg's map, does not exist, nor did it ever exist. Even if it had rusted away completely and the hole had become buried with debris, there would still be a corresponding drill hole through the ceiling, and there is not. Little Minnehaha Falls or something like it, it seemed to me, could have provided the source of water.

Something else was conspicuous by its absence. Where were all the cockroaches? I had been sold on that point! Not a single one, not even a dead roach, anywhere. Nor were there any bats or rats, for that matter. Instead, the cave was dominated by a sort of fly-and-worm ecosystem that, I later learned, has been found in other polluted urban caves around the country. The Schieks Cave biota is basically a guano-phile (excrement-loving) community. Fungus gardens were fed upon by swarms of fungus gnats that in turn supported the spiders in the cave, and earthworms covered the floor like spaghetti near the broken sewer lines.

The flood history of Schieks Cave was enough to concern the most intrepid sewer explorer. One source said, "After heavy rains the sewer backs up leaving water and debris scattered around the cave." Indeed, we found plastic soda straws and tampon applicators (by far the two most abundant types of detritus) on ledges several feet above the cave floor.

Two weeks later we returned to Schieks Cave to get video footage and continue our exploration. To maintain a coherent narrative in the sandstone maze we filmed the cave in a clockwise direction, following Dornberg's 1939 "route of camera exploration," using the survey maps as a basis for commentary. The whole thing went quite well, except for a few expletives, and I showed the resulting video in my geology courses at a local college for years afterward.

One of our goals during the second trip was to explore what Lund's 1904 map called the North Western National Bank tunnel, which appeared to run under the floor of Schieks Cave. The notion of explor-ing an obscure tunnel under an obscure cave appealed to my sense of the utterly remote, and I wanted to take a stroll down there. I finally located the rusted manhole lid in the floor of the cave and banged away until it came loose. Unfortunately, the passage was filled to the brim with a nauseous, yellow-gray liquid. The bank tunnel was really a sewer tunnel. The video guy recorded my disgust.

After the first trip to Schieks Cave, I was convulsed with a violent illness that I initially attributed to food poisoning. But it was becoming apparent that similar episodes had followed by a day or two any visit to the North Minneapolis Tunnel. The symptoms involved rolling about on the bathroom floor for six hours while puking my guts out. I could barely hoist myself onto the pot for the diarrhea part. My cats would stroll through occasionally to use their litter box and seemed to view me with great pity. One time, worse than the rest, I went down in the cellar for buckets and was disgusted to observe that vomit had dripped through the floorboards. Have you ever been that sick?

Having perceived the pattern, I determined to at least have the honor of giving the sewage sickness a name, Rinker's Revenge. Andrew Rinker, Minneapolis city engineer for thirty-six years, was the Father of the North Minneapolis Tunnel. Entering NMT—or even getting near it—assured that I would come down with the ailment. Never on any occasion that I became sick did I recall having actually swallowed sewage while in the tunnel. I did notice, however, that whenever a beam of light illuminated the tunnel, the air was laced with shining droplets and rainbows. And once, leaning down near the surface of the stream, I got a soapy taste, as if the air I inhaled contained enough droplets to generate taste. I later learned that these infectious droplets are well known to aerobiologists as coliform aerosols and contain fecal bacteria, among other things. The NMT rainbows were not friendly harbingers.

Who could tell what other evil bugs lay in wait for us in the depths of the hexagonal abysses? To stave off the agonies of Rinker's Revenge on our second trip to Schieks Cave, I devised elaborate precautions worthy of the *Andromeda Strain*. I wore a full-face respirator with chemical cartridges while walking through the NMT. I packed a decon kit consisting of a hydrogen peroxide spritz bottle, latex gloves, clean towels, and so forth. I wore a raincoat, neoprene chest waders, rubber gloves, and rubber boots.

Wearing a mask in NMT had its downside. While I was protected from the infectious mist, the face piece fogged over and was unbearably hot. But the cartridges were so effective that I didn't even smell hydrogen sulfide, the Chanel No. 5 of sewer scents, at any time I was down there. Nor did I get sick.

After our second visit to Schieks Cave and descending into the murky NMT, I decided to ride the stream all the way down to the Wash-Port regulator instead of returning via the break in the storm drain. I was curious to see what was down those six blocks of dark tunnel. John, less foolhardy, thought there was too much risk of getting swept away and ending up at the treatment plant and agreed to meet me back at the regulator, where the two systems crossed paths for the last time.

Entering NMT for the home lap—respirator firmly clamped over my face—I abandoned myself to the powerful current, which carried me along on tiptoes. The consequences of losing my balance or passing out in raw sewage up to my neck were too hideous to contemplate, even with a respirator. Within a short time, John's light had faded away and I was alone in the world, or rather under it. I could hear a muffled roar ahead of me in the darkness, where the sewage plunged into the regulator. After a while I got used to it and was able to stop myself and explore a few interesting side passages along the way.

The enormous sewer break that allowed us to portage from the deep storm tunnels to Schieks Cave was soon found and sealed by Public Works. The task required drilling a special-purpose four-foot diameter shaft down to the tunnel. The fortuitous connection had existed less than a year, but I had no doubt that new portals would develop in the future as the mortar decayed.

Apart from the intrinsic interest of Dornberg's "Lost World," Schieks Cave was important because it gave us access to a system of voids that ran along the tops of the tunnels under the Loop. Consulting Peele, the mining engineer's bible, I found that these voids, called overbreaks, are a by-product of tunnel construction. Located outside the concrete tunnel linings in the surrounding sandrock, overbreaks are the most remote physical spaces under the city of Minneapolis. The overbreaks range in size from tight belly crawls to Gothic cathedral passages fifteen feet high, but most of them involve painful creeping on hands and knees, for which I evolved a special marsupial pack that slung from my belly to carry basic supplies. My hope was to use this secret system of dry passages to get from Schieks Cave to other caves depicted on the sewer plats, such as the Nicollet Mall cave, mentioned in a 1929 newspaper clipping.

Schieks Cave was thus an advanced base camp for exploring the far-flung archipelago of caves under the Loop. The old nightclub cave, ringed about by deadly sewage waterfalls, became the jumping-off place in the hunt for ice age caves among the cathedral overbreaks. In the years since, a talented explorer from Alaska took up this work, showing once again what a magnet the subterranean Twin Cities has become. Remember the days when people used to go *to* Alaska to explore the last frontier?

THE BIG WHITE
CHANNEL ROCK CAVERN

During the secret preparation of ropes and lights, some awkward
misgivings began to sneak into the castle of my determination.

PORTE CRAYON, *VIRGINIA ILLUSTRATED*

YEARS AGO I went prospecting for caves along the Winchell Trail in
Minneapolis. This rollercoastering pathway, officially designated by
the Park Board in 1915 and named after the pioneer geologist Newton
Horace Winchell, followed an old Indian trail. Presumably it was one
of the trails that Winchell himself had followed while making his classic studies of the postglacial retreat of St. Anthony Falls from what
is now Fort Snelling to its present location. While hiking this trail,
I noticed that the stretch of Mississippi River bluff south of the Lake
Street Bridge was highly deformed and strange looking. Every once in
a while I'd find an interesting little cave around there, like the one I
photographed one particularly cold winter—a deep limestone crevice
where baseball-bat-size ice stalagmites grew up from the reddish cave
soil. It's nothing to find ice stalactites (more commonly known as icicles), but the kind that grow up from the floor are much less common.
There was much bigger game in the vicinity, however: a great, whale-
shaped cavern in the whitish sandstone that would eventually become
our Big White.

By the 1920s, the contamination of the Mississippi River with raw
sewage was getting too serious to ignore. The cities of Minneapolis and
St. Paul got together to form a Sanitary District in 1933, with plans to
build a sewage treatment plant at Pig's Eye Lake, on the river below
St. Paul, which eventually opened in 1938. All the sewage that had formerly flowed into the river through separate outfalls was diverted by
sanitary sewers running parallel to the river along its banks. In order
to excavate these tunnels, called interceptors, hydraulic lances were

employed, jetting through the loosely consolidated St. Peter Sandstone. In some places, pressurized air locks were required.

One branch of this big system was the Minneapolis Southwest interceptor, draining sewage from as far away as Edina and carrying it to Lake Street, where it met the sewage coming from the downtown area, drained by the North Minneapolis Tunnel. At Lake Street, the two sewage streams converged and passed under the Mississippi River by means of an inverted siphon, a cast iron tube laid on the riverbed, reemerging on the St. Paul side. From there, the sewage flowed through an even larger tunnel, along the line of Marshall Street, about two hundred feet underground, going another ten miles to the treatment plant.

In the summer of 1935, while constructing the Minneapolis Southwest interceptor, workmen by chance dug into what remains the largest-known cave under Minneapolis. (Several other sandstone caves, albeit smaller, were discovered during this same interceptor project in the 1930s, so it might even be dubbed the golden age of sewer caves.) Located near East Thirty-fourth Street and West River Road, the cave is eight hundred feet long, twenty feet high, and fifty feet wide. In shape it's roughly like a whale or, I thought, like Moby Dick, arching back into one of his poses in the classic Rockwell Kent illustrations. Although the name Channel Rock Cavern was suggested for it years ago, this name has no historical roots that I am aware of. Many cavers to this day simply call it the Thirty-fourth Street cave and leave it at

Photograph of divers working on the Mississippi River near the Lake Street Bridge during the construction of the sewage siphon under the river, November 10, 1937.

that. Most of this cave lies within the St. Peter Sandstone, but its ceiling has migrated upward into the overlying Platteville Limestone. To the sandhogs, or tunnel workmen, the cave was a blessing because it gave them a convenient place to dump their sand as they continued digging the tunnel. In ancient times the cave had opened onto the river banks and had slumped shut with material sloughing from the slopes above, so it was fairly easy for them to create a timbered work tunnel to the outside world.

After the discovery of the great cavern, word got around, and it attracted curious visitors. For a time, it was thought it might be converted into an underground city park, but it was finally decided to seal the timbered work tunnel on the river banks. Standing on the spot today, there is nothing whatever to suggest there's a cave nearby. A new access point for the cave was created, a fifty-two-foot shaft down from West River Road, capped with a hexagonal lid, and just under that, a heavy slab of concrete that requires a winch to remove. The cave was only rarely visited after that, so any visit became newsworthy, as in 1972, when sewer workers discovered several fake graves that someone had set up inside the cave, probably in the 1930s. In 1979, WCCO broadcast the first televised visit to the cave on the *Moore on Sunday* show. In 1980, the National Speleological Society held its annual convention in the Twin Cities, and this cave was one of the featured stops, again generating newspaper publicity. There were several trips in the 1990s for the benefit of visiting Canadian researchers, allowing them to collect samples of flowstone inside the cave for the purpose of dating it. But any visit was a big production because the road had to be blocked off temporarily so the lid could be safely removed.

My friends John and Mike became interested in this cavern. Our first project, which had nothing to do with visiting the cave but which gave us valuable clues when the time came, we called RUR, in the spirit of text messaging. It meant "River Under the River." One of the barrels of the sewage siphon is kept in reserve while the other two are active, and we thought that we could walk through the dry barrel, under the bed of the Mississippi River, and up onto the St. Paul side. When we actually examined the siphon, however, it was found that this barrel is full of sewage at all times even when it's not moving, until more sewage comes flooding in, starting it up. We found the place incredibly dangerous and left it alone after that. One slip would have meant a horrible death, a human sacrifice to the Great Siphon god, as we called it.

I could plainly see from sewer maps that the underlying interceptor could be used to walk to the cavern. The potential upstream access points were too far away from the cave, so it looked as if the much closer downstream access was the better option in this case, if only we could breast the current and traverse the slippery bottom. While visiting one of these access points and as we were discussing the matter without having actually entered the interceptor, we heard a buzzing noise and saw a guillotine-style hydraulic gate descending. Thus blockaded, the sewage in the interceptor rose to chest height in a matter of minutes. That gave us pause; what if the interceptor were to sump completely? You could imagine your anguished last moments as the terrible meniscus crept up the sides of the tunnel until your last gulp of air was gone.

After that, we confined our attempts to reach the cave to the middle of the night on weekends, because that's when the sewage flow was least (everyone's asleep). The flow was three feet lower at the siphon at such times, making it much easier to walk upstream against the current. We encouraged ourselves with the reflection that the warm gray fluid we were treading was, after all, mostly just bathwater. But in recognition that the interceptor reached past the Minneapolis–St. Paul

KSTP Broadcasts From 200 Feet Underground

"An unusual radio broadcast conducted by KSTP originated 200 feet below the streets of St. Paul in the new Minneapolis–St. Paul sewage disposal tunnel," depicted in this 1930s clipping from a Twin Cities newspaper.

FROM METROPOLITAN WASTE CONTROL COMMISSION, *50 YEARS.*

International Airport, we joked that in the middle of the night the tunnel was running mostly pilot's piss.

I met the others in the agreed-upon place along the riverbanks while it was still dark. One of them was not told what the real goal was until the last minute. We were playing the cards close to our chest this time, having learned the hard way what happens when you share too much information with others. We went loaded for bear, carrying every item we thought we could potentially use. In the end, we needed very little of the gear, but it was hard to predict what we would be up against when we got to the cave itself.

Opening the lid, the hole blew out sewer gas like a volcanic vent, scattering dried leaves every which way. Ducking down belowground and banging the manhole lid over us, we changed into our sewer garb, already standardized from the Schieks Cave expeditions. It was the Apollo moon suit of the deep sewers.

Entering the interceptor tunnel, six feet high, the sewage was flowing at a brisk three feet per second. Even at this optimal time in the diurnal sewage cycle, heading upstream was very, very fatiguing, requiring a rest stop every few hundred feet. We had to brace ourselves against the walls as we walked, leaving our arms bloodless. The respirators, whose cartridges seemed to have worn out, were hard to breathe through, causing us to re-inhale our own exhalations, causing further fatigue, so we let the masks flop, potentially exposing ourselves to aerosolized intestinal pathogens. The monotonous concrete tube seemed to stretch out ahead of us forever, and the rest stops became even more frequent. Thankfully, there were no floor sediments to impede motion because the fast flow kept the bottom flushed clean.

Secretly, despite our precautions, I was so fearful of drowning in the sewage from the dropping of the guillotine gates that I had stowed several clear plastic bags in an easy-to-reach pouch on my rucksack. They could be used as escape hoods in the event of surges in the pipe. The idea was that if we quickly wrapped them over our heads, we would have precious extra moments of breathing time, during which the sewage level might drop again.

After nearly a mile of this agonized progress, the lead man let out a whoop. It was our Big White at long last, accessed through a hexagonal hole in the ceiling of the tunnel. Owing to the configuration of the floor, the sewage was traveling exceptionally fast here, creating a haystack wave. We rigged a rope ladder and climbed up into the largest natural cavern under Minneapolis. Directly above us, a steel ladder led up to West River Boulevard through a round hole in the ceiling of the cave, the access point used by normal visitors.

We removed our respirators. It felt good to get out of the fog of toxic aerosols into the cool, pure air of the cave. The top of the tunnel was covered with strange flowstone formations that looked like the entrails of animals: intestines, kidneys, and livers. Taking my first step off the top of the tunnel, which ran like a hump through the floor of the cave, I nearly sprained my ankle, which would have spelled disaster in this remote setting.

The absence of footprints on the sandy floor, as well as the dense covering of delicate drip pockets, which take time to form, told us that no one had visited the cave in a long time, perhaps a decade. We were certainly the first to get to this place through the sewers. On the wall next to us there was a large old graffito, "Remember Pearl Harbor," a phrase that seemed especially fitting to me at the time, as we had just outlived the embarrassment of not having reached Schieks Cave first. We took our classic expedition shot and even had a flag of sorts.

Channel Rock Cavern, the largest cave under Minneapolis, was discovered by sewer workers in 1935. This photograph of the cave from 1961 gives a good idea of its enormous size. This primarily sandstone cave has a limestone ceiling.

Physically, the cave is basically a great L-shaped hall, eight hundred feet long. The cave may have formed by forces similar to those that caused the Eastman Tunnel disaster of 1869, where river water had been pirated underground through a subterranean channel and back into the river again below the falls. That's apparently what happened here, eight or nine thousand years ago, as St. Anthony Falls migrated upstream.

We examined the old bluff entrance to the cave, with its timbered access portal, now totally collapsed. Railroad tie beams held up the cave ceiling at this point. Originally, we had thought of bringing a shovel and digging it out to the riverbanks, to create a shortcut for future trips, but we could now see that it would have required many trips to do this, and it would have been an unstable excavation, liable to collapse on us at any time. It's just as well we left the shovel at home.

The sewer obviously overflowed into the cave occasionally. The two halves of the hexagonal lids were lying apart on the floor as if they had been blown off by a volcanic surcharge from the underlying tunnel. The debris field of the sewer, its overflow zone, extended out to the big elbow in the cave, several hundred feet away. While over most of this area we found the traditional sanitary tokens—rockets and white mice, polite names for the two most common feminine hygiene products—we also found plastic water bottles and intact Styrofoam cups, suggesting that storm water had been involved. (They didn't get here by being flushed down a toilet.). This would not be the case if the storm drains and sanitary sewers were completely separated, again emphasizing that it was not safe to be in the interceptor during a rainstorm.

At the elbow of the cave, but well within the overflow zone, we found the faux cemetery mentioned in the 1972 newspaper clipping. The cemetery consisted of half a dozen elongated soil mounds with a "headstone" at one end and tennis shoes sticking out the other.

The life of the cave was confined to the overflow zone because that's where the organic detritus was, providing things to eat. Enormous black spiders plied their trade here, hoping to catch a flying feast. Beyond the sewage line at the elbow, the cave was floored with pristine white sand, like a beach, roomy enough to lay out several volleyball courts, but quite sterile. The width of the flat limestone ceiling here was amazing—how could it exist without collapsing, we wondered, when houses were built on top, and vehicles thundered overhead? Here we found areas that had been taped off by researchers so that visitors would not step on them. They protected the cave's most distinctive formation, the calcite-lined drip pocket in sand. Most of the pockets followed a linear trend, extending under the main ceiling joint, which oozed water.

Toward the end of the cave we came to a steep declivity, like the edge of a great sand dune. It did not occur to us until this point that the sand we had been walking on all along was fill material left by the sandhogs as they excavated the interceptor in the 1930s. In one place, we found the corroded remnants of their narrow-gauge railroad, complete with steel rails and wooden cross ties. The best estimate is that there is about fifteen feet of sand fill; unfortunately, it hides the original floor. In the 1935 photos you can see this floor, covered with limestone breakdown slabs, and how much roomier the cave was then than it is today. Almost certainly, the fill had buried side passages that we would have liked to explore. We would especially have liked to find a connection between the cave and the giant sinkhole in Seven Oaks Oval Park, which I had probed on the surface years earlier.

At the very end of the cave, at the very lowest point down at the bottom of the sand hill, there was a sapphire pool of cold, pure water. In earlier published accounts this was called "a small pool of green-ish water," the word "greenish" suggesting contamination, but this pool appeared so clean you could drink from it, although the experiment was not attempted. The water derived from seepage through the ceiling, which left hundreds of flexible mud stalactites several inches long, another unique formation for this cave that I hadn't seen else-where. I found no amphipods or other creatures in this pool, again because there was no organic matter.

Our time in the cave was limited because the sewage level in the interceptor would soon begin rising again as morning approached, trapping us in the cave. We did not relish having to lower ourselves back into that murky pipe, so odorous was it, with its dense cloud of coliform aerosol droplets. After a long hike back, almost effort-less because the sewage was pushing us from behind this time, we put everything back the way it was, pushed off the manhole lid, and entered the smiling, golden morning sunshine.

SOURCES AND FURTHER READING

Alexander, E. Calvin, Jr., ed. *An Introduction to Caves of Minnesota, Iowa, and Wisconsin: Guidebook for the 1980 NSS Convention.* Huntsville, Ala.: National Speleological Society, 1980.

Anfinson, Scott F. "Archaeology of the Central Minneapolis Riverfront." *Minnesota Archaeologist* 48, no. 1–2 (1989): 1–160.

Armstrong, Ellis L., ed. *History of Public Works in the United States.* Chicago: American Public Works Association, 1976.

Bobrick, Benson. *Labyrinths of Iron.* New York: Henry Holt, 1981.

Brick, Greg. "Anthropogenic Caves in St. Peter Sandstone at Minneapolis, Minnesota." *Journal of Cave and Karst Studies* 62, no. 3 (2000): 194.

———. "Beyond the Sump: The Burnley Map of Carver's Cave." *Journal of Cave and Karst Studies* 62, no. 1 (2000): 40.

———. "Bizarre Journalism at Fountain Cave and Its Lessons for the Speleohistorian." *Journal of Spelean History* 40, no. 2 (2006): 53–55.

———. "Cave Hoaxes and Nineteenth Century Archaeological Theory." *Journal of Cave and Karst Studies* 66, no. 3 (2004): 116.

———. "'Charon Trimmed His Lamp': Carver's Cave and the Definition of a Show Cave." *Journal of Spelean History* 41, no. 1 (2007): 23–26.

———. "Classification and Morphology of St. Peter Sandstone Piping Caves in Minnesota." Geological Society of America, Northeastern Section, Valley Forge, Pennsylvania, *Abstracts with Programs* 29, no. 1 (1997): 33.

———."Little Minnehaha Falls: The Great Subterranean Spring of Minneapolis." *Minnesota Ground Water Association Newsletter* 25, no. 1 (2006): 17–19.

———. "The Old Bank Cave." *Infiltration* (Toronto), no. 20 (2003): 25–32.

———. "A Piping Voice: Theories of Cave Genesis in Minnesota Prior to 1880." *Minnesota Ground Water Association Newsletter* 24, no. 3 (2005): 24–25.

———. "The Rediscovery of Minnesota's First Commercial Cave." *NSS News* 50, no. 7 (1992): 182–83.

———. "Sanitary Abyss: The Schieks Cave Adventure." In National Speleological Society, *2001 Speleo Digest*, 143–47. Huntsville, Ala.: National Speleological Society, 2004.

———. "Stahlmann's Cellars: The Cave under the Castle." *Ramsey County History* 41, no. 1 (2006): 12–19.

———. "Stairway to the Abyss: The Diverting Story of Cascade Creek." *Ramsey County History* 33, no. 1 (1998): 4–8, 27.

———. "The University Farm Experimental Cave and How St. Paul Became the Blue Cheese Capital of the World." *Ramsey County History* 36, no. 3 (2003): 4–10.

———. "What Happened to Fountain Cave—The Real Birthplace of St. Paul?" *Ramsey County History* 29, no. 4 (1995): 4–15.

Brick, Greg, and Penny A. Petersen. "Ten-Cent Tour: The Story of Chute's Cave." *Hennepin History* 63, no. 2 (2004): 4–25.

Brueggemann, Gary J. "Beer Capital of the State: St. Paul's Historic Family Breweries." *Ramsey County History* 16, no. 2 (1981): 3–15.

Carver, Jonathan. *Travels through the Interior Parts of North America.* Minneapolis: Ross & Haines, 1956. Facsimile reprint of the third London edition, 1781.

Chaney, Josiah B. "Early Bridges and Changes of the Land and Water Surface in the City of St. Paul." *Collections of the Minnesota Historical Society* 12 (1908): 131–48.

Cohen, William A., and Ryan Johnson, eds. *Filth: Dirt, Disgust, and Modern Life.* Minneapolis: University of Minnesota Press, 2005.

Culver, David C., and William B. White, eds. *Encyclopedia of Caves.* Boston: Elsevier Academic Press, 2005.

Donahue, William. "Notes from Underground." *National Geographic Adventure*, Winter 1999, 75–77, 79.

Dornberg, David. "Camera Safari Explores 'Lost World' Under Loop." *Minneapolis Journal*, April 16, 1939.

Empson, Don. *The Street Where You Live.* Minneapolis: University of Minnesota Press, 2006.

Eveleigh, David J. *Bogs, Baths, and Basins: The Story of Domestic Sanitation.* Thrupp, Gloucestershire, UK: Sutton Publishing, 2003.

Ford, Trevor D., and Cecil H. D. Cullingford, eds. *The Science of Speleology*. London: Academic Press, 1976.

Granick, Harry. *Underneath New York*. New York: Fordham University Press, 1947.

Gunn, John, ed. *Encyclopedia of Caves and Karst Science*. New York: Fitzroy Dearborn, 2004.

Gustafson, Neil C. "Bassett's Creek: A Case Study of the Changing Concepts in Urban Land Use." Master's thesis, University of Minnesota, Minneapolis, 1959.

Haga, Chuck. "Cave Man Sheds Light on City's Deep Secrets." *Minneapolis Star Tribune*, September 6, 1993.

Hodgson, Barbara. *The Rat: A Perverse Miscellany*. Vancouver, B.C.: Greystone Books, 1997.

Hogberg, Rudolph K. *Environmental Geology of the Twin Cities Metropolitan Area*. St. Paul: Minnesota Geological Survey, 1971.

Hogberg, Rudolph K., and T. N. Bayer. *Guide to the Caves of Minnesota*. St. Paul: Minnesota Geological Survey, 1967.

Hollingshead, John. *Underground London*. London: Groombridge & Sons, 1862.

Hovey, Horace C. *Celebrated American Caverns*. Cincinnati, Ohio: Robert Clarke Co., 1896.

Jones, Pamela. *Under the City Streets: A History of Subterranean New York*. New York: Holt, Rinehart & Winston, 1978.

Kane, Lucile M. *The Falls of St. Anthony: The Waterfall That Built Minneapolis*. St. Paul: Minnesota Historical Society Press, 1987.

Keating, Ann D. *Invisible Networks: Exploring the History of Local Utilities and Public Works*. Malabar, Fla.: Krieger Publishing Co., 1994.

Kehret, Roger. *Minnesota Caves of History and Legend*. Chatfield, Minn.: Superior Printing, 1974.

Koeppel, Gerard T. *Water for Gotham: A History*. Princeton, N.J.: Princeton University Press, 2000.

Legget, Robert F. *Cities and Geology*. New York: McGraw-Hill, 1973.

Maccabee, Paul. *John Dillinger Slept Here: A Crook's Tour of Crime and Corruption in St. Paul, 1920–1936*. St. Paul: Minnesota Historical Society Press, 1995.

Matthews, William H. *Mazes and Labyrinths: Their History and Development*. New York: Dover Publications, 1970.

Mayhew, Henry. *Mayhew's London*. London: Spring Books, 1964. Originally published in 1851.

Metcalf, Leonard, and Harrison P. Eddy. *Sewerage and Sewage Disposal: A Textbook.* 2nd ed. New York: McGraw-Hill. 1930.

Metropolitan Waste Control Commission. *50 Years: Treating the Mississippi Right.* St. Paul, Minn.: Metropolitan Waste Control Commission, 1988.

Meyer, Herbert W. *Builders of Northern States Power Company.* St. Paul: Northern States Power Company, 1972.

Miller, Kay. "Way Down in Minnesota." *Minneapolis Star-Tribune Sunday Magazine*, January 29, 1989.

Millett, Larry. "Muck, Bats, Gas: Only the Brave Plunge into Caves." *St. Paul Pioneer Press*, October 19, 1992.

Moffat, Bruce G. *The Chicago Tunnel Story: Exploring the Railroad Forty Feet Below.* Bulletin 135. Chicago: Central Electric Railfan's Association, 2002.

Mosedale, Mike. "Notes from Underground." *City Pages*, October 17, 2001.

Munsey, Cecil. *The Illustrated Guide to Collecting Bottles.* New York: Hawthorn Books, 1970.

New York Steam Corporation. *Fifty Years of New York Steam Service: The Story of the Founding and Development of a Public Utility.* New York: New York Steam Corporation, 1932.

Ojakangas, Richard W., and Charles L. Matsch. *Minnesota's Geology.* Minneapolis: University of Minnesota Press, 1982.

Palmer, Arthur N. *Cave Geology.* Dayton, Ohio: Cave Books, 2007.

Peele, Robert. *Mining Engineers' Handbook.* 3rd ed. New York: John Wiley & Sons, 1941.

Potter, Merle. *101 Best Stories of Minnesota.* Minneapolis, Minn.: Harrison and Smith, 1931.

Reid, Donald. *Paris Sewers and Sewermen: Realities and Representation.* Cambridge, Mass.: Harvard University Press, 1991.

Rinker, Andrew. "The Development of the Minneapolis Sewer System." *Bulletin of the Minnesota Academy of Sciences* 4, no. 3 (1910): 422–27.

Rother, Hubert, and Charlotte Rother. *Lost Caves of St. Louis: A History of the City's Forgotten Caves.* St. Louis, Mo.: Virginia Publishing, 1996.

Sandstrom, Gosta E. *Tunnels.* New York: Holt, Rinehart, and Winston, 1963.

Scarpino, Philip V. *Great River: An Environmental History of the Upper Mississippi, 1890-1950*. Columbia: University of Missouri Press, 1985.

Schwartz, George M. *The Geology of the Minneapolis–St. Paul Metropolitan Area*. St. Paul: Minnesota Geological Survey, 1936.

Schwartz, George M., and George A. Thiel. *Minnesota's Rocks and Waters*. Minneapolis: University of Minnesota Press, 1963.

Shortland, Michael. "Darkness Visible: Underground Culture in the Golden Age of Geology." *History of Science* 32 (1994): 1–61.

Sloan, R. E., ed. *Middle and Late Ordovician Lithostratigraphy and Biostratigraphy of the Upper Mississippi Valley*. Report of Investigations 35. St. Paul: Minnesota Geological Survey, 1987.

Smith, Stephen. *Underground London: Travels beneath the City Streets*. London: Little, Brown, 2004.

Solis, Julia. *New York Underground: The Anatomy of a City*. New York: Routledge, 2004.

Sullivan, Robert. *Rats: Observations on the History and Habitat of the City's Most Unwanted Inhabitants*. New York: Bloomsbury, 2004.

Toth, Jennifer. *The Mole People: Life in the Tunnels beneath New York City*. Chicago: Chicago Review Press, 1993.

Trench, Richard, and Ellis Hillman. *London under London: A Subterranean Guide*. London: John Murray, 1984.

Westbrook, Nicholas, ed. *A Guide to the Industrial Archeology of the Twin Cities*. St. Paul: Society for Industrial Archeology, 1983.

Whitfield, John W. *Underground Space Resources in Missouri*. Report of Investigations no. 65. Rolla: Missouri Department of Natural Resources, 1981.

Williams, John Fletcher. *A History of the City of Saint Paul to 1875*. St. Paul: Minnesota Historical Society Press, 1983. With an introduction by Lucile M. Kane. Originally published in 1876.

PUBLICATION HISTORY

Portions of "A Wild Goose Chase through the Sewers" previously appeared as "What Happened to Fountain Cave—The Real Birthplace of St. Paul?" *Ramsey County History* 29, no. 4 (1995): 4–15.

Portions of "The Urban Nile" were previously published as "Stairway to the Abyss: The Diverting Story of Cascade Creek," *Ramsey County History* 33, no. 1 (1998): 4–8, 27.

Portions of "The Cave under the Castle" were previously published as "Stahlmann's Cellars: The Cave under the Castle," *Ramsey County History* 41, no. 1 (2006): 12–19.

Portions of "The Medieval Temples of Mushroom Valley" appeared as "Terrific Battles: Pests, Diseases, and Technological Change at St. Paul's Mushroom Caves," *Journal of Spelean History* 37, no. 2 (2003): 49–50.

Portions of "Boat Ride to Oblivion" were published as Greg Brick and P. A. Petersen, "Ten Cent Tour: The Story of Chute's Cave," *Hennepin County History* 63, no. 2 (2004): 4–25.

Portions of "A Lonely Day under the Mortuary" previously appeared as "Deep Down Under—Exploring Fort Road Sewers," *West Seventh Community Reporter* (August 2007): 5, 7.

Portions of "Lost World" were previously published as "Sanitary Abyss: The Schieks Cave Adventure," in *2001 Speleo Digest* (Huntsville, Ala.: National Speleological Society, 2004), 143–47.

INDEX